Economic Theory in a Changing World

Economic Theory in a Changing World
Policymaking for Growth

Edited by

Sajal Lahiri

Pradip Maiti

OXFORD
UNIVERSITY PRESS

OXFORD
UNIVERSITY PRESS

YMCA Library Building, Jai Singh Road, New Delhi 110001

Oxford University Press is a department of the University of Oxford.
It furthers the University's objective of excellence in research,
scholarship, and education by publishing worldwide in

Oxford New York

Auckland Cape Town Dar es Salaam Hong Kong Karachi
Kuala Lumpur Madrid Melbourne Mexico City Nairobi
New Delhi Shanghai Taipei Toronto

With offices in

Argentina Austria Brazil Chile Czech Republic France Greece
Guatemala Hungary Italy Japan Poland Portugal Singapore
South Korea Switzerland Thailand Turkey Ukraine Vietnam

Oxford is a registered trade mark of Oxford University Press
in the UK and in certain other countries

Published in India
by Oxford University Press, New Delhi

© Oxford University Press 2005

The moral rights of the author have been asserted
Database right Oxford University Press (maker)

First published 2005

ISBN-13: 978-0-19-567230-5
ISBN-10: 0-19-567230-5

Typeset by Excel Publishing Services, 62/1, Laxmi Market, Munirka, New Delhi
Printed in India at Pauls Press, New Delhi 110 020
Published by Manzar Khan, Oxford University Press
YMCA Library Building, Jai Singh Road, New Delhi 110 001

Dedicated to
Sanjit Bose,
an independent and original mind

Sanjit Bose

Sanjit Bose's interests in economics over the years have covered a broad spectrum of areas in economic theory and policy making, many of which are as relevant and topical today as they were in the 1960s and 1970s. Models of economic growth and technical progress, his early interests, are now back as important areas of research, albeit with a widened focus incorporating effects of accumulation of knowledge and human capital.[1]

Born on 12 September 1940 to Debjani and Atul Bose, Sanjit Bose's undergraduate degree was a combined honours in economics and political science from the well-known Presidency College, Kolkata. It is possibly this interdisciplinary training that nurtured his interests in political–economic issues throughout his academic life. For his postgraduate degree (from Calcutta University) he chose to specialize in economics, motivated as he was by a number of factors. He was particularly inspired by his professor Bhabatosh Datta, amongst the greatest teachers in economics at the time. Further he had periodic discussions with his peers, particularly Amit Bhaduri, Tapan Lahiri, as also Ashok Sanjay Guha, a few years' his senior at Presidency. Such interactions with Ashok Sanjay Guha helped him develop his analytical mind and crystallize his thinking in economics. During his Master's he came to appreciate the width, depth, and above all, significance of economics as a discipline in impacting human existence.

While still an MA student, Sanjit Bose displayed clear signs of an original mind and wrote a technical paper in 1961 on investment allocation and the choice of techniques in a diagrammatic framework. This was a remarkable achievement by any standards worldwide. He sent it to Amartya Sen who wrote back with his detailed comments and appreciation. The work was published later in *Economia Internazionale*.[2] After completing his MA, he joined Presidency College as a faculty. In

---

[1] The following book discusses the new literature: R.J. Barro, and X. Sala-i-Martin, 2003, *Economic Growth: Second Edition*, MIT Press, Cambridge, MA.

[2] Sanjit Bose, 1965, 'Economic Growth in a Two-sector Planning Model', *Economia Internazionale*, 18, August, pp. 431–7.

1963 he married Uttara, daughter of Pranati and Bishnu De. They now have two sons Sayantan and Saraswat. He taught at the Presidency during 1963 to 1965 and some of his early students included Mukul Majumdar, now at Cornell University. This was one of the most exciting periods of his academic life. He started working on a dual economy model involving marketed surplus and the price of food. During this period he was also a regular participant in informal meetings organized by reputed economists like Tapas Majumdar, Ajit Biswas, Amiya Bagchi, Nabendu Sen, and Ashok Mitra. Such interactions helped him to formalize his thinking on issues such as embodied technical progress/vintage capital model, and other works of Robert Solow on technical progress. His close contact with Ajit Biswas during this time, had a great influence on him and regular discussions with Ajit Biswas helped Bose narrow down the areas in which he could think of working further.

Sanjit Bose got a scholarship from the MIT in 1965 and went there to work on his PhD. He took a number of courses such as one on capital theory by Robert Solow, on general equilibrium by Kenneth Arrow, and one on Russian economic history in the nineteenth century from Evsey Domar. His peer group at MIT included Tony Atkinson, George Akerlof, Avinash Dixit, Joseph Stiglitz, and Martin Weitzman. He completed his PhD in May 1967 under the guidance of Robert Solow well within two years of arriving at MIT. He worked on the theoretical aspects/extensions of the Mahalanobis model of economic growth and two of the chapters of his dissertation were published in *Econometrica* and the *Review of Economic Studies*.[3] While studying economic growth models, he also got deeply interested in issues related to economic welfare, and income distributions in a general-equilibrium dual-economy framework. One of his unpublished papers on this subject has received a lot of attention in the literature.[4] According to Avinash Dixit, this unpublished paper of Sanjit Bose was the first to emphasize the need for a general-equilibrium analysis of the dual economy.[5] He returned to India after his PhD and a brief teaching tenure at Brandeis University in Boston, mulling over a number of

[3] Sanjit Bose, 1970, 'Optimal Growth in a Non-shiftable Capital Model, *Econometrica*, 38, 128–52; and Sanjit Bose, 1968, 'Optimal Growth and Investment Allocation', *Review of Economic Studies*, 35, 465–80.

[4] *See* contribution by Anthony B. Atkinson (Chapter 6) for a discussion on that paper.

[5] A.K. Dixit, 1971, 'Short-run Equilibrium and Shadow Prices in the Dual Economy', *Oxford Economic Papers*, 23, 384–400.

interesting economic problems many of which were later sought to be resolved by his PhD students.

Sanjit Bose joined as a faculty at the Delhi Centre of the Indian Statistical Institute (ISI) in April 1969, and later moved to the Kolkata Centre where he stayed until his retirement in September 2003. He first started work on multi-sectoral linear economic models and activity analysis—an area in which he maintained a long-lasting interest.[6] This was also the time that his interests shifted away from mainstream economics into areas and ideas that were yet to get crystallized. This process started as he exchanged thoughts with some leftist economists such as Krishna Bharadwaj, Sukhamay Ganguly, Ashok Rudra, Amiya Bagchi, and Ashok Mitra. He also got interested in works of Michal Kalecki and was highly influenced by Nicholas Georgescu-Roegen and Karl Polanyi. He became concerned with issues such as price formation, agrarian relations, relations prevalent in the formal sector, and the three facets of the relational structure of a formal sector firm involving labour, capital/finance, and marketing, both from a domestic and an international perspective.

Sanjit Bose supervised successfully PhD works of a large number of graduate students on a variety of topics. Over a period of time he developed a most remarkable understanding of the concepts of time, production, distinction between stock and flows or between circulating and fixed capital. All his students have benefited immensely from his clarity of thought and dexterity in imparting this conceptual understanding to them. This is especially important as most of the commonly used basic concepts such as income, production, time, etc., receive less attention than they deserve in classroom instruction although no one will disagree that without a proper emphasis on these concepts the understanding economic science can remain murky.

Apart from linear economic structure and related models, Bose's students also worked on input-output models in a non-linear structure. Sanjit Bose has always felt that the classical model including its concept of annual cycle of production has not yet been properly formalized, at

---

[6] A large number of papers were written on linear models then. Apart from many papers written by his students, he himself wrote two quite important papers on the topic and these are: Sanjit Bose, 1972, 'A New Proof of the Non-substitution Theory', *International Economic Review*, 13, 183–6; and Deb Kumar Bose and Sanjit Bose, 1972, 'An Algorithm for Computing the von Neuman Balanced Growth Path', *Econometrica*, 40, 763–6.

least not by the Sraffa system. In fact, he supervised research in some of these areas as a critique of Sraffa. However, since he tried to examine all these issues from an entirely new and unorthodox perspective, his success in this area has so far been only limited.

His work in the area of economic growth has not only been pivotal in increasing our understanding of the process of growth, but has also helped in advancing many conceptual and methodological issues such as the different types of technical progress, the concept of income, the dynamics of income distribution, etc. This has furthered the advancing of mathematical techniques for analysing growth processes such as the calculus of variation, optimal control theory and dynamic programming.

A number of graduate students at ISI (including ourselves) have benefited from his leadership. His friendly manner, liberal views and willingness to help students and younger colleagues endeared him with everyone. We still have fond memories of the one-to-one meetings that we frequently had with him. He was a young man bubbling with new ideas. What we learnt from him was not just economics, but how one should approach research and, above all, how to supervise graduate students. It is therefore not just us who benefited from his wisdom, but also all our graduate students have a lot for which they should be thankful to him.

Contributors

Anthony B. Atkinson Warden, Nuffield College, University of Oxford, UK.

Amit Bhaduri Senior Fellow, Institute of Advanced Study, University of Bologna.

Dipankar Dasgupta Professor of Economics, Indian Statistical Institute, Kolkata.

Avinash Dixit John J.F. Sherrerd '52 University Professor of Economics, Princeton University.

Sajal Lahiri Vandeveer Professor of Economics, Southern Illinois University at Carbondale.

Pradip Maiti Professor of Economics, Indian Statistical Institute, Kolkata.

Mukul Majumdar H.T. Warshow and Robert I. Warshow Professor of Economics, Cornell University.

Sugata Marjit Professor of Economics, Centre for Studies in Social Sciences, Kolkata.

Sandip Mitra Economic Research Unit, Indian Statistical Institute, Kolkata.

Anjan Mukherji Professor of Economics, School of Social Sciences, Jawaharlal Nehru University, New Delhi.

Ilaria Ossella-Durbal Assistant Professor of Economics, Illinois Wesleyan University.

Mihir Rakshit Emeritus Professor of Economics, Indian Statistical Institute, Kolkata.

Abhirup Sarkar Professor of Economics, Indian Statistical Institute, Kolkata.

Robert M. Solow Emeritus Professor of Economics, Massachusetts Institute of Technology.

Kevin Sylwester Associate Professor of Economics, Southern Illinois University at Carbondale.

Martin L. Weitzman Ernest E. Monrad Professor of Economics, Harvard University.

Contents

Figures

Tables

Overview

SAJAL LAHIRI AND PRADIP MAITI

In the context of Sanjit Bose's interest and work on growth theory and the conceptual issues therein, Robert Solow—Bose's PhD supervisor at MIT—in Chapter 1, returns to the analytical issues relating to embodied technical change and discusses how the interplay of theory and fact has nurtured this concept which remains important even today for the interpretation of productivity statistics and growth-oriented public policies.[1] Another conceptual issue is dealt with in Chapter 2 by Martin Weitzman who attempts to answer the question 'what is income?' using a model developed by Sanjit Bose.[2] Income being such a basic concept in economics, it is of vital importance that it be clearly understood.[3] In Chapter 3, Amit Bhaduri takes a radically different approach to the phenomenon of endogenous growth by introducing the Keynesian distinction between investment and savings behaviour. Dipankar Dasgupta in Chapter 4 examines in depth optimal control theory as an analytical tool for the analysis of the neoclassical growth model a la Solow for an infinite-horizon objective function. Since these analytical tools are also applicable to the new growth theory, this chapter would provide students of growth theory, old and new, with a single source for the development of the subject from first principles.

Dynamic economic models are obviously essential for the analysis

---

[1] *See* J. Greenwood and B. Jovanovic, 2001, 'Accounting for Growth', in C. Hulten, E. Dean, and M. Harper, eds., *New Developments in Productivity Analysis*, University of Chicago Press, Chicago, 179–224.

[2] Sanjit Bose, 1968, 'Optimal Growth and Investment Allocation', *Review of Economic Studies*, 35, 465–80.

[3] For a fuller analysis of the issues, *see* M.L. Weitzman, 2003, *Income, Wealth, and the Maximum Principle*, Harvard University Press, Cambridge, Massachusetts.

of growth processes. However, such analytical tools have also been used to study many other interesting issues which require a dynamic framework. As Debraj Ray noted, identifying key sectors to lead the process of growth and development has been an issue of lasting importance in development economics.[4] Mukul Majumdar and Ilaria Ossella-Durbal provide in Chapter 5 an analytical solution to the problem in the context of a multi-sectoral linear model of economic growth. Another lasting topic of importance in development economics literature has been the question of determinants of income distribution. In Chapter 6, Anthony Atkinson examines the interrelationship between structural change and income distribution in a dynamic dual-economy model. His analysis would help researchers understand better the vast empirical literature on the well-known Kuznets curve and recent studies which use data from a panel of countries.[5] The formation of commodity prices is another topic that has been receiving a lot of attention in development literature with the seminal works by Raul Prebisch and Hans Singer on the secular decline of the South's terms of trade.[6] A related issue is why commodity prices may differ within an economy between sellers.[7] In particular, Abhirup Sarkar and Sandip Mitra develop a dynamic model of price formation in Chapter 7 in order to explain why large sellers get a better price for their products than small sellers in backward agricultural markets. They test the prediction of their theory with data on selected potato markets in West Bengal, India.

Finally, on the topic of dynamics, it is well recognized in the literature that many economic variables show a cyclical bevaviour. Since the classic

[4] *See* Chapter 5 in Debraj Ray, 1998, *Development Economics*, Princeton University Press.

[5] *See*, S. Anand and S.M.R. Kanbur, 1993, 'The Kuznets Process and the Inequality–Development Relationship', *Journal of Development Economics*, 40, 25–52.

[6] The early contributions are R. Prebisch, 1959, 'Commercial Policy in Under-developed Countries', *American Economic Review Papers and Proceedings*, 49, 251–73; and H.W. Singer, 1950, 'The Distribution of Gains between Investing and Borrowing Countries', *American Economic Review Papers and Proceedings*, 40, 473–85. A recent contribution is A. Deaton and G. Laroque, 2003, 'A Model of Commodity Prices after Sir Arthur Lewis', *Journal of Development Economics*, 71, 289–310.

[7] *See*, Amit Bhaduri, 1983, *Economic Structure of Backward Agriculture*, Macmillan, New York.

work by Richard Goodwin,[8] a lot has been written to explain and analyse this phenomenon.[9] In Chapter 8, Anjan Mukherji analyses a class of predator–prey models and the results are applied to the special case of the Goodwin growth model. He shows that the cyclical behaviour noticed by Goodwin lacks robustness in the more general context. In particular, cyclical behaviour is obtained only for a very specific value of the parameter.

As mentioned before, the present focus in the literature on economic growth is the accumulation (or the lack of it) of human capital. Education and training are two important tools for the development of human capital. Chapters 9 and 10 deal with the topic of education in two different ways. In Chapter 9, Avinash Dixit examines the efficacy of public services such as education being provided by faith-based organizations. This issue has immediate policy relevance in countries such as the USA and the UK where the current administrations are trying to promote faith-based initiatives against strong opposition (sometimes from the very faith-based organizations). In secular democracies such as India, where there are many large organized religions, this issue would become important sooner or later. Avinash Dixit approaches this problem by developing a principal–agent model where the principal, the government, designs an optimal incentive scheme.[10] Sajal Lahiri and Kevin Sylwester, in Chapter 10, focus on both the demand for and the supply of education, and the interaction between private capital and human capital. In their analysis, a family decides whether to send a child to school or to send it to work, and this decision depends, inter alia, on the quality of education available.[11] More expenditure on education can lead to a lower investment in physical capital and more investment in physical capital can affect education expenditure and thus the quality of education by altering the tax base for such expenditure programme.

[8] R.M. Goodwin, 1950, 'A Non-linear Theory of the Cycle, *Review of Economics and Statistics*, 32, 316–20.

[9] *See* G. Gandolfo, 1997, *Economic Dynamics*, Study edition, Springer Verlag, Berlin.

[10] The model is based on George Baker, 2000, 'The Use of Performance Measure in Incentive Contracting', *American Economic Review Papers and Proceedings*, 90, 415–20.

[11] This work extends the emerging literature on education and child labour, in particular, the paper S. Jafarey and S. Lahiri, 2002, 'Will Trade Sanction Reduce Child Labour? The Role of Credit Markets, *Journal of Development Economics*, 68, 137–56.

In the context of the long-lasting interest of Sanjit Bose in linear economic models, as mentioned above, Mukul Majumdar and Ilaria Ossella-Durbal, in Chapter 5, analyse a dynamic linear model. The analytics of linear models can have very unusual and neat applications. For example, in his classic book David Gale proves the existence and uniqueness of a solution of the well-known two-person zero-sum game using the technique of linear programming models.[12] Similarly, in Chapter 11, Pradip Maiti synthesizes the standard theory of individual choice under uncertainty in a unified and rigorous way using the tools of linear economic models, providing simpler proofs and useful illustrations. The importance of this topic for current policy discussions cannot be overemphasized. Since the existence of uncertainty is pervasive in almost all walks of life, it is of vital importance to policymakers to know how in market economies individual agents act in the face of uncertainty and also to formulate policies when it does not have all the information it needs with certainty.[13]

The role of international trade in both goods and factors in economic growth and welfare is possibly one of the areas that have been receiving the most attention from academic economists and policy makers. In particular, multilateral negotiations for trade liberalizations at the behest of the WTO and unilateral actions by many developing countries have brought the issue at the centre of policy discussions at national and inter-national levels.[14] The last two chapters of this volume examine this question in two different frameworks. In Chapter 12, Mihir Rakshit examines the effect of the removal of trade barriers on income and employment in a Keynesian model of North–South trade and the intersectoral differences in the operation of demand and supply constraints which play an important role in determining if trade is expansionary or contractionary for the countries. He finds trade can in principle be contractionary for both countries and it will be expansionary for both countries if each country imports goods that are supply constraints in the domestic market against commodities the

---

[12] David Gale, 1960, *Linear Economic Models*, McGraw Hill, New York.

[13] For a recent survey of the literature, *see* Chris Starmer, 2000, 'Developments in Non-expected Utility Theory: The Hunt for a Descriptive Theory of Choice Under Risk', *Journal of Economic Literature*, 38, 332–82.

[14] For a discussion on unilateral trade policy reforms, *see* J.N. Bhagwati (ed.), 2002, *Going Alone: The Case for Relaxed Reciprocity in Freeing Trade*, MIT Press. For a robust case for trade liberalization in India, *see* J.N. Bhagwati, 1993, *India in Transition: Freeing the Economy*, Clarendon Press, Oxford.

production of which is limited by demand. In Chapter 13, Sugata Marjit considers general neoclassical trade models of higher dimension, that is, where there are more than one exportable and importable, and examines the role of complementarity between sectors of production in deriving results on trade protection and well-being. Having developed a general framework, he then considers specific examples of models of trade and development to focus on issues such as foreign investment and welfare, and trade and unemployment in the presence of complementarity in production. One of the results he reports is that the presence of complementarity puts to serious test the conventional wisdom that foreign investment is unambiguously welfare-reducing in the presence of tariff distortion.[15]

As should be clear from what we have written above, the volume contains a wide variety of contribution on topics that have interested Sanjit Bose over the years and which remain relevant even today in discussions on theoretical development and policy making. The contributions vary not only in the area of coverage but also on the tradition of economics that they belong to. In other words, one would get a sense of how different traditions of economics view some of the current debates in economic theory and policy. This diversity in the contributions is a fitting tribute to the man who, according to Avinash Dixit—a fellow graduate student with Sanjit Bose at the MIT, is 'seriously interested in everything' (Chapter 9). Many of the contributions also take rather non-conventional approaches to problems at hand and question conventional wisdom. This is again only appropriate in a volume dedicated to a man who taught many of us including Amit Bhaduri 'to think independently about economic problems without taking conventional wisdom too seriously' (Chapter 3).

---

[15] For the conventional wisdom, *see* R. Brecher and Diaz-Alejandro Carlos, 1977, 'Tariff, Foreign Capital and Immiserizing Growth', *Journal of International Economics*, 7, 317–22.

Part I: Growth and Dynamics

1. Embodied Technical Change Reconsidered

ROBERT M. SOLOW

Sanjit Bose was my student at MIT—and an outstanding one—in the 1960s, and finished his PhD in 1967. For better or worse, when I think of him now I see him as the modest young man he was then. As my small contribution in his honour, I want to reconsider an analytical issue that concerned us in those days in an intellectual environment that I remember with the greatest pleasure.

I shall begin by retracing the path that led me to the 'embodiment' question. The story, which began more than forty years ago, still seems interesting for three reasons. (1) The substance remains important for the interpretation of productivity statistics and for growth-oriented policy. (2) There may be a lesson about the way economics develops from the interplay of theory and fact. (3) It is a connection between then and now that is still alive.

One startling consequence of neoclassical growth theory (with diminishing returns to capital goods) was that sustained growth of productivity rests primarily on continued technological change, except under certain limiting circumstances. That result has given rise to a tradition of research on human capital and other endogenous sources of rising 'total factor productivity'. A less startling, but still striking, result was the calculation that even large increases in the rate of capital investment would generate disappointingly small increases in the *level* of output along a steady-state growth path. To be precise, a sustained increase in the share of output saved and invested leads only to a temporary speed-up in growth, and eventually to a new steady state path at the pre-existing growth rate, but at a permanently higher level. After reasonable calibration, the estimated elasticity of steady-state output per worker with respect to the saving-investment quota turned out to be so small that a policy of increased investment seemed to be unpromising.

This surprise led me and others to wonder if the standard model might be hiding or suppressing part of the contribution of tangible investment to productivity. One possible candidate explanation was the 'embodiment hypothesis', reflecting the obvious fact that new technology often requires the installation of new physical capital before it can have any effect on productivity. Examples were everywhere: the invention of the jet engine can have no effect on airline productivity until old propeller-driven aircraft are replaced by newly built jets; the invention of electronically controlled machinery can have no effect on user productivity until investment in elaborate control modules takes place. The volume of investment limits the speed of introduction of new technology; and this effect was omitted from the standard models.

In response to this common sense observation, vintage models were developed. In them, capital goods were distinguished by their date of birth. Newly installed capital equipment 'embodies' the newest technology, and is thus more productive than older capital goods. New capital depreciates over time, but holds its original productivity until it is retired. At each instant of time, labour is allocated optimally over vintages: the *marginal* product of labour must be the same regardless of the age of the capital with which it works (although *average* productivity will be higher with newer capital). In a one-sector model of this kind, each instant's output is divided between immediate consumption and investment in latest vintage capital with a one-to-one marginal rate of transformation.

Two conclusions emerged from this sort of vintage model. First, embodiment does not affect the steady-state growth rate, which is still primarily determined by the rate of technological progress. Second, embodiment does increase the sensitivity of the steady-state level of output or productivity to the maintained rate of investment, but very modestly. The embodiment effect works because a larger investment quota leads to an eventual steady state in which the capital stock is on average younger and, therefore, more productive than before. (The mechanism is familiar from demography. A higher birth rate leads to a younger population.) But the effect on the average age of capital is fairly small, and thus, so is the response of productivity.

This connection between investment and productivity seemed so natural that I expected it would show up in many empirical applications.

But in fact it did not. The embodiment effect proved very difficult to detect, either non-existent or unimportant, and certainly more trouble some than it was worth. It played at best a minor role in the empirical analysis of productivity. One can think of reasons why that might be so. First, it might in fact be unimportant: I was told, for example, that innovations in chemical engineering were often planned to allow for the cheap retrofitting of old equipment. Second, since the embodiment effect works through the influence of current investment on the age distribution of equipment, it is bound to be slow and easily obscured in data. Finally, large sustained changes in the investment quota are rarely observed anyway. The embodiment idea never caught on; nearly all serious empirical work on growth models got along with unembodied technological change. (The one exception is that the ubiquitous cross-country growth regressions usually include the rate of investment as a right-hand-side (RHS) variable, and find that faster-growing countries invest more. But this regularity could arise in several ways, including reverse causation.)

Just recently the embodiment issue has been revived in a number of papers, and approached from a different angle. *See*, the paper by Greenwood, Hercowitz, and Krusell (1997) and the brief review article by Hercowitz (1998). Two recent working papers are Licandro, Ruiz-Castillo and Durán (2001) and Boucekkine, del Rio, and Licandro (2001). I am not going to review their approach, but instead look at its basis from my own, perhaps old-fashioned, point of view. In effect, I shall make a quick comparison of three models, one of which is my old version of 1960, and the other two are chosen for their transparency.

It is useful to imagine an economy with two sectors, one producing consumption goods and the other investment goods. Investment goods are produced from labour alone under constant returns, so $L_I = xI$, where L_I is the amount of labour allocated to the investment-goods sector. Investment goods do not change in productivity, so $C = F(K, L_C)$ and $dK/dt = I - aK$, a being the rate of depreciation; thus the cumulated stock of investment goods is used as an input in the consumption-goods sector, along with the rest of the labour. All the technological progress is concentrated in the *production* of investment goods. (This is reminiscent of the 1990s in the US, when dramatic gains in efficiency in the computer-producing industry was the main source of increasing productivity on the national scale.) So I shall set $x = x_0 e^{-mt}$.

It is easy to complete this model under competitive assumptions (with obvious modifications for imperfect competition). Thus

$p_I/p_C = xw/p_C$ and $w/p_C = F_L(K, N - L_I)$. This is already five equations in the six unknowns L_I, I, K, C, p_I/p_C, and w/p_C, taking N, the total supply of labour, as given. The sixth equation must come from the demand side; one convention in growth theory is to add a consumption function. There is room for much more sophistication here, but I shall choose the simplest linear case: $p_C C = b(p_C C + p_I I)$, which leads at once to $C = [b/(1 - b)]p_I I/p_C$. (It is easily checked that this nominal formulation is equivalent to making real consumption or real saving proportional to real income.)

Again for simplicity, I choose the Cobb-Douglas function for the consumption sector, so $C = K^b(N - L_I)^{1-b}$. Finally, for ease of notation, let $q = p_I/p_C$ and $v = w/p_C$, so that $q = xv$; the real wage and the relative price of investment goods are expressed in terms of consumption goods. We can also define the real GDP as $Y = C + qI$, again expressed in terms of consumption goods.

Let the labour force (N) grow exponentially at rate n. Then it is straightforward to calculate the steady-state growth rates of the endogenous variables C, I, K, q, v: they are, in order, $n + hm$, $n + m$, $n + m$, $-(1 - h)m$, and hm. This is clearly a model with embodiment; if there is no investment, there is no effective technological progress. The model also has the expected property that steady-state growth rates depend only on the demographic and technological parameters (n, m, h) and are independent of the investment quota $(1 - b)$. An interesting, but obvious, property of this model is that the price of investment goods *falls* relative to the price of consumption goods; this is empirically correct for the US economy, but I am not sure about other industrial countries. Keep in mind that a *constant-quality* price index is required here. In this model the quality of investment goods does not change, but their cost of production does. This observation will be more important later.

With a little more tedious calculation it is possible to solve this model explicitly. For example, steady-state GDP per worker (Y/N) grows exponentially at rate hm, with the level of the path (at $t = 0$) given by $(1 - h)A^{-h}/(1 - bh)$ where A is shorthand for $(1 - h)x_0(m + n + a)b/(1 - b)$. I do not think it is worth elaborating on these formulae. The model is too simple to be calibrated; it is designed to illustrate a point, not to describe the world.

The particular point that I have in mind will be clearer when I change the model slightly. In the first model, investment goods of unchanging quality are produced more and more efficiently by virtue of technological change. Now I want to allow the quality of capital goods to change, but I need a notion of quantity to go along with the quality. So I think of the investment good as 'a box'. It is produced by labour alone, and always one unit of labour produces one box (per unit time). But *capital-augmenting* technological change takes place in the şense that newer boxes are more productive than older ones, as inputs in the consumption-goods sector.

This can be represented in the following way. Let I be the output of boxes, and $L_I = I$. But now $dK/dt = y(t)I - aK$; that is to say, a box produced at time t acts like $y(t)$ standard boxes, and K is a stock of quality-adjusted capital goods. Then, as before, $C = F(K, L_C) = K^h L_C^{1-h}$ in the Cobb-Douglas case. Under competition the nominal price of a box on legs equals the nominal wage, so $p_I = w$, and $v = w/p_C = F_L = q = p_I/p_C$. But now we have to distinguish between the price of a box and the price of a quality-adjusted box. The latter is $p_I' = p_I/y = w/y$, so in the obvious notation $q' = q/y = v/y$. The symmetry with the first model is clearer if we write $J = yI$ for quality-adjusted investment and observe that $L_I = J/y$ and p_J is just what a moment ago I called $p_I' = w/y$. Now it can be checked directly that Model One *becomes* Model Two if I is replaced by J, q by q', and x by $1/y$. So all the calculations made for Model One can be carried over to Model Two with a change of notation.

The steady-state behaviour of this model is therefore exactly like the first model with $1/y$ playing the role of x, and q' playing the role of q. In this second version, a time series for p_J or for q' is all that is needed to reveal the course of (embodied) technological progress. Near steady state, it would be very hard to distinguish between the two models. Of course, in historical time we know by direct observation what is actually happening. We know, for instance, that the real price of a unit of computer power has been falling like a stone, and that the 'boxes' are of higher and higher quality.

At first I thought it odd that these two, 'physically' rather different ways of describing technological progress should produce essentially the same model. The underlying intuition may be essentially classical: if investment is a process of transforming labour into productive capacity, it may not matter whether technological progress allows the making of unchanged capital goods with less labour or the making of more productive capital goods with unchanged labour. Either way, the effectiveness of labour is enhanced as a source of productive capacity.

These two-sector models can be compared with the one-sector model of 1958 (published in 1960). Because the consumption and investment goods are identical in the latter, it would be artificial to try to model a cost reduction limited strictly to the investment goods; $p_I/p_C = 1$ always. So Model Two is the relevant comparison. In the one-sector vintage model I introduced a new concept that I shall call H. (It was J in the original paper.) H is a quality-adjusted capital stock; it is a weighted sum of past values of I, where the weight on I_v is $e^{mv}e^{-a(t-v)}$; the first factor corresponds to $y(v)$ and the second is depreciation. Thus $H(t) = \int I(v)e^{(m + a)v-at}dv$, with the integral extending in principle over vintages from $-\infty$ to t. So $dH/dt = e^{mt}I(t) - aH$. The parallel to Model Two is quite exact. We could get evidence about the rate of capital-embodied technological progress by looking at a price index for *quality-adjusted* capital goods relative to consumer goods.

In reality there is both technological progress in the production of capital goods and capital-embodied (and unembodied) technological progress in the use of capital goods in the consumption sector (and in the investment sector, for that matter). A more general two-sector model would be complicated; but clearly the relative price of capital goods would fall for both reasons. Boxes are produced more cheaply, and the price of a box has to be adjusted down to account for improved quality. The computer is the obvious contemporary example, but the automobile was once the paradigmatic case.

An advantage of this formulation is that it clarifies the theoretical role of q or q' (the price of capital goods relative to consumer goods) as an aggregative indicator of the rate of technological progress. A closely related advantage is that, whereas in the past we have had to infer—or fail to infer—the presence and significance of capital-embodied technological change indirectly from aggregate data, we now have available a more direct approach through the calculation of q or q/q'. More direct, but not necessarily easy: the path from q to q' through a process of quality adjustment is a major undertaking. For the US, we have the monumental individual effort by R.J. Gordon (1990). More recently, the spectacular evolution of the computer has forced the Bureau of Labour Statistics into the tricky business of constructing hedonic price indexes for selected items in the Consumer Price Index. We must hope for the continuation and extension of this project. This is certainly a case where it is better to be roughly right than to be precisely wrong. So far as I know, Europe has made little progress in this direction, but perhaps, I am merely out of touch.

A third possible advantage of the approach I have been sketching has not yet been the object of serious research. It should be possible in this framework to get a better empirical evaluation of the elasticity of steady-state output with respect to the rate of investment and saving. A reliable rule of thumb would be an indispensable reference point for the making of reasonable medium- and long-run macro-policy. This is both a theoretical and an empirical task. Even at a very high level of aggregation it requires more complex and flexible models than those used here, together with extension and continuation of quality adjustment and hedonic pricing as an important part of national income accounting.

The broad picture for the US is striking, to say the least. Think of q as being the price of equipment (i.e., excluding structures) relative to the price of non-durable consumer goods. Then, from 1969–9, q falls quite steadily at just under 2 per cent per year, as reported by the Bureau of Economic Analysis (the agency responsible for the National Income and Product Accounts). The rate of decline actually speeds up towards the end of the period. The similarly-deflated price of durable consumer goods follows a roughly parallel path. I do not know how much quality adjustment or hedonic pricing is already embedded in these data. Robert Gordon's explicitly quality-adjusted series, which ends before 1990, falls at about 4 per cent a year. It is certainly possible that the accelerated fall in the last decade of the BEA series represents increased coverage of hedonic pricing. In that case, one might consider the working hypothesis that q' has been falling in the US at about 4 per cent a year for the past forty years. If we put the Cobb-Douglas parameter h at its conventional value of 0.3–0.4, we can account in this way for growth of total factor productivity of something like 1.3 per cent per year, which would be a large fraction of what has been measured in more conventional ways.

I shall mention one other remarkable observation: according to Greenwood and Jovanovic (2001), interpretation of technological progress along these lines shows no sign of the usual slowdown after 1973. This question deserves analysis and explanation. I do not know if it is relevant that the slowdown in conventionally calculated total factor productivity in US manufacturing is less pronounced than in other parts of the economy, but this is worth exploring.

An interesting question is whether the pattern observed in the US is duplicated in other industrial economies. I have looked casually at data for the European Union. At least from 1990 on, the producer price index for investment goods has risen more slowly than that for non-durable consumer goods, but the difference is slightly less than one per cent per year. The European price series are probably not quality-adjusted, at least not as fully as the American. So the equivalent of q' may be decreasing noticeably. It would be useful to piece together comparable price series for a considerably longer time interval, so that a meaningful comparison can be made.

It is too soon to ask if this revival of the embodiment model leads to new conclusions about the supply-side effects of investment on aggregate output and productivity. One can hope that further research will narrow down the possibilities. Methodological implications are cheaper, and I shall suggest two. Ideas with a strong appeal to common sense should not be abandoned easily. And economists should never limit arbitrarily the kind of evidence they are willing to consider.

REFERENCES

BOUCEKKINE, R., F. DEL RIO, and O. LICANDRO, (2001), 'Obsolescence and Modernization in the Growth Process', European University Institute Working Paper No. 2001/18.

GORDON, ROBERT J., (1990), *The Measurement of Durable Goods Prices*, Chicago: University of Chicago Press.

GREENWOOD, J. and B. JOVANOVIC, (2001), 'Accounting for Growth', in C. Hulten, E. Dean, and M. Harper (eds), *New Developments in Productivity Analysis*, Chicago: University of Chicago Press, pp. 179–224.

GREENWOOD, J., Z. HERCOWITZ, and P. KRUSELL, (1997), 'Long-run Implications of Investment-Specific Technological Change', *American Economic Review*, 87, Stanford, pp. 342–62.

HERCOWITZ, Z., (1998), 'The Embodiment Controversy: A Review Essay', *Journal of Monetary Economics*, 41, pp. 217–24.

LICANDRO, O., J. RUIZ-CASTILLO, and J. DURÁN, (2001), 'The Measurement of Growth under Embodied Technical Change', European University Institute Working Paper No. 2001/14.

SOLOW, R., (1960), 'Investment and Technical Progress', in K. Arrow, S. Karlin, and P. Suyppes (eds), (1959), *Mathematical Methods in the Social Sciences*, Stanford: Stanford University Press, pp. 89–104.

2. The Bose Model and National Income

MARTIN L. WEITZMAN

In 1966, Sanjit Bose published the first optimal-growth version of the famous Fel'dman–Mahalanobis model. In a pioneering application of the maximum principle, Bose showed how the consumption- and investment-goods sectors of an economy should optimally be developed over time. Essentially, the optimal growth trajectory consists of two phases. In phase one, investment goods go to increase the capacity of whichever sector is 'under-balanced' relative to the other. In phase two, which begins as soon as balance has been achieved between the two sectors, balanced growth is thereafter maintained by allocating new investment goods to the two sectors in proportions that maintain the balance.

In this paper, I seek to redo an especially simple version of the 'Bose model' in order to emphasize the connection with a basic conceptual issue of national income accounting. For reasons that will become apparent, the Bose model is an ideal construct for examining the fundamental question 'what is income?'.

Let us first solve a one-sector growth model for a situation where homogeneous aggregate output is linearly proportional to aggregate capital (with output/capital coefficient a) and utility is a logarithmic function of consumption. Then we seek to pose and solve a natural two-sector generalization of the same problem, which is a special form of the model Bose solved in 1966.

We write the one-sector version here as being the optimal control problem to

$$\text{maximize } \int_0^\infty U(C(t))\, e^{-\rho t}\, dt \tag{2.1}$$

subject to

$$C(t) + I(t) = aK(t), \tag{2.2}$$

and

$$\dot{K}(t) = I(t), \tag{2.3}$$

and with the given initial condition

$$K(0) = K_0, \tag{2.4}$$

where the utility function is of the logarithmic from

$$U(C) = \log(C). \tag{2.5}$$

The 'net savings rate' at time t for the above model is defined as

$$s(t) \equiv \frac{I(t)}{C(t) + I(t)}. \tag{2.6}$$

As is well known, we can completely characterize the solution to (2.1)–(2.6) as being to follow a policy of saving always at the constant rate

$$s^* = \frac{a - \rho}{a}, \tag{2.7}$$

which corresponds to having every part of the economy grow exponentially at the constant rate $g^* = a - \rho$.

The non-shiftable-capital model we shall analyse here consists of two sectors: the consumption-goods sector (Department 2), and the investment-goods sector (Department 1). We make the plausible assumption that at any given instant of time the productive capacity of each sector is quasi-fixed and non-shiftable, but that over time the proportions can be continuously altered by directing *new* investments to one or the other of the two sectors. Such a description accords well with the familiar putty-clay nature of real-world investment. The cement and steel of the investment-goods sector are pliable general-purpose construction materials that can be used to increase the capacity of either sector until they are hardened into concrete shells and bolted-down specific machinery dedicated to producing either more consumption (bread bakeries, urban housing, and so forth) or more investment (steel mills, cement factories, and so forth), at which point the two types of capital are considered to be as if frozen in place and are no longer shiftable.

To make the one- and two-sector versions comparable here, we assume that the utility of consumption for both models is the same logarithmic function (2.5), and that the output/capital coefficient is the same value a in *both* sectors of the two-sector model (as well as for the single aggregated sector of the one-sector model). In his pioneering paper, Bose considered the more general case of an iso-elastic utility function and allowed capital to depreciate. The model we are considering here is thus a special case of the Bose model.

The simplest two-sector putty-clay analogue of the problem (2.1)–(2.6) is to

$$\text{maximize} \int_0^\infty U(C(t))\, e^{-\rho t}\, dt \tag{2.8}$$

subject to

$$C(t) = aK_2(t), \tag{2.9}$$

$$I(t) = aK_1(t), \tag{2.10}$$

and

$$\dot{K}_1(t) = I_1(t), \tag{2.11}$$

$$\dot{K}_2(t) = I_2(t), \tag{2.12}$$

and

$$I_1(t) + I_2(t) = I(t), \tag{2.13}$$

and

$$0 \le I_1(t) \le I(t), \tag{2.14}$$

$$0 \le I_2(t) \le I(t), \tag{2.15}$$

and with the given initial conditions

$$K_1(0) = K_0^1, \tag{2.16}$$

$$K_2(0) = K_0^2. \tag{2.17}$$

What is the relationship between the one-sector optimal growth model (2.1)–(2.6) and its two-sector putty-clay generalization (2.12)–(2.17)? To make both models tightly conformable, let us assume

$$K(0) = K_1(0) + K_2(0). \qquad (2.18)$$

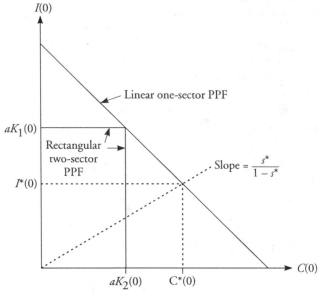

Figure 2.1: Shiftable versus Nonshiftable Capital
(PPF: production possibility frontier)

In Figure 2.1 is depicted the relationship between the two models when (2.18) holds. At time zero (now), the one-sector version has a straight-line production possibilities frontier with a slope of -1, and the decision maker is free to choose *any* non-negative values of $C(0)$ and $I(0)$ satisfying

$$C(0) + I(0) = aK(0). \qquad (2.19)$$

By contrast, the two-sector putty-clay version is 'stuck' at time zero with its historically inherited as-if-fixed-coefficient values of $C(0)$ and $I(0)$, which satisfy

$$C(0) = aK_2(0) \qquad (2.20)$$

and

$$I(0) = aK_1(0). \qquad (2.21)$$

Thus, the two-sector model here has a *rectangular*-shaped production possibilities frontier in Figure 2.1 [described by (2.20), (2.21)], while the one-sector aggregated version has a *line*-shaped production possibilities frontier in Figure 2.1 [described by (2.19)]. We know that the currently producible, historically given two-sector combination $(C(0), I(0)) = (aK_1(0), aK_2(0))$ is a point lying on the linear production possibilities frontier of the one-sector version. This *particular* point, however, need not represent an *optimal* combination of consumption and investment for the aggregate one-sector model. Imagine, though, that it *does*. Suppose, by pure coincidence, that the initial capital stocks of the two-sector model just so happen to satisfy the one-sector optimal savings condition, that is,

$$\frac{K_1(0)}{K_1(0) + K_2(0)} = s^*, \tag{2.22}$$

where s^* is given by (2.7).

Notice that the one-sector aggregate version always has more production possibility options than the two-sector putty-clay version because the rectangular production possibilities set represented by (2.20), (2.21) is contained within the corresponding linear production possibilities set represented by (2.18). Notice too that, when (2.22) holds initially, the two-sector putty-clay model can choose to 'imitate' exactly the optimal one-sector constant-saving policy by selecting $I_1(t)$ at all times $t \geq 0$ so that

$$\frac{I_1(t)}{I(t)} = s^*. \tag{2.23}$$

Therefore, it follows, if (2.22) holds then both the one- and two-sector models have the identical optimal consumption trajectory and the same optimal value of the objective function. The relevant Hamiltonian for the two-sector optimal control problem is

$$H = U(aK_2) + p_1 I_1 + p_2 I_2. \tag{2.24}$$

Even without getting deeply involved in the details of the maximum principle here, it is now possible to make an 'educated guess' about the form of an optimal policy. If condition (2.22) holds initially, the optimal two-sector policy is to maintain these same ideal capital stock proportions forever thereafter by always obeying (2.23). If condition (2.22) does *not* hold initially, an 'educated guess' here might be that the optimal two-sector investment policy is a *most rapid approach* to the ideal savings ratio of capital stocks, which satisfies

$$\frac{K_1(t)}{K_1(t) + K_2(t)} = s^*, \tag{2.25}$$

and then, once condition (2.24) has been attained, the optimal policy remains forever in a state where (2.24) holds by following thereafter investment policy (2.23). A formal proof of the optimality of such a most rapid approach to the 'ideal proportions' (2.24) hinges on showing that the conditions

$$\frac{K_1(t)}{K_1(t) + K_2(t)} < s^*, \quad p_1(t) > p_2(t), \quad I_1^*(t) = aK_1(t), \quad I_2^*(t) = 0 \tag{2.26}$$

and

$$\frac{K_1(t)}{K_1(t) + K_2(t)} > s^*, \quad p_1(t) < p_2(t), \quad I_1^*(t) = 0, \quad I_2^*(t) = aK_1(t) \tag{2.27}$$

are mutually consistent with the corresponding price-differential equations of motion

$$\dot{p}_1(t) = \rho p_1(t) - a \max\{p_1(t), p_2(t)\}, \tag{2.28a}$$

$$\dot{p}_2(t) = \rho p_2(t) - U'(aK_2(t)), \tag{2.28b}$$

and also with the appropriate transversality conditions

$$\lim_{t \to \infty} p_1(t) K_1(t) e^{-\rho t} = \lim_{t \to \infty} p_2(t) K_2(t) e^{-\rho t} = 0. \tag{2.29}$$

(We leave the formal proof as an exercise with the additional hint that if $t = T$ is the *first time* when condition (2.24) holds, $p_1(t) = p_2(t)$ for all $t \geq T$.)

Having employed the relatively simple device of the two-sector non-shiftable-capital dynamic problem (2.12)–(2.17) to indicate how the maximum principle may be used to clarify the relationship between one- and two-sector versions of an optimal growth problem, we now utilize this same apparatus to explore in a very tentative way some aspects of the concept of national income. Let us observe first what emerges when we attempt to apply a standard well-known income concept here to both of our model economies.

For the sake of argument, suppose we are at time zero in a state of the two-sector putty-clay model where the two capital stocks $K_1(0)$ and are $K_2(0)$ are 'ideally balanced' in the sense that (2.22) holds. Then we know that with initial conditions satisfying (2.18) and (2.22), the optimal trajectories of the one- and two-sector models are identical and both yield exactly the same dynamic welfare.

A well-known concept of income can perhaps be paraphrased as saying that income is 'the maximum amount that can presently be consumed without compromising future ability to consume at the same level'. I think this is a fair phrasing of a widespread notion of income that finds implicit expression throughout a broad range of contexts— from being a free translation of such populist public sources as the report on *Our Common Future* issued by the Bruntland Commission,[1] to being a transliteration of the financial/business concept of 'economic earnings',[2] to being a particular mutual strand of the conceptual apparatus used by three great economists who did fundamental theoretical work on the concept of income: Fisher, Lindahl, and Hicks.[3]

Irving Fisher (1930) was the first economist to note clearly that 'earnings' (what others would call 'income'—the headstrong Fisher had already appropriated the term 'income' for what others would call 'consumption') can fruitfully be conceptualized as a form of interest-like return paid on capital or wealth. Erik Lindahl (1933) argued cogently that the income of a period should be identified with the sum of consumption plus the net increase of capital value over the period. John Hicks (1946) introduced the modern idea, expressed in the definition of the previous paragraph, that income measures maximum present consumption subject to the sustainability-like condition of leaving intact future ability to consume at the same level. In the world of a Robinson Crusoe–like person whose single homogeneous capital good acts like a deposit in a bank account paying a constant interest rate, all three definitions (Fisher's 'income as interest on capital', Lindahl's 'income as consumption plus net capital increment', and Hicks's 'income as maximum sustainable consumption') coincide. But in almost any other world with even slightly more realistic complications, these three definitions generally differ, and it is not at all clear which one is better—or even, for what purposes it might be better. For the sake of

[1] World Commission on Environment and Development, 1987, p. 43, which defines 'sustainable development' as being 'development that meets the needs of the present without compromising the ability of future generations to meet their own needs'.

[2] *See*, Bodie, Kane, and Marcus, 2002, p. 611, who define 'economic earnings' as 'the sustainable cash flow that can be paid out to stockholders without impairing the productive capacity of the firm'.

[3] I hasten to add that several other concepts of income were also explored by them.

specificity, let us concentrate here on trying to apply the popular Hicksian concept ('the maximum amount that can presently be consumed without compromising future ability to consume at the same level') to this modified Bose model.

A glance at Figure 2.1 reveals that for the one-sector aggregate economy (with straight-line production possibilities), the Hicksian definition of income yields

$$aK(0), \tag{2.30}$$

while for the equivalent two-sector putty-clay version, the same definition of income gives

$$aK_2(0). \tag{2.31}$$

With conditions (2.22) and (2.25) holding, both economies are essentially equivalent, yet the *difference* in income (as defined above) between the one- and two-sector versions is

$$aK_1(0) = s^* aK(0). \tag{2.32}$$

Now, it should be apparent that something seems very puzzling about the fact that the above seemingly reasonable standard definition of income yields very different values for what are essentially identical economic situations. From Figure 2.1, the core problem here seems to be that such a definition of income effectively forces us to compare the hypothetical consumption-producing ability of economies in the region where net investment is zero (that is, where $s = 0$) even when we most emphatically prefer *not* to locate ourselves in such a region whenever $s^* > 0$.

'The maximum amount that can presently be consumed without compromising future ability to consume at the same level' might be a fine definition of income *if* we happen to *want* presently to be consuming at such a maximum sustainable rate in the sense that we *choose* $s^* = 0$. Otherwise, unfortunately, this definition of income depends artificially, and arbitrarily, on the elasticity of short-run substitution between the production of consumption and investment, which (at least in this example) is *not* related to the economy's ability to produce well-being over time. Such a definition, as Samuelson (1961) put it, essentially defines income as 'capacity to produce emergency consumption'—and this feature makes it quite idiosyncratically peculiar in any setting other than a situation where consumption and investment are infinitely substitutable. It seems natural enough to want income to be measuring some 'sustainable-like' property of 'present' and 'future' consumption possibilities; but this model is hinting very strongly that income should *not* be defined literally as the highest permanently maintainable level of consumption, and that a proper definition of income (if one exists) may have almost nothing to do with literal sustainability.

Without revealing all of the details, we merely state here what is the resolution of the seeming paradox, and which is the subject of a forthcoming book.

Let V represent the maximized value of the objective function (2.8) subject to the constraints (2.9)–(2.17). It is V that we are really interested in, because it is measuring welfare.

A natural definition of 'utility income' here is the Hamiltonian expression (2.24). The fundamental relationship between wealth or welfare and income is here

$$H = \rho V. \tag{2.33}$$

To make a long story short, it is (2.33) that gives the proper welfare underpinning for using here the natural definition of income H. The Hicksian parable is not literally true, but it is figuratively true. Although the constant utility income level H is not literally attainable, because the production possibilities frontier is a rectangle instead of a straight line, it has the same allegorical meaning as Hicks intended. Income H represents the *sustainable equivalent* or the *stationary equivalent* of the welfare that an optimal programme is actually able to deliver. That is to say, the present discounted utility of the optimal solution to the Bose model is exactly the same as the present discounted utility of the hypothetical constant utility level H. Because the relation (2.33) holds in a very broad class of economic models, this result is generic. To know H is to know V. Hamiltonian income is the return on wealth (or welfare).

REFERENCES

BODIE, Z., A. KANE, and A.J. MARCUS, (2002), *Investments*, 5th ed., New York: McGraw-Hill, Irwin.

BOSE, S., (1968), 'Optimal Growth and Investment Allocation', *Review of Economic Studies*, 35, no 4, pp. 465–80.

DASGUPTA, P.S., (1969), 'Optimal Growth when Capital is Non-Transferable', *Review of Economic Studies*, 36, January, pp. 77–88.

DOMAR, E.D., (1957), 'A Soviet Model of Growth', in E.D. Domar, *Essays in the Theory of Economic Growth*, New York: Oxford University Press.

FEL'DMAN, G.A., (1928), 'On the Theory of Growth Rates of National Income', *Planovoe Khoziaistovo*, translated in N. Spulber (ed.), (1964), *Foundations of Soviet Strategy for Economic Growth*, Bloomington, Indiana.

FISHER, I. (1930), *The Theory of Interest*, New York: Macmillan.

HICKS, J.R., (1946), *Value and Capital*, 2nd ed., Oxford: Oxford University Press.

LINDAHL, E., (1933), 'The Concept of Income', in G. Bagge (ed.), *Economic Essays in Honor of Gustaf Cassel*, London: George Allen and Unwin.

MAHALANOBIS, P.C., (1953), 'Some Observations on the Process of Growth of National Income', *Sankhya*, 12, Part 4, pp. 307–12.

SAMUELSON, P.A., (1961), 'The evaluation of "social income": Capital formation and wealth', in F.A. Lutz and D.C. Hague (eds), *The Theory of Capital*, New York: St. Martin's Press.

WEITZMAN, M.L., (1971), 'Shiftable Versus Non-Shiftable Capital: a Synthesis', *Econometrica*, 39, pp. 511–29.

——, (2003), *Income, Wealth, and the Maximum Principle*, Cambridge, Massachusettes: Harvard University Press.

3. A Keynesian Model of Endogenous Growth with Some Classical Features

Amit Bhaduri

NEOCLASSICAL GROWTH THEORY: AN ASSESSMENT

The aim of this paper is to develop a model of endogenous economic growth, by rectifying two serious defects which seem generic to the entire intellectual tradition of neoclassical growth models initiated by Solow (1956) and Swan (1956). First, as Solow (1970) himself had recognized, this framework ignores the Keynesian problem of effective demand, by assuming a version of Say's Law in which the full employment level of saving is automatically reinvested in each period. Thus, while full employment is maintained, no separation between saving and investment decision is permitted. In Solow's own words, one tends 'to be neoclassical in the long run and Keynesian in the short run' (Solow 2000: 352). Since the problem posed originally by Harrod (1939) about the problem of the equality between the 'actual' and the 'warranted' rate of growth hinges on the Keynesian distinction between investment and saving decision, it cannot be discussed meaningfully in this scheme of analysis.

Sanjit Bose was, and still remains one of my closest friends from our college days. He might be surprised to learn that he was the first one to teach me how to think independently about economic problems without taking conventional wisdom too seriously. This is a small tribute to a friend, and an independent mind.

Subsequent models of economic growth became formally more sophisticated by introducing the assumption of a single representative household, endowed with perfect foresight over infinite life (Koopmans 1965; Cass 1965), in which the saving behaviour is derived as the optimum choice between present and future consumption (and perhaps leisure). Although posited originally as a normative planning problem of optimum saving (Ramsey 1928), it began to be treated increasingly as identical with descriptive saving behaviour by households in a market economy. Thus, not only was the separation of investment from saving decision obliterated, but even the distinction between normative and descriptive growth models disappeared. Similarly, while the overlapping generation model (Samuelson 1958) might be argued to provide a more plausible description of the saving behaviour of the households, its integration with growth theory came to be achieved by returning to the pre-Keynesian world governed by Say's Law, where all markets always clear, facing no problem of effective demand (Diamond 1965).

The *second* major defect of neoclassical growth models is their dependence on the concept of an aggregate production function in terms of which the analysis is usually conducted. It should have been understood and accepted by now that this concept is logically indefensible outside a one-commodity world due to capital-theoretic problems (Robinson 1956; Sraffa 1960; Samuelson 1966; Pasinetti 2000). Although Swan (1956) had recognized this problem explicitly, it has subsequently been ignored, except in passing references (for example, Lucas 1988; Malinvaud 1993). Nevertheless, the logical limitation of a framework which cannot be extended beyond the one-commodity world is simply far too glaring to ignore.

These two serious defects of neoclassical growth analysis tend to reinforce one another. In a one-commodity world, where the same good serves the purpose of saving as well as investment, it is easy to slip into a habit of thinking in which these two decisions are identical. Thus, in the popular Solow–Swan framework, with all the saving of the economy automatically reinvested in each period, the stock of capital grows from the supply side. When the capital stock accumulates faster than labour, the capital–labour ratio also rises through substitution between capital and labour. Under the assumption of constant returns to scale, the marginal product of capital falls, and this process continues until capital grows at the same steady rate as that of labour to keep the capital–labour ratio, and consequently, the marginal product of capital constant along a long-run steady-state growth path, dictated by an exogenously specified growth rate of labour. A higher (or lower) savings ratio has merely transitory impact, in so far it raises (or lowers) the capital-labour ratio and output per worker out of the steady state; but it cannot influence the steady-state rate of growth itself, which is determined entirely by the exogenously given rate of growth of the labour force, either in natural units, or in efficiency units of labour with (Harrod-neutral) technical progress. Despite capital being a reproducible factor of production, this scheme may be said to have reinvented the Ricardian stationary state as a long-run steady-state rate of growth, in which diminishing returns to capital plays a crucial role, similar to Ricardian land, in guiding the economy to its ultimate fate.

The view that economies tend to converge to their predetermined, long-run growth rates dictated entirely by their exogenous growth rates of labour seems questionable, especially because it implies that the long-run growth rates are immune to variations in the investment and saving rate. Consequently, an escape route is sought. Unsurprisingly, attention is focussed in the neoclassical scheme on finding a way for the marginal productivity of capital from falling in the course of rising capital–labour ratio through accumulation. Perhaps, the most obvious candidate is endogenous technical progress, generated continuously by the process of economic growth itself. This is an old idea. Adam Smith (1776, Book 1: Chs 1–3), and even before him Willam Petty (1662 [1963]: 471–2) had recognized that the reduction in unit production cost through the division of labour on the one hand, and the extension of the size of the market on the other, set in motion an interactive process which drives economic growth. Later writers like Marshall (1890 [1920]: Appendix H), Young (1928) and Kaldor (1985) tried to recapture this idea as an endogenously driven process of industrial growth through 'dynamic increasing returns to scale', in contrast to static economies of scale (especially emphasized by Babbage [1832]).

Ignoring capital-theoretic objections to the validity of any aggregate measure of 'capital' as a factor of production, modern neoclassical growth theory tries to reach a similar objective by compounding the problem! It introduces yet another accumulable stock as an additional argument in the aggregate production function—the intangible intellectual stock of knowledge of a society which accumulates along with the physical stock of capital over time. Frequently described as 'human capital', it is similar to the tangible, physical stock of capital in every respect, except for its public goods characteristics of at least partial non-excludability and non-rivalry. This makes the regime of intellectual property rights imperfect; individual firms generating technical knowledge cannot appropriate all the benefits of innovation by excluding rivals altogether. Benefits that are external to individual firms as spillover of knowledge arise. Therefore, even in a competitive set-up, each firm tends to underestimate the social benefit of generating knowledge, and private investment in research and development falls short of its socially optimal level. Thus, this result hinges on human capital as public good being differentiated from physical capital as private good.

Although the specific mechanics may differ from model to model, most endogenous growth models using the notion of human capital require very special assumptions for constructing a composite stock of capital, consisting of both the tangible, physical and the intangible, intellectual component. The typical assumption is that the accumulation of human capital occurs *exclusively* through the accumulation of physical capital requiring no direct assistance from labour. In effect, this assumption makes human capital a function only of physical capital; and the stock of composite capital, consisting both of the physical and the intellectual component, becomes reducible to some measure of physical capital alone (Arrow 1962; Frankel 1962; Romer 1986; Barro and Sala-i-Martin, 1995). Assuming that the intellectual component of composite capital has rising, but its physical component has falling marginal productivity, their relative strengths determine whether the marginal productivity of successive doses of composite capital falls, as in the traditional Solow–Swan or Arrow's model; stays constant, resembling the Harrod–Domar model of constant marginal capital–output ratio; or even rises in the course of accumulation. In the last case, however, unless the rising marginal product of capital is bounded sufficiently from above (Romer, 1986), runaway growth might occur through the indefinitely rising marginal product of composite capital.

Attempts at relaxing the extreme assumption that human capital is a function exclusively of physical capital have not been particularly successful. The models constructed along these lines so far have required going to the other extreme, by assuming that the accumulation of human capital (Uzawa 1965; Lucas 1988) or, of 'new designs' (Romer 1990) is feasible only by means of human capital or old designs, that is, again requiring no assistance directly from raw labour or physical capital. This case would make the growth of human capital or designs self-reproducing in a sense similar to Sraffa's 'basic' commodity separable from the production of output in the rest of the economy. It becomes formally analogous to the old-fashioned Hicks-neutral technical progress with the same consequence that the long-run growth rate of output also becomes semi-exogenous, that is, dependent on the self-reproducing growth rate of human capital.

AN ALTERNATIVE APPROACH TO ENDOGENOUS GROWTH

The present paper takes a radically different approach to the problem of endogenous growth. It is based essentially on a Keynesian interpretation of Adam Smith's vision (Smith 1776, Book 1: Ch. 3) that, the extent of division of labour is limited by the size of the market. It is also similar to the Young–Kaldor tradition, with the important difference that the dubious concept of a measurable stock of capital as a factor of production, physical or human, is avoided in our formulation. On the other hand, effective demand as the critical factor in determining the size of the market plays a central role to make the interplay between an expanding market size and increasing division of labour the propelling force, endogenously driving economic growth.

A simple index of the extent of division of labour is output per worker, or simply productivity. Smith had taken it for granted that, higher productivity, resulting in more surplus per worker at a given wage rate, would get automatically reinvested through competition among the capitalists themselves. The higher investment, in turn, would lead to further division of labour, setting in motion a self-reinforcing dynamic process. Or, as Young (1928: 533) put it, this 'amounts to the theorem that the division of labour depends in large part upon the division of labour'.

With Keynesian hindsight, the flaw in this argument is easy to detect. Like in modern neoclassical growth theory, saving is treated as identical with investment by Smith, as in Say's Law. Or, to emphasize the same flaw differently, higher saving per worker need not entail higher *total* saving; because the latter depends also on the level of employment, which is determined, in turn, by the level of effective demand through independent investment decisions, and the resulting multiplier mechanism.

We capture the Smithian self-reinforcing mechanism of division of labour sketched above by letting both saving (S) and investment (I) depend on the level of output (Y), as well as on labour productivity (x).

Definitionally,

$$x = Y/L \qquad (3.1)$$

implying,

$$g_x = g_Y - g_L \qquad (3.2)$$

where g_j = rate of growth of variable j, and L is the amount of labour. However, unlike in the case of Smith or, of later neoclassical growth theorists, investment needs to be distinguished from saving in a Keynesian manner by means of separate functions, but with identical arguments, that is

$$I = I(Y, x),\ I_Y > 0,\ I_x > 0 \qquad (3.3)$$

and,

$$S = S(Y, x),\ S_Y > 0,\ S_x \text{ is unsigned} \qquad (3.4)$$

with subscripts denoting partial derivatives. Note that, in (3.4) saving might be assumed to respond positively to labour productivity on the Smithian assumption that the wage rate remains constant, or at least rises at a slower rate than productivity to distribute productivity gains more in favour of profit, while saving out of profit is also assumed to be higher than that of wages (Kaldor 1956 and Pasinetti 1962, for implications). When all income categories have the same saving propensity, as in Solow's and Swan's original models, $S_x = 0$, because technical change through income distribution does not affect saving by assumption.

Note that variables Y and x are not independent, but related through (3.1), so that, $x_Y = (1/L)$ and, $X_L = -(Y/L^2)$. Using these in the total differentiation of (3.3) with respect to time, and simplifying with the aid of (3.2), we obtain

$$g_I = a g_Y + p.g_x,\ a > 0,\ p > 0 \qquad (3.5)$$

and similarly, from (3.4)

$$g_S = b g_Y + q.g_x,\ b > 0,\ q > 0 \qquad (3.6)$$

where, a, p, b, and q are the relevant partial elasticities of investment and saving with respect to output and productivity respectively, that is,

$$a = (Y.I_Y / I),\ p = (x.I_x / I),\ b = (Y.S_Y / S) \text{ and } q = (x.S_x / S).$$

Starting with initial investment–saving equality, along a steady-state growth path, the growth rates of investment and saving must equal in order to clear continuously the commodity market to yield a dynamic version of Hicks's (1937) IS-curve in the output–productivity plane. This yields from (3.5) and (3.6), a Keynesian adjustment equation for income growth through aggregate demand as,

$$\dot{g}_Y = \alpha(g_I - g_S) = \alpha[-(b-a)g_Y + (p-q)g_x], \quad \alpha > 0 \qquad (3.7)$$

The Keynesian demand-determined model developed so far shows how the trend growth rate in output adjusts through saving-investment equality captured by (3.7). In conjunction with the definitional equation (3.2), the model has three trend rates, g_Y, g_x, and g_L and the equilibrium value of g_Y^* at $\dot{g}_Y = 0$ in (3.7) and (3.2). This provides the essential degree of freedom needed for the growth rate to be determined endogenously through further determining the behaviour of productivity or employment growth. Thus, if the condition for full employment is imposed, as in standard neoclassical models, we would close that degree of freedom directly. Although very different in economic conception of the labour market from the neoclassics, the Marxian idea of labour-saving technical progress as the driving force for maintaining a 'reserve army of labour' offers a convenient reference point for formal comparison with the neoclassical models.

Assume that a constant fraction of the labour force is maintained as the reserve army through adjustments in labour productivity, while the labour force grows at an exponential rate, n. This yields the adjustment equation for labour productivity as,

$$\dot{g}_x = \beta(g_L - n) = \beta[g_Y - g_x - n], \quad \beta > 0 \qquad (3.8)$$

where n = the natural rate of growth of labour force (*see*, however, Marglin [1984], which makes a plausible case against this standard assumption).

The equilibrium rate of growth of income is given from (3.2), (3.7), and (3.8) as,

$$g_Y^* = [n.(p-q)/\{(p-q)-(b-a)\}] \qquad (3.9)$$

Comparing (3.9) with the neoclassical growth models, it is clear that the long-run steady-state growth, g_Y^*, depends not only on the exogenous growth rate of the labour force (n), but also on the saving and investment behaviour of the economy due to the Keynesian influence of aggregate demand on long-run growth.

The stability of the system, given by (3.7) and (3.8), requires that the relevant Jacobian has a negative trace (T), and a positive determinant

(D), that is,

$$T = - [\alpha (b - a) + \beta], \quad T < 0 \tag{3.10}$$

and,

$$D = \alpha\beta [(b - a) - (p - q)], \quad D > 0 \tag{3.11}$$

The condition for a positive determinant in (3.11) requires the denominator of (3.9) to be negative. Therefore, positive long-run growth g_Y^* is possible only if

$$(p - q) < 0 \tag{3.12}$$

Technical progress, when it has the Marxian labour-saving bias of holding down the real wage rate through the continuous recreation of a reserve army of labour, would tend to redistribute income in favour of profit against wage. Under classical assumptions regarding the savings behaviour, total saving would respond positively to higher productivity achieved through labour-saving technical progress, because more is saved out of profit than out of wage, that is,

$$S_x > 0, \quad \text{implying } q > 0 \tag{3.13}$$

Thus, given $p > 0$ from (3.3) and (3.7) it follows that the positive response of saving in this case of labour-saving technical progress has to be stronger than that of investment to satisfy condition (3.12). On the other hand, if technical progress and savings behaviour are such that $q < 0$ (for example, labour-using technical progress raising wage share coupled with classical savings function), or $q = 0$ because the saving propensity is uniform across the classes (as in the Solow–Swan model) so that, any bias in technical change does not impact on saving, condition (3.12) would fail to be satisfied. In other words, long-run steady-state growth with a stable configuration of *positive* growth rates in employment and output is possible only if technical progress has a labour-saving bias in this scheme of Keynesian income adjustment according to effective demand (3.7) combined with Marxian productivity adjustment ensuring that a constant fraction of the labour force remains persistently unemployed as the reserve army of labour (3.8).

Moreover, since the equilibrium configuration of output and productivity growth is given from (3.7) as,

$$g_x^* = [(a - b)/(p - q)]g_Y^* \tag{3.14}$$

positive productivity growth in equilibrium requires from (3.12) and (3.14),

$$(b - a) < 0. \tag{3.15}$$

Inequality (3.15) reverses the usual stability condition for the one-variable Keynesian income adjustment process which needs saving to be more responsive than investment to changes in income. Nevertheless, note that the determinant condition (3.11) imposes a similar restriction in an extended form in this two-variable case, in so far as it requires the response of saving to the combined effect of income and productivity change to exceed that of investment, i.e. $(b + q) > (a + p)$, from (3.11). Thus, a stable (that is, conditions 3.10 and 3.11) equilibrium configuration characterized by positive employment, output (3.9), and labour-saving (condition 3.13) productivity growth (3.14) would be satisfied sufficiently in view of (3.10), (3.11), (3.12), and (3.15), if the following set of inequality conditions were satisfied :

$$(\beta/\alpha) > (q-p) > (a-b) > 0. \tag{3.16}$$

This captures analytically some of the difficulties inherent in maintaining endogenously long-run, steady-state growth driven by Keynesian effective demand, while maintaining a constant rate of unemployment as the Marxian 'reserve army of labour'.

CONCLUDING OBSERVATIONS

Three concluding observations related to the preceding exercise in growth theory might be in order. First, the first generation neoclassical growth models in the tradition of Solow and Swan had the apparently 'paradoxical' result that the long-run growth rate is not influenced by saving and investment behaviour, but depends only on the exogenous, natural rate of growth of the labour force. However, this is simply because they threw away the baby of effective demand with the bath water of Harrod's knife-edge instability problem! Since, by assumption the problem of effective demand arising from investment being separated from saving decision is not allowed to play any role, it is hardly paradoxical that investment or saving behaviour fails to influence the long-run growth rate. Non-diminishing marginal product of 'capital' through endogenous technical progress was the tortuous route followed by the second generation of neoclassical growth models to recapture the influence of saving (and investment) decisions on the long-run growth rate. Yet, this is both unnecessary and theoretically misleading. In contrast, as our exercise shows, the long-run equilibrium growth rate in output, given by (3.9), is influenced by both saving and investment decisions. Moreover, under restrictions imposed by (3.16), which make the long-run steady-state growth rates in output, employment, and productivity positive and stable, it is easy to see (from 3.9 and 3.16) that the output growth rate would be *higher* than the growth rate of the labour force. Thus the natural rate of growth of the labour force sets the lower limit to the stable, long-run growth rate of output; and, within this limit saving and investment decisions do affect its magnitude (3.9).

Second, the endogeneity of technical progress, or rising labour productivity can be viewed from different angles in the context of growth theory. The current approach of neoclassical economics has been to treat it as accumulation of 'human capital' which occurs concomitantly with the accumulation of 'physical capital' in a precisely specified functional form; or, a production technology for knowledge generation which depends only on 'physical capital' or 'human capital'. Not only unconvincing descriptively, these approaches can also be faulted on capital-theoretic grounds. This paper merely hints at an alternative approach typical of the classical economists of very different persuasions like Smith and Marx (and also later, Schumpeter). For Smith, rising labour productivity achieved through increasing division of labour is limited at each stage by the size of the market (demand) on the one hand, but is also driven by the competition among the capitalists, on the other. For Marx, rising labour productivity is achieved through the introduction of labour-saving technical progress, designed to maintain a reserve army of labour in the conflict of class interests between capitalists and the workers. In this classical approach, intra- or inter-class competition and conflict are the central themes for the introduction and diffusion of technological progress. This is in contrast to the neoclassical approach in which attention is focussed mostly on the method by which technological knowledge is produced, but not the socio-economic context which drives its introduction and diffusion.

Finally, it should be emphasized that the present paper only illustrates how the Keynesian approach to effective demand as the determinant of the market size and output could be combined with one *particular* classical approach to endogenous technical progress, namely that of Marx. It remains a matter of future research as to how other classical approaches to endogenous technical progress and their elaborations through dynamic increasing returns may be incorporated into the Keynesian effective demand framework.

REFERENCES

ARROW, K., (1962), 'The Economic Implications of Learning by Doing', *Review of Economic Studies*, 29, pp. 155–73.

BABBAGE, C., (1832), *On the Economy of Machinery and Manufactures* (2nd edition), London: Chaveles Knight.

BARRO, R. and X. SALA-I-MARTIN, (1995), *Economic Growth*, New York: McGraw-Hill.

CASS, D., (1965), 'Optimal Growth in an Aggregative Model of Capital Accumulation', *Review of Economic Studies*, 32, pp. 233–40.

DIAMOND, P., (1965), 'National Debt in a Neoclassical Growth Model', *American Economic Review*, 55, pp. 1126–50.

FRANKEL, M., (1962), 'The Production Function in Allocation and Growth: A Synthesis', *American Economic Review*, 52, pp. 995–1002.

HARROD, R., (1939), 'An Essay in Dynamic Theory', *Economic Journal*, 49, pp. 14–33

HICKS, J.R., 1937, 'Mr. Keynes and the Classics : A Suggested Interpretation', *Econometrica*, 4, 5147–59.

KALDOR, N., (1956),. 'Alternative Theories of Distribution', *Review of Economic Studies*, 23, pp. 83–100.

_____, (1966), *Causes of the Slow Rate of Growth of the United Kingdom*, Cambridge: Cambridge University Press.

_____, (1985), *Economics without Equilibrium*, University College, Cardiff: Cardiff Press.

KOOPMANS, T. C., (1965), 'On the Concept of Optimal Economic Growth', *The Econometric Approach to Development Planning*, Amsterdam: North-Holland (for Pontificia Academy).

LUCAS, R., (1988), 'On the Mechanics of Economic Development', *Journal of Monetary Economics*, 22, pp. 3–42.

MALINVAUD, E., (1993), 'Regard d'un Ancien Sur les Nouvelles The'ories de la Croissance', *Revue Economique*, 44, pp. 171–88.

MARGLIN, S.A., (1984), *Growth, Distribution and Prices*, Cambridge, Massachusetts: Harvard University Press.

MARSHALL, A., (1890), *Principles of Economics*, 8th edition (1920). Reprint (1977), London: Macmillan.

PASINETTI, L., (1962), 'Rate of Profit and Income Distribution in Relation to the Rate of Economic Growth', *Review of Economic Studies*, 29, pp. 267–79.

_____, (2000), 'Critique of the Neoclassical Theory of Growth and Distribution', *Banca Nazionale del Lavoro Quarterly Review*, 53, pp. 383–432.

PETTY, W., (1662), *A Treatise on Taxes and Contributions*, in C.H. Hull (ed.), *The Economic Writings of Sir Willam Petty*, Cambridge: Cambridge University Press, (1899), revised, M. Kelly edition (1963), New York.

RAMSEY, F., (1928), 'A Mathematical Theory of Saving', *Economic Journal*, 38, pp. 543–99.

ROBINSON, J., (1956), *The Accumulation of Capital*, London: Macmillan.

Romer, P., (1986), 'Increasing Returns and Long Run Growth', *Journal of Political Economy*, 94, pp. 1002–37.

_____, (1990), 'Endogenous Technical Change', *Journal of Political Economy*, 98, pp. S 71–102.

SAMUELSON, P., (1958), 'An Exact Consumption-loan Model of Interest, With or Without the Social Contrivance of Money', *Journal of Political Economy*, 66, pp. 467–82.

_____, (1966), 'A Summing Up', *Quarterly Journal of Economics*, 80, pp. 568–83.

SCHUMPETER, J., (1961), *Theory of Economic Development*, New York: Oxford University Press.

SMITH, A., (1776), *An Inquiry into the Nature and Causes of the Wealth of Nations*, in R.H. Cambell, A.S. Skinner, and W.B. Todd (eds), *Works and Correspondence of Adam Smith*, Glasgow edition in two Vols, Oxford: Oxford University Press, 1976, Book I, Chapters 1–3.

SRAFFA, P., (1960), *Production of Commodities by Means of Commodities: Prelude to a Critique of Economic Theory*, Cambridge, UK: Cambridge University Press.

SOLOW, R., (1956), 'A Contribution to the Theory of Economic Growth', *Quarterly Journal of Economics*, 70, pp. 65–94.

_____, (1970), *Growth Theory: An Exposition*, Oxford: Calendron Press.

_____, (2000), 'The Neoclassical Theory of Growth and Distribution', *Banca Nazionale del Lavoro Quarterly Review*, 53, pp. 349–82.

SWAN, T., (1956), 'Economic Growth and Capital Accumulation', *Economic Record*, 32, pp. 343–61.

UZAWA, H., (1965), 'Optimal Technical Change in an Aggregate Model of Economic Growth', *International Economic Review*, 6, pp. 18–31.

YOUNG, A., (1928), 'Increasing Returns and Economic Progress', *Economic Journal*, 38, pp. 527–4.

4. Notes on Optimal Control Theory for the Neoclassical Model of Growth

Dipankar Dasgupta

INTRODUCTION

At the time Professor Sanjit Bose was using control theory techniques (Bose 1970, 1971), the acadmic profession had a serious interest in problems of optimal economic growth in centrally planned economies. The need to compute undominated growth paths led one to optimization methods for function spaces and control theory turned out to be the favoured choice of the majority. A great deal has changed since then. First, the world has witnessed the effective demise of planned systems. Second, in the context of optimization techniques for function spaces, the popularity of control theory amongst economists has waned to some extent with the rise of dynamic programming methods in discrete time.

Despite these events, control theory has not altogether lost its usefulness. There has been a recent revival of interest in these methods,

The pages that follow represent the outcome of my attempts to come to grips with the basic ideas underlying optimal control theory. I have often used these for teaching and, to that extent, owe a note of thanks to all students who suffered willy-nilly through my lectures. I am partcularly indebted, however, to Vidya Atal, Ranajoy Basu, Arpita Chatterjee, Sayan Datta, Kaushik Gangopadhyay, Raman Khaddaria, and Shubhashis Modak Chaudhury, six wonderful students who kept me going. Amongst fellow professionals, Amitava Bose, Pradip Maiti, and Sugata Marjit helped me generously as I struggled to learn. A more comprehensive treatment of the ideas discussed here may be found in Chapter 2, Dasgupta (2005).

particularly so with the arrival of endogenous growth theory in the mid-1980s. These models typically assume, like their neoclassical predecessors Cass (1965), Koopmans (1965) and Ramsey (1928), a dynastic macro household, or a social planner, choosing a consumption (hence, saving) plan by maximizing a welfare integral over an infinite time domain. The mathematical theory as well as the economic interpretations underlying optimal control methods (as applied to neoclassical growth models of the pre-endogenous genre) has been discussed by authors such as Arrow and Kurz (1970), Aghion and Howitt (1998), Barro and Sala-i-Martin (1995/1999), Cass (1965), Chiang (1992), Dixit (1990), Dorfman (1968), Intrilligator (1971), Kamien and Schwartz (2000) and others. Since the same principles carry over mutatis mutandis to the new growth models, students who wish to embark upon a study of modern growth theory have a large and readily available literature to fall back upon for an introduction to optimal control techniques.

The advantage, however, is weighed down by that fact that while many of these references contain lucid presentations of the basic tenets of control theory, none of them provides a complete treatment of the necessary and sufficient conditions characterizing *infinite* horizon optimal paths for the standard neoclassical model. To the best of our knowledge, Cass (1965) contains the most satisfactory *sufficiency* proof for the optimality of the infinite-horizon Solow (1956) path. A comparable development of the *necessary* conditions, however, is hard to come by. Arrow and Kurz (1970) and Kamien and Schwartz (2000) provide alternative necessity proofs for the finite-horizon problem. By comparison, their discussions of the infinite-horizon case are sketchy. The same observation holds for the other references quoted above.[1] A little investigation reveals on the other hand, that the full set of results is scattered about in the literature like pieces of a jigsaw puzzle, though no single source presents them in a comprehensive manner. Consequently, students uninitiated to the subject often find it difficult to put these together on thier own. In this connection, matters are complicated further by a famous counter-example due to Halkin (1974), which demonstrated that the infinite-horizon necessary condition describing the value of a co-state variable in the limit need not constitute a straightforward generalization of its finite-horizon counterpart.

---

[1] The seminal reference on the subject is Pontryagin et al. (1962), which contains a rigorous treatment of necessary conditions. However, the treatment there is not ideal as a first exposure to the problem. Also, the proofs in that work are not directly motivated by economic arguments.

A second lacuna in the literature lies in the economic interpretation accorded to the differential equation describing the evolution of the co-state variable(s) over time when investment is assumed to be irreversible. The general form of this equation (covering both reversible and irreversible investments) undergoes a change to account for the possibility of corner solutions. Cass (1965), once again, contains a clear statement of this condition (for a model without technical progress). The intuitive arguments underlying the Cass equation, however, are not readily available in the literature. Yet, this equation constitutes one of the main pillars of optimal control theory and it is important to clarify its economic content.

The purpose of these notes is to present the control-theoretic necessary and sufficient conditions for the optimal path associated with Solow model in the presence of exogenous technical progress.[2] This is done partly by collecting proofs and explanations from existing sources and partly by filling out the lacunae where they exist. The mathematics used to develop the conditions is mostly rigorous, though it does not go beyond the use of elementary calculus. Hopefully, this will enable students to obtain a quick grasp of control theory techniques without having to consult several references involving varying degrees of mathematical complexity. By deliberate choice, the treatment is restricted to the one-sector Solow model. This is mainly to ensure easy communication. The approach, however, is readily extendable to simple two-sector versions of the Solow exercise.

For expositional ease, the main body of these notes restricts attention to the case of reversible investment only and problems connected with irreversibility are relegated to the appendices. The second section is a description of the economic model. The third section presents an intuitive discussion of the necessary conditions for the existence of an optimal path in a centrally planned economy. The fourth section extends the discussion of the third section to the case of a private ownership system. This is followed by a comparison of the private and the planned economy optimality conditions in the last section. Appendices A4.1 and A4.2 discuss the material of the third section more rigorously and present a unified treatment of reversible and irreversible investment models. Appendix A4.3 generalizes Cass's (Cass 1965) result that the necessary conditions for an optimum are also

---

[2] We allow here for exogenous technical change alone, but it serves to highlight the alterations in earlier growth exercises that endogeneity will cause.

sufficient in the presence of technical progress for the existence of a unique optimum path for the infinite-horizon problem. Appendix A4.4 presents a proof of a vitally important result underlying the so-called transversality condition. The proof is a generalization of a theorem due to Koopmans (1965) to incorporate the case of technical progress. Finally, Appendix A4.5 produces a counter-example to the standard form of the transversality condition constructed by Halkin (1974) and indicates why it is inapplicable to the neoclassical growth model.

THE MODEL

The description of the economic model relies on Arrow and Kurz (1970), Cass (1965, 1966), Koopmans (1965), Ramsey (1928) and Solow (1956). Let us begin by summarizing the essential components of this model. It is standard practice nowadays to develop the model under two alternative assumptions about economic organization. The first assumes a single decision maker, say a planner, who allocates all resources at each point of time as well as across time. It does not recognize private claim to economic property. To the extent that the omnipotent planner is in a position to achieve all possible allocations of existing resources, he may attain the best one amongst these according to some criterion or the other (to be specified subsequently). We may refer to this set-up as a Command Economy and view it as a theoretical device for locating the best possible allocation of resources in a growing economy. The alternative to the Command Economy is the Private Economy where resources are privately owned and allocated by private incentive-driven forces. A large part of these forces assume the shape of competitive markets, though modern growth economics recognizes other market forms also. The scope of these notes, however, does not permit us to elaborate on these other market forms. The Private Economy will represent the way an economy is actually likely to function. It evolves over time through the interaction of the agents constituting it, namely, the households and the firms. As in most macro-models, we shall abstract completely from interactions between households alone or those between producers alone at any point of time. Consequently, we shall pretend that there is a single aggregative or representative household (H) and a single representative business firm (B) in the economy. The household increases in size over time and its rate of growth is captured by the equation

$$L(t) = L_0 e^{nt}, \tag{4.1}$$

where n is the exponential growth rate of the household size over time and $L(t)$ is the size of H at t. In what follows, $L(t)$ will be referred to as population at t.

Denoting the capital stock at t by $K(t)$, the economy faces an instantaneous constraint on consumption and capital accumulation or investment, $Z(t)$, given by

$$C(t) + Z(t) = Y(t), \tag{4.2}$$

where $Y(t)$ stands for the flow of output at t. The decision maker cannot borrow against future to enhance current expenditure. It is standard practice to refer to $Z(t)$ as gross investment. A fraction $\delta > 0$ of the capital stock depreciates through use per instant of time. Hence, $Z(t)$ leads to a *net* addition of

$$\dot{K}(t) = Z(t) - \delta K(t) \tag{4.3}$$

to the capital stock at each t. Accordingly, $\dot{K}(t)$ is referred to as net investment. Here (4.2) is rewritten as

$$C(t) + \dot{K}(t) = Y(t) - \delta K(t). \tag{4.4}$$

The technology for producing Y is represented by an aggregate production function

$$Y(t) = F(K(t), A(t)L(t)), \tag{4.5}$$

where $K(t)$ and $L(t)$ are the flows of capital and labour services entering the production process at t. Note that the use of the same notations for capital stock and services as well as for population size and labour services implies that the stock–flow ratios for both factors are assumed to be constants (normalized to unity). The coefficient $A(t)$ of $L(t)$ represents technological progress and satisfies

Assumption T $\dot{A}(t) / A(t) = \mu > 0$.

There are different ways in which the notion of technical progress may be formalized. The (4.5) in particular captures it by introducing a distinction between the apparent size of the labour force and its effective size. An improvement in work efficiency is tantamount to a reduction in the time taken to complete a given job. Alternatively, a worker finishes two jobs (say) as opposed to one during any fixed interval of time as her/his efficiency improves. Consequently, from the point of view of work performed, the efficient worker may be treated as two less efficient ones. Viewed this way, technical progress is referred to as factor augmenting. Assumption T says that the labour force is effectively augmented at the rate μ on account of a rise in work efficiency generated by technological change.[3]

Henceforth, particular values attained by variables at a point of time such as t_0 will be represented by C_{t_0}, K_{t_0}, etc. Nonetheless, the time index will often be dropped to achieve notational simplicity, unless essential for the argument. The function $F(.,.)$ satisfies the standard neoclassical properties, namely,

Assumption $PF - 1$: $F(.,.)$ is continuous and differentiable. $F(0, AL) = 0 = F(K, 0)$, and F displays constant returns to scale in K and AL.

Assumption $PF - 2$: $F_1 > 0$, $F_2 > 0$, $F_{11} < 0$, $F_{22} < 0$.

The assumptions $F_{11} < 0$ and $F_{22} < 0$ imply the law of diminishing returns. In a static environment, the assumption predicts diminishing marginal product of a factor as increasing doses of the factor are combined with constant quantities of the other factor. For a growing economy, however, the factor services K and AL would be increasing simultaneously. In this case, what diminishing returns imply is that the marginal product of capital (say) will rise if AL grows faster than K. In particular, a faster growth in A relative to that in K (as of given L) causes the marginal product of K to increase. In other words, it is the direction of change in K/AL that will determine how marginal products of factors respond to improvements in the size of labour-augmenting technical change.

Henceforth, we shall denote per capita variables by the corresponding small letters. Thus, $y = Y/L$, $c = C/L$, $k = K/L$ and $z = Z/L$. Also, it will be usefull to rewrite (4.5) in terms of quantities per unit of *effective labour* (i.e., AL). Thus, denoting Y/AL and K/AL by $\hat{y}$ and $\hat{k}$ respectively and using Assumption $PF - 1$, we obtain

$$\hat{y} = F(\hat{k}, 1) = f(\hat{k}), f(0) = 0, \; f \text{ is continuous and differentiable.}$$
$$(4.6)$$

Assumption $PF - 2$ implies

Property $f1$: f is a strictly concave function with $f'(\hat{k}) > 0$.

---

[3] For a useful introduction to the nature of technical change, *see* Burmeister and Dobell (1970), Chapter 3. Neoclassical growth theory has undergone significant changes since the writing of that book. Nonetheless, its discussion continues to be useful. *See* Barro and Sala-i-Martin (2004), Chapter 1, Appendix.

In addition to Assumption $PF-1$ and $PF-2$, we shall impose Assumption $f2$: $f'(\hat{k}) \to \infty$ as $\hat{k} \to 0$ and $f'(\hat{k}) \to 0$ as $\hat{k} \to \infty$.

It is easy to verify (using the assumption of constant returns to scale) that $\partial F/\partial K = f'(\hat{k})$ and $\partial F/\partial AL = f(\hat{k}) - \hat{k}f'(\hat{k})$. Thus, Assumption $f2$ means that the marginal product of capital increases without bound as capital becomes indefinitely scarce relative to the factor AL. On the other hand, using Euler's theorem, we see that

$$\frac{\hat{k}f'(\hat{k})}{\hat{y}} + \frac{f(\hat{k}) - \hat{k}f'(\hat{k})}{\hat{y}} = 1.$$

This means that $0 \le (f(\hat{k}) - \hat{k}f'(\hat{k}))/\hat{y} = 1 - \hat{k}f'(\hat{k})/\hat{y} \le 1$. Hence, $\partial F/\partial AL = f(\hat{k}) - \hat{k}f'(\hat{k}) = f(\hat{k})\{1 - \hat{k}f'(\hat{k})/\hat{y}\} \to 0$ as $\hat{k} \to 0$. In other words, as $\hat{k} \to 0$, the marignal product of effective labour turns indefinitely small. Put differently, the marginal product of capital rises and that of effective labour falls boundlessly as K *relative to AL* becomes indefinitely scarce (irrespective of the *absolute* values of K and AL).

Assumption $f2$ is referred to as an Inada condition and constitutes a regularity requirement. It guarantees that the model has mathematically meaningful solutions.

Using (4.5), we rewrite (4.2) as

$$C(t) + Z(t) = F(K(t), A_t L_t). \tag{4.7}$$

At each t, this equation can be viewed as the transformation frontier between $C(t)$ and $Z(t)$, given $K(t)$. Deflating both sides by $A_t L_t$, (4.7) reduces to

$$\frac{c(t)}{A_t} + \hat{z}(t) = f(\hat{k}(t)), \tag{4.8}$$

where $\hat{z}(t) = Z(t)/A_t L_t$. Since

$$\hat{z} = \frac{\dot{K} + \delta K}{AL} = \frac{\dot{K}}{K}\frac{K}{AL} + \delta\hat{k}$$

$$= \left(\frac{\dot{K}}{K} - (\mu + n)\right)\hat{k} + (\mu + \delta + n)\hat{k}$$

$$= \frac{\dot{\hat{k}}}{\hat{k}}\hat{k} + (\mu + n + \delta)\hat{k} = \dot{\hat{k}} + (\mu + n + \delta)\hat{k}, \tag{4.9}$$

an alternative representation of (4.8) is

$$\frac{\dot{c}(t)}{At} + \dot{\hat{k}}(t) + (\mu + n + \delta)\hat{k}(t) = f(\hat{k}(t)),$$

$$\text{or,} \quad c(t) + A_t\dot{\hat{k}}(t) = A_t\{f(\hat{k}(t)) - (\mu + n + \delta)\hat{k}(t)\}, \tag{4.10}$$

where, according to (4.9), $(\mu + n + \delta)\hat{k}(t)$ represents the minimum level of gross investment per unit of effective labour, (that is, $\hat{z}$), that leaves $\hat{k}(t)$ unchanged.

It is convenient at this stage to consider two cases depending on whether investment is reversible or irreversible. When investment is irreversible, installed capital cannot be 'eaten into' except through depreciation. Reversible investment permits direct capital consumption. The literature on growth theory has developed mostly under the assumption of reversible investment. Accordingly, we shall not present the case of irreversible investment in any depth. However, in the interest of students who wish to follow the technicalities of irreversible investment, the appendices will prove a few results on optimal growth with irreversible investment. Reversible investment permits $Z < 0$, so that it is possible to have $\dot{K} < -\delta K$. Since δK stands for physical depreciation of capital, the maximum amount of the capital stock that can be directly consumed by the household is $(1-\delta)K$. Hence, the maximum sustainable net disinvestment equals $\dot{K} = -[(1-\delta)K + \delta K]$ $= -K$. Consequently, $Z = \dot{K} + \delta K = -(1-\delta)K$. Alternatively, $\hat{z} = -(1-\delta)\hat{k}$ and $\dot{\hat{k}} = -(1+\mu+n)\hat{k}$. The corresponding maximum possible level of per capita consumption is $c = A(f(\hat{k}) + (1-\delta)\hat{k})$. The transformation locus between c and $\hat{k}$ is illustrated in Figure 4.1.

A consumption path c must satisfy the condition

$$0 \le c \le A(f(\hat{k}) + (1-\delta)\hat{k}), \tag{4.11}$$

if investment is reversible. For later use, we may prove the following elementary property of the Solow model.

Proposition 1: Any feasible path $\hat{k}(t)$ satisfying (4.10) is bounded above.

Proof: Referring back to (4.10), the maximum value of $\hat{k}(t)$ possible at each t is found by equating c/A to zero for all t. This may be called the path of pure capital accumulation. Denote the path by $\hat{k}_p(t)$. It satisfies the equation

$$\dot{\hat{k}}_p(t) = f(\hat{k}_p(t)) - \lambda\hat{k}_p(t).$$

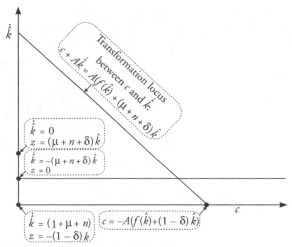

Figure 4.1: A Transformation Locus

By virtue of Assumption $f2, \exists$ a $\bar{\hat{k}}$ such that $\hat{k}_p(t) > \bar{\hat{k}} \Rightarrow \dot{\hat{k}}_p(t) < 0$. Thus, max $\{\hat{k}(0), \bar{\hat{k}}\}$ is the claimed upper bound on $\hat{k}(t)$.

The intuitive argument underlying Proposition 1 is as follows. If $\hat{k}(t)$ is not bounded above, K must forever be increasing faster than AL. Therefore, on account of diminishing returns (strengthened by the Inada conditions), GDP per unit of effective labour (that is, $\hat{y}$) approaches zero as $\hat{k}$ approaches infinity. On the other hand, the minimum investment per unit of effective labour (that is, $\hat{z}$) necessary to maintain $\hat{k}$ at any given level is $\lambda \hat{k} > 0$. The latter gets arbitrarily large with $\hat{k}$, while $\hat{y}$ gets arbitrarily small. Since $\hat{y}$ must cover $\lambda \hat{k}$, there is a contradiction.

The economy, being infinitely lived in principle, the decision maker too will be assumed to have infinite life. This does not literally mean that he lives forever. It means rather that he, even though finitely lived, cares for future generations of individuals. The agent at $t = 0$ is assumed to plan for the entire future of the economy. In other words, he decides about an optimal consumption path $C(t)$, $t \in [0, \infty]$, where $C(t)$ is the aggregate consumption enjoyed by $L(t)$. Optimality of the path is judged with reference to an inter-temporal welfare function of the form

$$U = \int_0^\infty u(c(t)) e^{nt} \cdot e^{-\rho t} \, dt$$

$$= \int_0^\infty u(c(t)) e^{-(\rho - n)t} \, dt, \tag{4.12}$$

which is a weighted sum of instantaneous utilities derived from $c(t)$. The weights reflect two facts. First, e^{nt} shows that utilities from per capita consumption receive exponentially higher weights with time to take account of the fact that the household size increases at the rate n. Secondly, $\rho > 0$ stands for the rate of time preference arising out of the fact that utilities further down in time are valued less than utilities enjoyed earlier on. This leads to an exponentially decaying weight $e^{-\rho t}$ with the passage of time. The function U is assumed to reflect the inter-temporal preferences of the planner as well as H and satisfy the following assumptions:

Assumption u1 $u'(c) > 0, u''(c) < 0,$
Assumption u2 $u'(c) \to \infty$ as $c \to 0$ and $u'(c) \to 0$ as $c \to \infty,$
Assumption u3 $\rho > n.$

In other words, instantaneous utility is a strictly concave function of c, the marginal utility is unboundedly high for small values of c, while it is as close to zero as possible for large c. The first part of Assumption u2 rules out zero consumption at each point of time. Assumption u3 ensures that U is well defined.[4] In view of Assumption T, the convergence of (4.12) will generally call for a strengthening of Assumption u3. (Appendix A4.4).

We noted that (4.7) can be viewed as the transformation frontier between $C(t)$ and $Z(t)$, given $K(t)$. With reversible investment, the optimal value of c must necessarily be an interior point of the transformation frontier. If not, suppose

$$c = A(f(\hat{k}) + (1-\delta)\hat{k}) \tag{4.13}$$

holds for some t. This means that all capital gets exhausted at t and the economy cannot produce positive output beyond t. Hence, $C = 0$ subsequent to t. Given Assumption u2, however, a small decrease in consumption at t accompanied by an increase at a later point of time must be welfare improving. Consequently, any optimal consumption path c must satisfy the condition

$$0 < c < A(f(\hat{k}) + (1-\delta)\hat{k}). \tag{4.14}$$

---

[4] When $\rho < n$, the function U could be unbounded.

Necessary Conditions for an Optimum in a Command Economy: An Intuitive Discussion

We begin with the planner's optimization exercise, which may be stated as follows:

Optimization under Reversible Investment

Find $\{c^*(t)\}_0^\infty$ to maximize (4.12) subject to (4.10) and $\hat{k}(0) = \hat{k}_0$. In standard terminology, $c(t)$ is referred to as a control variable and $\hat{k}(t)$ as a state variable.

We assume that the planner has chosen an optimum path $\{c_t^*, \hat{k}_t^*\}_0^\infty$ of per capita consumptin and capital per unit of effective labour over time and derive intuitively the properties to be satisfied by that path. Let us fix any time point t. From his own past decisions, the planner has inherited an unalterable level of $\hat{k}(t) = \hat{k}_t^*$. This determines the size of net resources (namely, the RHS of (4.10)) the planner must allocate between $c(t)$ and $\dot{\hat{k}}(t)$. To find the allocation, we define a reduced-form welfare function governing the planner's behaviour at t. The function, commonly called the Hamiltonian, is written[5]

$$\mathcal{H}(c(t), \hat{k}(t), q_t) = u(c(t)) + q_t \dot{\hat{k}}(t). \qquad (4.15)$$

where $\hat{k}$ enters the function $\mathcal{H}$ as an argument, since $\dot{\hat{k}}$ is a function of $\hat{k}$ and c on account of (4.10). The variable q_t is called a co-state variable and represents the shadow price of $\hat{K}$ at t. It is measured in utils and may be calculated as follows. Consider any path $\{c_t, \hat{k}_t\}_0^\infty$. We imagine that the best possible value of aggregate utility across growth paths starting from $\hat{k}_t$ is given by the function $V(\hat{k}_t)$. Then, q_t is the marginal social productivity (measured in utils) of $\hat{k}$ at t, that is, $q_t = dV(\hat{k}_t)/d\hat{k}_t$. It represents the efficient or shadow price to be assigned to a marginal change in $\hat{k}$ at t. In what follows, we shall loosely refer to $\hat{k}$ as investment in $\hat{k}$. Thus, $\mathcal{H}$ stands for the utility derived by the planner from the choice $(c(t), \hat{k}(t))$, *under the assumption that the path from t onwards brought about by the investment is optimal.* As defined therefore, $\mathcal{H}$ already incorporates an element of optimality as far as the future is concerned. It says, whatever may be the value of $\hat{k}$, the future course of the economy will be optimal.

---

5 Appendix A4.2 presents a rigorous treatment of this function as well as the following intuitive discussion.

Different choices of the value of investment, however, will give rise to different optimal values for the future. Which of these should the planner pick up? To answer this question, we have to compare the social productivity of a marginal change in $\hat{k}$ with the marginal utility of c at t. This boils down to computing the marginal rate of substitution (MRS) along level curves generated by the Hamiltonian. Differentiate $\mathcal{H}$ totally to get

$$\frac{d\,c(t)}{d\,\hat{k}(t)} = -\frac{q_t}{u'(c(t))} < 0$$

and

$$\frac{d^2 c(t)}{d\,\hat{k}(t)^2} = q_t \frac{1}{u'(c(t))^2} u''(c(t)) \frac{d c(t)}{d\,\hat{k}(t)} > 0.$$

Thus, the level curves corresponding to $\mathcal{H}$ are downward falling and strictly convex to the origin. As in any constrained optimization problem, optimum choice implies equating the MRS with the slope of the constraint. The slope of the linear constraint (4.10) is $-1/A_t$. Hence, a necessary FOC to be satisfied by the optimal path $\{c_t^*, \hat{k}_t^*\}_0^\infty$ is[6]

$$\frac{q_t^*}{u'(c_t^*)} = \frac{1}{A_t},$$

or,

$$u'(c_t^*) = \frac{q_t^*}{A_t}, \tag{4.16}$$

where $q_t^* = d\,V(\hat{k}_t^*)/d\,\hat{k}(t)$. Here (4.16) may also be written as

$$\frac{\partial \mathcal{H}(c_t^*, \hat{k}_t^*, q_t^*)}{\partial c(t)} = 0 \text{ at each } t. \tag{4.17}$$

In view of the shape of the level curves of $\mathcal{H}$, (4.17) implies that $\mathcal{H}$ is maximized subject to (4.10) at each t. The equilibrium is described in Figure 4.2. Note that the Hamiltonian $\mathcal{H}$ can be interpreted approximately as the value in utils imputed to per capita net national product at t.[7] Thus, an optimal path $\{c_t^*, \hat{k}_t^*\}_0^\infty$ has associated with it a

---

[6] The shape of the level curves of $\mathcal{H}$ tells us further that c_t^* is a unique solution to the optimization problem.

[7] The qualification 'approximate' is needed since $\hat{k}$ is investment per unit of effective labour AL, rather than per capita investment.

path of $\{\hat{q}^*(t)\}_0^\infty$ such that the corresponding inputed value of per capita net national product is maximized with respect to $c(t)$ at each point of time. In view of this implication, (4.17) is often referred to as the *Maximal Principle*.

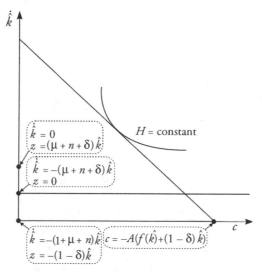

Figure 4.2: The Static Equilibrium

To complete the characterization of the optimal path, we derive another property that q^* must satisfy. This second property is a necessary condition for the optimality of investment at each t. It says that along the optimal path, the cost of a net marginal increase in $\hat{k}$ brought about at any t and maintained ever afterwards must be equal to the discounted present value of the stream of utility returns it brings forth forever. Let us suppose then that $\hat{k}^*$ is raised by Δ at t and that this rise is maintained for all subsequent time points. This will cause a parallel shift in the path of $\hat{k}_s^*$, $s \geq t$ as in Figure 4.3.

The cost of the initial rise is $q_t^* \Delta$. Since $q_t^* = A_t u'(c_t^*)$, we have $q_t^* \Delta = u'(c_t^*) A_t \Delta$. Now, $A_t \Delta$ being the per capita equivalent of Δ, we may view it as the loss in per capita consumption at t necessitated by the rise in $\hat{k}$. Thus, the cost $q_t^* \Delta$ is the utility loss $u'(c_t^*) A_t \Delta$ associated with the net fall $A_t \Delta$ in c at t. We shall weigh it against the discounted stream of utility gains to be made forever after netting out the costs of maintenance.

The extra *per capita* output produced by Δ at any $s > t$ is $A_s f'(\hat{k}_s^*) \Delta$,

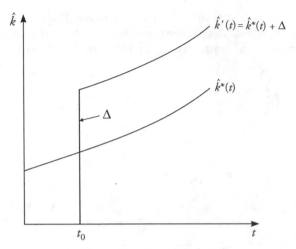

Figure 4.3: Comparison Paths

whereas the *per capita* investment necessary to maintain Δ is $A_s(\mu + n + \delta)\Delta$. Hence, the net per capita extra output produced by the additional Δ at each $s > t$ is $A_s(f'(\hat{k}_s^*) - (\mu + n + \delta))\Delta$. The extra utility it gives rise to at s is $u'(c_s^*)A_s(f'(\hat{k}_s^*) - (\mu + n + \delta))\Delta$ $= q_s^*\{f'(\hat{k}_s^*) - (\mu + n + \delta)\}\Delta$. The discounted present value of the stream of utilities is $\int_t^\infty e^{-(\rho - n)(s-t)}q_s^*\{f'(\hat{k}_s^*) - (\mu + n + \delta)\}\Delta\, ds$. Equating the cost to the discounted returns as explained above, we have

$$q_t^* = \int_t^\infty e^{-(\rho-n)(s-t)}q_s^*\{f'(\hat{k}_s^*) - (\mu + n + \delta)\}\, ds. \qquad (4.18)$$

The above calculation may be expressed in terms of the Hamiltonian function. Note in this context that

$$\frac{\partial \mathcal{H}(c_s^*, \hat{k}_s^*, q_s^*)}{\partial \hat{k}(s)} = u'(c_s^*)\frac{\partial c_s^*}{\partial \hat{k}(s)} + q_s^*\left\{ f'(\hat{k}_s^* - (\mu + n + \delta)\right.$$

$$\left. - \frac{1}{A_s}\frac{\partial c_s^*}{\partial \hat{k}(s)}\right\}$$

$$= q_s^*\{f'(\hat{k}_s^*) - (\mu + n + \delta)\}, \qquad (4.19)$$

using (4.10) and (4.16). Consequently, (4.18) reduces to

$$q_t^* = \int_t^\infty \partial \mathcal{H}(c_s^*, \hat{k}_s^*, q_s^*) / \partial \hat{k}(s) e^{-(\rho-n)(s-t)} ds. \tag{4.20}$$

For q_t^* to be well defined in (4.18) or (4.20), the integral on the RHS must exist for each t. We shall demonstrate in Appendix A4.4 that the optimality of $\{c_t^*, \hat{k}_t^*\}_0^\infty$ implies that $f'(\hat{k}_s^*) - (\mu + n + \delta)$ is bounded strictly away from zero for s sufficiently large.[8] Anticipating this result, the intergral can exist $\forall\, t$ only if

$$e^{-(\rho-n)t} q_t^* \to 0 \text{ as } t \to \infty. \tag{4.21}$$

Equation (4.21) is called the transversality condition and constitutes a restriction on an optimal path. Intuitively, (4.21) implies that efficient paths view capital stocks far out in the future to be increasingly useless relative to present stocks.[9]

The balance between cost and benefits in (4.18) implies a restriction on the optimal path. This is seen by differentiating (4.18) with respect to t to get[10]

$$\dot{q}_t^* = -q_t^* \{ f'(\hat{k}_t^*) - (\mu + n + \delta) \}$$
$$+ (\rho - n) \int_t^\infty e^{-(\rho-n)(s-t)} q_s^* \{ f'(\hat{k}_s^*)$$
$$- (\mu + n + \delta) \} ds.$$

[8] Proposition (J) of Koopmans (1965) proves the result for a model without technical progress. Proposition *A4* may be viewed as an extension of Koopmans' result to the case where the production function exhibits technical progress.

[9] It is worth noting here that the transversality condition follows from the fact that $f'(\hat{k}_s^*) - (\mu + n + \delta)$ is bounded strictly away from zero, rather than the other way round. Certain sources liken the transeversality condition to a no-Ponzi game restriction. The latter is a vacuous restriction for the present model, since it assumes a single macro household or planner which can neither be a net borrower nor a net lender. In any case, as we have demonstrated, optimality implies this condition. It is *not* an exogenous stipulation on the model. In Appendix A4.5 we shall encounter a counter-example (constructed by Halkin (1974)) to the necessity of the transversality condition. Contrary to the problem we are now discussing, the objective function for the counter-example will assign a disproportionately high weight on capital in the distant future.

[10] The formula for differentiating a definite integral of the form

$$K(x) = \int_a^{b(x)} F(t, x) dt$$

is

$$\frac{dK(x)}{dx} = \int_a^{b(x)} F_x(t, x) dt + F(b(x), x) b'(x).$$

See Chiang (1992), p. 31, also this volume A4.2.11, p.67.

Substituting from (4.18), The last equation reduces to

$$\dot{q}_t^* = -q_t^*\{f'(\hat{k}_t^*) - (\mu + n + \delta)\} + (\rho - n)q_t^*. \tag{4.22}$$

Alternatively, using (4.20) and (4.19) in succession, (4.22) may be expressed as

$$\dot{q}_t^* = \frac{d\left(\int_t^\infty \partial\mathcal{H}(c_s^*, \hat{k}_s^*, q_s^*)/\partial\hat{k}(s)e^{-(\rho-n)(s-t)}ds\right)}{dt}$$

$$= -\frac{\partial\mathcal{H}(c_t^*, \hat{k}_t^*, q_t^*)}{\partial\hat{k}(t)} + (\rho - n)q_t^*$$

$$= -f'(\hat{k}_t^*)q_t^* + (\mu + \rho + \delta)q_t^*, \tag{4.23}$$

In order to interpret (4.22), consider a different scenario where p is the money price of a unit of the commodity that acts both as a consumption and a capital good.[11] For simplicity, the capital good is assumed to be non-depreciating. Suppose further that there exists, alongside the capital good, an alternative monetary asset, a long-term bond, yielding a nominal rate of interest $i(t)$ for each t. An infinitely lived agent is engaged in evaluating a chosen path of capital accumulation $\{k(t)\}_0^\infty$. When p units of money are invested in a unit of the capital good at time t, the marginal product is $f'(k(s)) \, \forall s \geq t$, assuming as before that the agent maintains the extra unit of capital for all $s \geq t$ and consumes any residual output brought forth by the extra capital. Then, the agent's return from maintaining an extra unit of k forever from s onwards is $f'(k(s)) \, \forall s \geq t$. In nominal terms, the return equals $p(s)f'(k(s))$ at each s. For the agent to be indifferent between investing in the physical capital and the bond, the two investments must yield the same rate of return per instant of time. The rate of return from the physical capital investment, $r(s)$, is given by

$$p(t) = \int_t^\infty p(s)f'(k(s))e^{-\int_t^s r(x)dx}ds.$$

If the two rates of return are equal, $r(s) = i(s) \, \forall s$. Hence,

$$p(t) = \int_t^\infty p(s)f'(k(s)) \, e^{-\int_t^s i(x)dx}ds. \tag{4.24}$$

Differentiation of (4.24) with respect to t gives

---

[11] This interpretation is based on Solow (1956).

$$\dot{p}(t) = -p(t)f'(k(t)) + i(t)p(t),$$

or,

$$p(t)f'(k(t)) + \dot{p}(t) = i(t)p(t), \tag{4.25}$$

The first term on the LHS of (4.25) stands for the value of the instantaneous marginal product of investment in k in nominal terms, while the second term represents capital gain (or loss) on account of price change. The LHS then gives the *net* instantaneous nominal return from investing in k. The RHS, on the other hand, is the nominl return at t from holding the bond. The equality implies that the agent is indifferent between the two ways of investing.[12]

The logic underlying (4.25) may be applied to (4.22), which we rewrite as

$$q_t^*\{f'(\hat{k}_t^*) - (\mu + n + \delta)\} + \dot{q}_t^* = (\rho - n)q_t^*. \tag{4.26}$$

The LHS now gives the instantaneous net return in utils of a unit of investment in $\hat{k}(t)$, where $\dot{q}_t^*$ is the capital gain or loss measured in utils. On the RHS, the term $\rho - n$ is the rate at which utils ought to grow in the planner's judgement. It is the counterpart of $i(t)$ in (4.25). This rate applied to the shadow price of capital yields the instantaneous return that the planner finds acceptable, the imputed opportunity cost of investment in physical capital. Hence, (4.26) says that the rate of return from investment along the optimal path equals the household's minimum acceptable return. When (4.22) or (4.26) holds, therefore, the planner has no incentive to divert away from the chosen path of asset accumulation.

Both (4.16) and (4.18) have been restated above with reference to the Hamiltonian function. Here (4.10) too may be similarly rewritten. Since (4.10) implies

$$\dot{\hat{k}}_t^* = f(\hat{k}_t^*) - \frac{c_t^*}{A_t} - (\mu + n + \delta)\hat{k}_t^*, \tag{4.27}$$

it follows that (4.27) is reproduced by finding a stationary value of $\mathcal{H}$ with respect to $q(t)$:

$$\frac{\partial \mathcal{H}(c_t^*, \hat{k}_t^*, q_t^*)}{\partial q(t)} = \dot{\hat{k}}_t^*. \tag{4.28}$$

---

[12] A more common way of writing (4.25) is $f'(k(t)) + \dot{p}(t)/p(t) = i(t)$, usually called the Fisher equation, after Irving Fisher.

Let us collect the necessary conditions stated in terms of the Hamiltonian function as[13]

Proposition 2:   Suppose $\{c_t^*, \hat{k}_t^*\}_0^\infty$ solves the problem. Then, there exists a path of co-state variables q_t^* such that (4.17), (4.28), (4.23) and (4.21) are satisfied.

Neessary Conditions for an Optimum in a Private Economy

We proceed now to a discussion of the functioning of a Private Economy and compare its optimality properties with those derived for the Command Economy. The Private Economy is characterized by two aggregative or macro agents H and B. As opposed to the centralized decision making by the planner, the Private Economy's resource allocation exercise is carried out in a decentralized manner on the basis of independent actions taken by H and B. Agent H is viewed as a dynastic household that cares for all subsequent generations in the same way as the planner. Thus, the planner and H have identically the same preference function (4.12). The household is the ultimate owner of all capital, but it holds them in the form of shares issued by B. These will be referred to as assets and denoted by $\mathcal{A}$ in units of the numeraire commodity Y. Thus, each unit of $\mathcal{A}$ represents the ownership right over a unit of K. Agent B is supposed to treat all prices parametrically and maximize net profits (that is, profits net of capital depreciation) at each t, thus implying that the identical firms it subsumes behave competitively in factor and product markets. Denoting the competitive wage rate and rental (or interest rate) by $w(t)$ and $r(t)$, the household's budget constraint at t is

$$\dot{\mathcal{A}}(t) = w(t)\mathcal{L}(t) + r(t)\ \mathcal{A}(t) - C(t), \tag{4.29}$$

where $\dot{\mathcal{A}}(t)$ stands for investment or disinvestment in $\mathcal{A}(t)$, $w(t)L(t)$ the income from inelastically supplied labour, and $r(t)\mathcal{A}(t)$ the income from

---

[13]   The conditions resemble standard represnetations of the necessary conditons, except for the first line of (4.23). This is borrowed from Cass (1965, 1966). The advantage of choosing this form is that it makes direct reference to the economic interpretation of a co-state variable. Moreover, as will be evident from Appendix A4.3, it uses a single differential equation to describe the evolution of the co-state variable for both reversible and irreversible investment.

asset holdings. Denoting per capita asset holding by $a(t)$, (4.29) reduces to

$$\dot{a}(t) = w(t) + r(t)a(t) - c(t) - n\, a(t),\qquad (4.30)$$

where, following the arguments of (4.9), $n\, a(t)$ is the per capita investment in $\mathcal{A}(t)$ necessary to keep $a(t)$ unchanged. The business firm is assumed to choose $L(t)$ and $K(t)$ to maximize net profit

$$\Pi(t) = F(K(t), A(t)L(t)) - w(t)L(t) - r(t)K(t) - \delta K(t)\qquad (4.31)$$

at all t. The First Order Conditions (*FOC*'s) for this exercise are

$$r(t) = \frac{\partial F}{\partial K(t)} - \delta$$
$$= f'(\hat{k}(t)) - \delta,$$
$$w(t) = \frac{\delta F}{\delta L_t}$$
$$= A_t\{f(\hat{k}(t)) - \hat{k}f'(\hat{k}(t))\}.\qquad (4.32)$$

Given these preliminaries, let $\{\bar{c}_t^*, \bar{a}_t^*\}_0^\infty$ denote an optimal path of $\{c(t), a(t)\}$ chosen by $\mathcal{H}$. Suppose, moreover, that the associated path of $\{r(t), w(t)\}$ is $\{r_t^*, w_t^*\}_0^\infty$ and that $\{\hat{k}_t^*\}_0^\infty$ satisfies (4.32). As was the case for the planner, we are interested in deriving the necessary conditions for the optimality of the path. This is a relatively simple exercise now, given our derivation of the conditions for the Command Economy. All we need to do is replace (4.10) by (4.30) and treat a rather than $\hat{k}$ as the state variable. The control variable for both problems is c. The necessary condition for a static optimum thus turns out to be

$$u'(\bar{c}^*) - \bar{q}^* = 0,\qquad (4.33)$$

where $\bar{q}(t)$ is the co-state variable for the problem, that is, the shadow price of a unit of a and $\bar{q}^*$ its value along the chosen path.

The derivation of the dynamic optmization condition too mimics the corresponding derivation for the Command Economy. For H to be willing to hold $\bar{a}$ at each t, the optimal price of a unit of a at each t should equal the discounted present value of the stream of returns from the investment, after correction for depreciation on account of population growth. In other words,

$$\bar{q}_t = \int_t^\infty e^{-(\rho-n)(s-t)}(r_s - n)\bar{q}_s\, ds.\qquad (4.34)$$

Differentiating this equation, we get

$$\dot{\bar{q}}_t = -\bar{q}_t\, r_t + \bar{q}_t\, \rho. \tag{4.35}$$

The conditions (4.33),(4.34), and (4.35) correspond to (4.16), (4.18) and (4.22) respectively. Conditions (4.33)and (4.35) can be written with reference to the relevant Hamiltonian for the market economy:

$$\mathcal{H}_m(c(t), a(t), \bar{q}\,(t)) = u(c(t)) + \bar{q}(t)$$
$$[w(t) + (r(t)-n)a(t)-c(t)]. \tag{4.36}$$

Condition (4.33) turns out to be

$$\frac{\partial \mathcal{H}_m(\bar{c}_t^*, a_t^*, \bar{q}_t^*)}{\partial c(t)} = 0. \tag{4.37}$$

Similarly, (4.35) follows from

$$\dot{q}_t^* = \frac{d\int_t^\infty \partial \mathcal{H}_m(\bar{c}_s^*,\, a_s^*,\, \bar{q}_s^*)/\partial a(s)e^{-(\rho-n)(s-t)}ds}{dt}. \tag{4.38}$$

Finally,

$$\frac{\partial \mathcal{H}_m(\bar{c}_t^*,\, a_t^*,\, \bar{q}_t^*)}{\partial \bar{q}(t)} = \dot{a}^*\,(t) \tag{4.39}$$

yields (4.30).

Comparison of Optimal Growth Paths: Command Economy Versus Private Economy

The purpose of this section is to derive the complete set of optimality conditions for the household's dynamic optimization exercise in a Private Economy and establish that the equilibrium growth path of the Private Economy is unique and identically the same as the optimal growth path for the Command Economy. The latter result is the dynamic counterpart of the First Fundamental Theorem of Welfare Economics, which states that a competitive equilibrium is Pareto optimal.

Define a new variable p^* such that $p_t^*/A_t = \bar{q}_t^*$ at each t. Then, (4.34) reduces to

$$\frac{p_t^*}{A_t} = \int_t^\infty e^{-(\rho-n)(s-t)}(r_s^* - n)\frac{p_s^*}{A_s}\, ds. \tag{4.40}$$

Differentiating with respect to t and taking account of (4.32), we obtain

$$\dot{p}_t^* = -f'(\overline{\hat{k}}_t^*)p_t^* + (\mu + \rho + \delta)p_t^*. \tag{4.41}$$

Here (4.33) reduces to

$$u'(\overline{c}_t^*) = \frac{p_t^*}{A_t}. \tag{4.42}$$

Also, (4.30) implies (4.2) under constant returns to scale and the latter boils down [as with (4.10)] to

$$\overline{c}_t^* + A_t \dot{\overline{\hat{k}}}_t^* = A_t \left\{ f(\overline{\hat{k}}_t^*) - (\mu + n + \delta)\overline{\hat{k}}_t^* \right\}. \tag{4.43}$$

As indicated in the derivation of (4.21), $f'(\overline{\hat{k}}_t^*) - (\mu + \delta + n)$ stays bounded away from 0 as $t \to \infty$. Let us now solve (4.41) to obtain[14]

$$p_t^* = p_0^* \, e^{-\int_0^t (f'(\overline{\hat{k}}_s^*) - (\mu + \rho + \delta))ds}.$$

Multiplying both sides by $e^{-(\rho - n)t}$ and simplifying, we get

$$p_t^* e^{-(\rho - n)t} = p_0^* e^{-\int_0^t (f'(\overline{\hat{k}}_s^*) - (\mu + \delta + n))ds}. \tag{4.44}$$

Since, according to *Proposition A4.4.1*, $f'(\overline{\hat{k}}_t^*) - (\mu + \delta + n)$ is strictly positive from some t onwards and stays bounded away from 0 as $t \to \infty$, it follows that the RHS of the last equation converges to 0 as $t \to \infty$. Hence, p_t^* satisfies (4.21). We now refer to Appendix A4.3 to claim that (4.41), 4.42), (4.43), and (4.44) imply that the path $\{\overline{c}_t^*, \hat{k}_t^*\}_0^\infty$ is unique and solves the Command Economy's problem. Hence, the path of $\{r_t^*, w_t^*\}_0^\infty$ determined by (4.32) is unique also.

We may further note that (4.34) is rewritten as

$$\overline{q}_t^* = \int_t^\infty e^{-(\rho - n)(s-t)} (f'(\overline{\hat{k}}_t^*) - \delta - n)\overline{q}_s^* \, ds. \tag{4.45}$$

Moreover, *Proposition A4.4.1* implies once again that $f'(\overline{\hat{k}}_t^*) - (\delta + n)$ is strictly positive from some t onwards and stays bounded away from 0 as $t \to \infty$. Hence, the variable $\overline{q}_t^*$ must satisfy the transversality condition for (4.45) to hold at each t. Our results for the Private Economy may now be collected with reference to the Hamiltonian function $\mathcal{H}_m$:

---

[14] *See* Appendix 1.1.2 of Barro and Sala-i-Martin (2004) for a clear exposition of the method of solution of this differential equation.

Propositon 3:   Suppose $\{\bar{c}_t^*, \bar{a}_t^*\}_0^\infty$ and $\{r_t^*, w_t^*\}_0^\infty$ is an equilibrium path for the Private Economy. Then, there exists a path of co-state variables $\bar{q}_t^*$ such that (4.37), (4.38), (4.39), and the transversality condition

$$e^{-(\rho-n)t}\bar{q}_t^* \to 0 \text{ as } t \to \infty \tag{4.46}$$

are satisfied. The equilibrium paths of the variables chosen by the Private Economy are unique. Moreover, the paths of per capita consumption and capital chosen by the Private Economy are identically the same as the ones chosen by the Command Economy.

Thus, the decentralized decisions of a Private Economy produce a social optimum.[15] With this, we conclude the presentation of the main results.

Appendix A4.1
Irreversible Investment

Irreversible investment refers to the case where installed capital cannot be 'eaten into' except through depreciation. The smallest possible value $\dot{K}$ can assume is $-\delta K$. At this corner value of net investment, gross investment Z equals zero. This means that $z = 0$ and $\hat{k} = -(\mu + n + \delta)\hat{k}$. Consequently, from (4.10), the maximum possible per capita consumption is $c = Af(\hat{k})$. In this case, the consumption path will satisfy the condition

$$0 \le c \le Af(\hat{k}). \tag{A4.1.1}$$

Figure 4.1 indicates the maximum possible value of c corresponding to $\dot{\hat{k}} = -(\mu + n + \delta)\hat{k}$. The analytical consequences of c hitting its upper bound will be discussed further in Appendix A4.2.

---

[15] Recent literature on growth economics has prodced several examples of violation of this property.

Appendix A4.2
Optimality Conditions: General Treatment

This section has two objectives. First, it provides some of the mathematical details avoided by the intuitive discussion of the necessary first-order conditions for the Command Economy of the third section. Second, it gives an integrated analysis that applies to cases of reversible as well as irreversible investment. Note that for irreversible investment, it is not possible to rule out c hitting the upper bound. At the maximum possible value of c, all output is consumed away, but this does not exhaust the capital stock. The economy bequeaths $(1-\delta)K$ to posterity. Hence, positive production as well as consumption is feasible at subsequent points of time. However, Assumption u2 still rules out $c = 0$ at any t. Hence, for irreversible investment, (A4.1.1) reduces to

$$0 < c \leq Af(\hat{k}). \tag{A4.2.1}$$

Here (A4.2.1) shows that the optimum for the irreversible case could occur at a point where $\hat{k}$ can no longer be sacrificed to yield extra c. Consequently, the marginal rate of substitution between c and $\dot{\hat{k}}$ (as measured by the slope of the level curves of the Hamiltonian) may no longer equal the rate of technical substitution between them. At points such as these, the marginal rate of substitution will be treated as the correct price ratio. The implication of this observation will be clearer from subsequent discussion. The planner's optimization exercise for the case is:

Optimization under Irreversible Investment:

Find $\{c^*(t)\}_0^\infty$ to maximize (4.12)
subject to (4.10), (A4.2.1) and $\hat{k}(0) = \hat{k}_0$.

In what follows, we shall refer to the reversible and the irreversible investment versions of our problem as Version 1 and Version 2 respectively.

NECESSARY CONDITIONS FOR OPTIMUM

We begin our discussion with a

Definition: The function $c : R_+ \to R$ is piece-wise continuous if

(a) $c(\cdot)$ is continuous except over a finite set of points $\{a_1, ..., a_n\}$.

(b)   At each a_i, lim $c(t)$ exists for $t \uparrow a_i$ as well as for $t \downarrow a_i$, but the two limits are unequal.

In what follows, the control variable $c(t)$ will be restricted to piece-wise continuous functions satisfying (4.10). Any such $c(t)$ will be referred to as a *feasible path*.

At $t = 0$, the entire path $\{c(t)_0^\infty\}$ (leading to the associated path $\{\hat{k}(t)\}_{t>0}^\infty$) is the choice variable for the agent. To this extent, the agent is engaged in a dynamic exercise. However, we shall break up the analysis into two parts. The first part will be concerned with *static* optimality conditions, properties that must hold true for a given volume of output at t to be allocated optimally between consumption and investment. The second part will be concerned with *dynamic* conditions of optimal resource allocation across time, that is the way in which the optimal choice at a given point of time is linked to choices in the future.

Static optimization, the principle of optimality, and the functional equation

Strictly speaking of course, these exercises are not independent. The overall problem being dynamic in nature, even the static optimality conditions need to be derived with reference to a minimal set of dynamic considerations. In this context, we shall begin by developing Bellman's Principle of Optimality (Bellman 1957), a famous mathematical principle underlying multistage decisioin problems. Starting from any time point t_0, the best achievable value of welfare depends on $\hat{k}_{t_0}$. Notice that this is a deeper statement than might appear at first sight. If the planning horizon were finite, say T, the best value of welfare would depend on $\hat{k}_{t_0}$ as well as t_0, since the residual time horizon shrinks with the passage of time (that is, $T - t_0$ falls as t_0 rises). The infinite-horizon problem does not involve this complication. At any value of t, the residual horizon continues to be infinitely long.

Let $V(\hat{k}_{t_0})$ stand for the optimum welfare starting from $\hat{k}_{t_0}$. The function is normally referred to as the *value function*. Consider the truncated problem

$$\text{Maximize} \quad \int_{t_0}^{\infty} u(c(t))e^{-(\rho-n)(t-t_0)}dt$$

subject to (4.10), (4.14) [alternatively, (4.10), (A4.2.1)]

and

$$\hat{k}(t_0) = \hat{k}_{t_0}.$$ (A4.2.2)

If $\{\tilde{c}_t\}_{t_0}^{\infty}$ solves this problem,

$$V(\hat{k}_{t_0}) = \int_{t_0}^{\infty} u(\tilde{c}_t) e^{-(\rho-n)(t-t_0)} dt.$$

Bellman's Principle of Optimality says:

An optimal path has the property that whatever be the initial conditons and control variables over some initial period, the control variables over the remaining period must be optimal for the remaining problem, with the state resulting from the early decisions considered as the initial condition.

Let $\{c_t^*\}_0^{\infty}$ solve either Version 1 or Version 2 of our problem. Suppose, moreover, that it gives rise to the path $\hat{k}_t^*$. Then, according to the Principle of Optimality,

$$V(\hat{k}_{t_0}^*) = \int_{t_0}^{\infty} u(c_t^*) e^{-(\rho-n)(t-t_0)} dt.$$

Proof of the Principle of Optimality

Consider a small interval $0 \le t \le h$, $h > 0$. Denoting the truncated path $\{c(t)\}_0^h$ by $c_{0,h}$, it is clear that $\hat{k}_h$ is a function of $c_{0,h}$, given $\hat{k}_0$. Let $\hat{k}(h) = \phi(c_{0,h})$. Then, $V(\hat{k}(h)) = V(\phi(c_{0,h}))$. Suppose then that the agent chooses $c_{0,h}^*$ over the interval $[0, h]$, but that contrary to the Principle of Optimality, the aggregate utility from $\{c_t^*\}_h^{\infty}$ falls short of $V(\phi(c_0^*, h))$. If possible, let

$$V(\phi(c_0^*, h)) = \int_h^{\infty} u(\overline{c}_t) e^{?\,(\rho?\,n)(t?\,h)} dt$$

$$> \int_h^{\infty} u(c_t^*) e^{?\,(\rho?\,n)\,(t?\,h)} dt,$$

where $\overline{c}_t$ is feasible from $\phi(c_t^*, h)$ and $\overline{c}_t \ne c_t^*$ except possibly over a set of time points which is so small that it may be ignored. Define

$$c^{**}(t) = \begin{cases} c_t^*, & t \in [0,h] \\ \overline{c}_t & t \in (h,\infty). \end{cases}$$

Clearly, $c^{**}(t)$ is feasible, since $c^{**}(t)$ involves possibly a single point of discontinuity (at $t = h$) in addition to the finite number of discontinuities c_t^* or $\overline{c}_t$ might admit. Further,

$$\int_0^\infty u(c^{**}(t))\, e^{-(\rho-n)t}\, dt > \int_0^\infty u(c_t^*)\, e^{-(\rho-n)t}\, dt$$

by construction, which contradicts the presumed optimality of $\{c_t^*\}_0^\infty$.

According to the Principle of Optimality then,

$$V(\hat{k}_0) = \int_0^h u(c_t^*)\, e^{-(\rho-n)t}\, dt + V(\phi(c_t^*, h))$$

$$\geq \int_0^h u(c_t)\, e^{-(\rho-n)t}\, dt + V(\phi(c_{0,h})), \qquad (A4.2.3)$$

given any feasible path $\{c(t)\}_0^\infty$. Alternatively,

$$V(\hat{k}_0) = max_{c_0,h}\left\{\int_0^h u(c(t)) e^{-(\rho-n)t}\, dt + V(\phi(c_{0,h}))\right\}, \qquad (A4.2.4)$$

or, more generally,

$$V(\hat{k}_{t_0}) = max_{ct_0,t_0+h}\left\{\int_{t_0}^{t_0+h} u(c(t))\, e^{-(\rho-n)(t-t_0)}\, dt + V(\phi(c_{t_0,t_0+h}))\right\},$$
$$\qquad (A4.2.5)$$

where $max_{c_a,\,b}$ denotes maximization with respect to $c(t)$, $a \leq t \leq b$. (A4.2.4) [alternatively (A4.2.5)] is referred to as a *functional equation*. This completes our discussion of Bellman's Principle of Optimality.

NECESSARY CONDITIONS FOR STATIC OPTIMALITY

In what follows, we shall proceed under
Assumption V: $V(\hat{k})$ is continuously differentiable.

Assumption V allows us to make some approximations concerning the RHS of (A4.2.5). First, for h small,

$$u(c(t)) \cong u(c(t_0)), \quad t_0 \leq t \leq t_0 + h.$$

If t_0 is a point of discontinuity, we choose c_{t_0} as the right hand limit of $c(t)$ at t_0.[16]

---

[16] Note that replacing the optimal value of $c(t_0)$ by the right hand limit does not affect the value of the utility integral.

Therefore,

$$\int_{t_0}^{t_0+h} u(c(t))\, e^{-(\rho-n)(t-t_0)}\, dt \cong u(c(t_0)) \int_{t_0}^{t_0+h} e^{-(\rho-n)(t-t_0)}\, dt$$

$$= u(c(t_0))[-\frac{e^{-(\rho-n)(t-t_0)}}{\rho-n}]_{t_0}^{t_0+h}$$

$$= u(c(t_0))[-\frac{e^{-(\rho-n)h}}{\rho-n} + \frac{1}{\rho-n}]$$

$$= u(c(t_0))[\frac{1}{\rho-n}\{1 - e^{-(\rho-n)h}\}]$$

$$\cong u(c(t_0))[\frac{1}{\rho-n}\{1 - (1 - (\rho-n)h)\}]$$

by Taylor's approximation,

$$= u(c(t_0))h.$$

Thus, (A4.2.5) can be written as

$$V(\hat{k}_{t_0}) \cong \max_{c(t_0)} \left\{ h\, u(c(t_0)) + V(\hat{k}(t_0 + h)) \right\}, \tag{A4.2.6}$$

where $\hat{k}(t_0 + h)$ results from the choice of $c_{t_0,t_0+h} = c(t_0)$, $t_0 \le t \le t_0 + h$. A necessary condition for this optimum is

$$\frac{h\, \partial u(c(t_0))}{\partial c(t_0)} + \frac{\partial V(\hat{k}(t_0 + h))}{\partial c(t_0)} \ge 0. \tag{A4.2.7}$$

The *inequality* is explained by the fact that under irreversible investment, the optimum value of $c(t_0)$ might hit its upper bound given by (A4.2.1). This being a corner solution, the partial derivative may turn out to be strictly positive.

Next, note that

$$\frac{\partial V(\hat{k}(t_0 + h))}{\partial c(t_0)} = \frac{\partial V(\hat{k}(t_0 + h))}{\partial \hat{k}(t_0 + h)} \cdot \frac{\partial \hat{k}(t_0 + h)}{\partial c(t_0)}.$$

Linearizing again

$$\hat{k}(t_0 + h) \cong \hat{k}(t_0) + h\, \dot{\hat{k}}(t_0),$$

where, according to (4.10),

$$\dot{\hat{k}}(t_0) = f(\hat{k}(t_0)) - (\mu + n + \delta)\hat{k}(t_0) - \frac{c(t_0)}{A_{t_0}}.$$

Thus,

$$\frac{\partial \dot{\hat{k}}(t_0 + h)}{\partial c(t_0)} \cong -\frac{h}{A_{t_0}}.$$

Denote $\partial V(\hat{k}_t^*)/\partial \hat{k}(t)$ by q_t^*. The variable $q(t)$ stands for the maximum possible change in the social welfare from t onwards on account of a marginal change in $\hat{k}(t)$. In other words, it is the marginal value or shadow price of $\hat{k}$ at t along the optimal path. The assumption that V is differentiable implies that at any given value of $\hat{k}(t)$, the value of $q(t)$ is uniquely defined. Using these facts, the optimality of $\{c_t^*\}_{t_0}^{\infty}$, and the definition of q_t^*, (A4.2.7) reduces to

$$\frac{h \partial u(c_{t_0}^*)}{\partial c(t_0)} - q_{t_0+h}^* \frac{h}{A_{t_0}} = \frac{h \partial u(c_{t_0}^*)}{\partial c(t_0)} - \frac{h q_{t_0}^*}{A t_0} - \frac{h(q_{t_0+h}^* - q_{t_0}^*)}{A t_0} > 0$$

or,

$$\frac{\partial u(c_{t_0}^*)}{\partial c(t_0)} - \frac{q_{t_0}^*}{A_{t_0}} - \frac{(q_{t_0+h}^* - q_{t_0}^*)}{A_{t_0}} \geq 0.$$

Allowing $h \to 0$, replacing t_0 by t and using Assumption V, we see that for $\{c_t^*\}_0^{\infty}$ to be optimal,

$$\frac{\partial u(c_t^*)}{\partial c(t)} - \frac{q_t^*}{A_t} \geq 0, \quad \text{with equality}$$
$$\text{if } c_t^* \text{ is interior,} \tag{A4.2.8}$$

and

$$\left(\frac{\partial u(c_t^*)}{\partial c(t)} - \frac{q_t^*}{At} \right) z^*(t) = 0 \tag{A4.2.9}$$

must hold for all t.

THE MAXIMAL PRINCIPLE

The reader was introduced to the terminology Maximal Prinicple and the connection between the static optimization exercise and the auxiliary Hamiltonian function. We fill in some of the mathematical details of that discussion here and, in the process, generalize it to apply to the case of irreversible investment also.

Consider first the reversible investment case. We shall argue that in this case, c_t^* maximizes $\mathcal{H}$ subject to (4.10), $\hat{k}(t) = \hat{k}_t^*$ and $q(t) = q_t^*$ for each t. Moreover, the *FOC* characterizing such a solution is identically the same as the equality version of (A4.2.8). To see this, use (4.10) to get

$$\dot{\hat{k}}(t) = \left\{ f(\hat{k}^*(t)) - (\mu + n + \delta)\hat{k}^*(t) \right\} - \frac{c(t)}{At}.$$

Substituting in (4.15), $\mathcal{H}$ reduces to

$$\mathcal{H}(c(t), \hat{k}^*(t)q^*(t)) = u(c(t)) + q^*(t)[\{ f(\hat{k}^*(t)) - (\mu + n + \delta)\hat{k}^*(t) \} - \frac{c(t)}{A_t}],$$

which is a function of $c(t)$ alone. Differentiating $\mathcal{H}$ with respect to $c(t)$, we obtain $\partial u(c(t))/\partial c(t) - q^*(t)/A_t$. By assumption, $\exists$ a value c_t^* satisfying (4.10) and $\hat{k}(t) = \hat{k}_t^*$ such that

$$\frac{\partial u(c_t^*)}{\partial c(t)} - \frac{q_t^*}{A_t} = 0.$$

The shape of the level curves of $\mathcal{H}$ tells us further that c_t^* is a unique solution to the problem

Maximize $\mathcal{H}(c(t), \hat{k}_t^*, q_t^*)$ a subject to (4.10) (A4.2.10)

Next, consider a corner solution corresponding to irreversible investment. To relate it to the Hamiltonian, let us reformulate the relevant constraints in the Kuhn–Tucker form. Rewrite (4.10) as the inequality constraint

$$A_t\{ f(\hat{k}(t)) - (\mu + n + \delta)\hat{k}(t) \} - c(t) - A_t \dot{\hat{k}}(t) \geq 0 \quad (A4.2.11)$$

Similarly, note that

$$(\mu + n + \delta)\hat{k}(t) + \dot{\hat{k}}(t) \geq 0 \quad (A4.2.12)$$

must hold. The inequality (A4.2.8) may now be viewed as the *FOC* satisfying a corner solution to the problem

Maximize $\mathcal{H}(c(t), \hat{k}^*(t), q_t^*)$
subject to (A4.2.11) and (A4.2.12) . (A4.2.13)

Figure 4.4 shows that at the corner solution, both constraints are binding. The gradients to these constraints at the optimum point are

$(-1, -A_t)$ and $(0,1)$ respectively and the gradient to the objective function is $(u'(c_t^*), q_t^*)$. As per the Kuhn–Tucker conditions then, $\exists$ non-negative Lagrange multipliers λ_1 and λ_2 such that

$$(-u'(c_t^*), -q_t^*) = \lambda_1(-1, -A_t) + \lambda_2(0,1).$$

Moreover, it is easy to read from Figure 4.4 that (A4.2.8) must hold as a strict inequality.

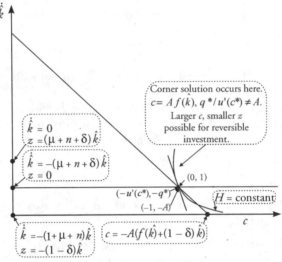

Figure 4.4: Corner Equilibrium

DYNAMIC OPTIMALITY

We shall consider the following perturbation in the optimal path (Figure 4.2):

(a) at t_0, consumption is lowered and investment increased marginally so as to raise $k_{t_0}^*$ to $\hat{k}'_{t_0}$, where $\hat{k}'_{t_0} - \hat{k}_{t_0}^* = \Delta$;

(b) $\hat{k}'_s = \hat{k}_s^* + \Delta \, \forall s > t_0$, or, as shown in Figure 4.2, $\hat{k}'_s$ is merely a parallel upward shift in $\hat{k}^*(s)$ for $s > t_0$;

(c) $\forall s > t_0$, the extra *per capita* output realized by the higher $\hat{k}'_s$ *after maintaining the additional* Δ *for all time* is consumed away.[17]

---

[17] The construction of the perturbed path follows Solow (2000).

The definition of $q(.)$ implies that the price of a unit of $\hat{k}(t_0)$ in units of $c(t_0)$ is $q_{t_0}^*/u'(c_{t_0}^*)$ along the optimal path. Thus, the sacrifice of $c(t_0)$ required to raise $k_{t_0}^*$ by Δ equals $(q_{t_0}^*/u'(c_{t_0}^*))\,\Delta$. This entails a loss of *utility* equal to $u'(c^*(t_0))\times\Delta(q_{t_0}^*/u'(c_{t_0}^*))=\Delta q_{t_0}^*$.

Let us now compute the extra utility provided by the new path $\forall s>t_0$. The extra per capita output brought forth by Δ at s equals $A_s f'(\hat{k}_s^*)\Delta$. This extra output is partly invested to maintain $\hat{k}(s)$ at the higher level. In units of z, the required investment is $(\mu+n+\delta)\,\Delta$, which equals $(q_s^*/u'(c_s^*))(\mu+n+\delta)\Delta$ in units of c. The extra per capita consumption permitted by the extra output after subtracting the investment is $A_s f'(\hat{k}_s^*)\Delta-(q_s^*/u'(c_s^*))(\mu+n+\delta)\Delta$. Multiplying out by $u'(c_s^*)$, the extra utility from the extra consumption at each s is given by $[A_s u'(c_s^*)f'(\hat{k}(s))-q_s^*(\mu+n+\delta)]\,\Delta$. Thus, the total discounted gain in utility at t_0 from the perturbation equals

$$\Delta\int_{t_0}^{\infty}e^{-(\rho-n)(s-t_0)}\{A_s u'(c_s^*)f'(\hat{k}_s^*)\ -q_s^*(\mu+n+\delta)\}ds\,.$$

Optimality, as noted, requires that the gain and the loss be equal. Hence,

$$\Delta\,q_{t_0}^*=\Delta\int_{t_0}^{\infty}e^{-(\rho-n)(s-t_0)}\{A_s u'(c_s^*)f'(\hat{k}_s^*)-q_s^*(\mu+n+\delta)\}ds$$

or, $\quad q_{t_0}^*=\int_{t_0}^{\infty}e^{-(\rho-n)(s-t_0)}\{A_s u'(c_s^*)f'(\hat{k}_s^*)-q_s^*(\mu+n+\delta)\}ds.$ (A4.2.14)

Replacing t_0 by t for notational ease, consistency between (A4.2.8) and (A4.2.14) implies

$$q_t^*\geq\int_t^{\infty}e^{-(\rho-n)(s-t)}q_s^*\{f'(\hat{k}_s^*)-(\mu+n+\delta)\}ds.\qquad\text{(A4.2.15)}$$

For q_t^* to be well defined, the integral on the RHS must exist for each t. We shall demonstrate in Appendix A 4.4 that the optimality of $\{c_t^*,\hat{k}_t^*\}_0^{\infty}$ implies $f'(\hat{k}_s^*)-(\mu+n+\delta)$ is bounded strictly away from zero for s sufficiently large. Anticipating this result, the integral can exist $\forall\,t$ only if the transversality condition (4.21) is satisfied. Differentiating (A4.2.14) with respect to t to get

$$\dot{q}_t^*=-\{A_t u'(c_t^*)f'(\hat{k}_t^*)-q_t^*(\mu+n+\delta)\}$$

$$+(\rho-n)\int_t^{\infty}e^{-(\rho-n)(s-t)}\{A_s u'(c_s^*)f'(\hat{k}_s^*)$$

$$-q_s^*(\mu+n+\delta)\}ds.$$

Using (A4.2.14), the last equation reduces to

$$\dot{q}_t^* = -\{A_t u'(c_t^*) f'(\hat{k}_t^*) - q_s^*(\mu + n + \delta)\} + (\rho - n)q_t^*. \qquad (A4.2.16)$$

The necessary conditions for static and dynamic optimality are renumbered and stated below for easy reference as

Proposition A.4.2.1:   If $\{c_t^*, \hat{k}_t^*\}_0^\infty$ is optimal, there exists a path of co-state variables $\{q_t^*\}_0^\infty$ such that

$$u'(c_t^*) \geq \frac{q_t^*}{A_t}, \text{ with equality for an interior } c_t^*; \qquad (A4.2.17)$$

$$\dot{\hat{k}}_t^* = f(\hat{k}_t^*) - \frac{c_t^*}{A_t} - (\mu + n + \delta)\hat{k}_t^*; \qquad (A4.2.18)$$

$$\dot{q}_t^* = -\{A_t u'(c_t^*) f'(\hat{k}_t^*) - q_t^*(\mu + n + \delta)\} + (\rho - n)q_t^*$$

$$= -A_t u'(c_t^*) f'(\hat{k}_t^*) + (\mu + \rho + \delta)q_t^*; \qquad (A4.2.19)$$

and $e^{-(\rho - n)t} q_t^* \to 0$ as $t \to \infty$. $\qquad (A4.2.20)$

THE HAMILTONIAN FUNCTION AGAIN

The link between (A4.2.17) of *Proposition A4.2.1* and the Hamiltonian was already indicated by (A4.2.10) and (A4.2.13). The remaining parts of this proposition can also be stated in terms of the same Hamiltonian function. Also (A4.2.18) follows from (4.28).

Here (4.23) established the link between (A4.2.19) and the Hamiltonian for the reversible investment case. For irreversible investment, use (4.10) and (A4.2.1) to get

$\mathcal{H} = u(A f(\hat{k})) - q(\mu + n + \delta)\hat{k}$, when c has a corner solution.

Differentiating $\mathcal{H}$ with respect to $\hat{k}$, we see that

$$\frac{\partial \mathcal{H}(c_s^*, \hat{k}_t^*, q_t^*)}{\partial \hat{k}(s)} = u'(c_s^*) A_s f'(\hat{k}_s^*) - q_t^*(\mu + n + \delta).$$

Using (A4.2.14) now, $q_t^* = \int_t^\infty (\partial \mathcal{H} / \partial \hat{k}(s)) e^{-(\rho - n)(s - t)} ds$. Thus,

$$\dot{q}_t^* = \frac{d(\int_t^\infty (\partial \mathcal{H}(c_s^*, \hat{k}_s^*, q_s^*) / \partial \hat{k}(s)) e^{-(\rho - n)(s - t)} ds)}{dt}$$

$$= -\frac{\partial \mathcal{H}(c_t^*, \hat{k}_t^*, q_t^*)}{\partial \hat{k}(t)} + (\rho - n)q_t^*$$

$$= -A_t\, u'(c_t^*) f'(\hat{k}_t^*) + (\mu + \rho + \delta)q_t^*, \qquad (A4.2.21)$$

which is none other than (A4.2.19). Let us collect the necessary conditions stated in terms of the Hamiltonian function as[18]

Proposition A4.2.2: Suppose $\{c_t^*,\, \hat{k}_t^*\}_0^\infty$ solves Version 1 or Version 2 of the problem. Then, there exists a path of co-state variables q_t^* such that (A4.2.10) (alternatively (A4.2.13)), (4.28), (A.4.2.21) and (A.4.2.20) are satisfied.

Appendix A4.3

Sufficient Conditions for an Optimum

We proceed to prove that under Assumptions u1 and f1, any path $\{c_t^*,\, \hat{k}_t^*,\, q_t^*\}_0^\infty$ satisfying (4.17), (4.28), (4.23), and (4.21) constitutes a unique solution to the problems stated as Version 1 and Version 2 above. Assume then that $\{c(t),\, \hat{k}(t)\}_0^\infty$ is any feasible path. Then (4.8), gives

$$A(f(\hat{k}) - \hat{z}) - c = 0, \qquad (A4.3.1)$$

where the time index t has been dropped for convenience. In what follows, we shall also use the fact u1 and f1 imply

$$u(c^*) - u(c) - u'(c^*)(c^* - c) > 0$$
$$f(\hat{k}^*) - f(\hat{k}) - f'(\hat{k}^*)(\hat{k}^* - \hat{k}) > 0. \qquad (A4.3.2)$$

Our claim is established if we can show that

$$D = \int_0^\infty \{u(c^*) - u(c)\} e^{-(\rho - n)t}\, dt > 0.$$

By adding and subtracting terms, we may use (A4.3.1) and the identity $\hat{z} = \hat{k} + (\mu + n + \delta)\hat{k}$ to write

---

[18] The conditions resemble standard representations of the first three necessary conditions, except for (A4.2.21). Also (A4.2.21) is borrowed from Cass (1965, 1966). The advantage of choosing the form (A4.2.21) is that it makes direct reference to the economic interpretation of a co-state variable. Moreover, it uses a single differential equation to describe the evolution of the co-state variable for both reversible and irreversible investment.

$$D = \int_0^\infty [\{u(c^*) - u(c)\} + u'(c^*)\{(A(f(\hat{k}^*) - \hat{z}^*) - c^*) - (A(f(\hat{k}) - \hat{z}) - c)\}$$
$$+ q^*\{(\hat{z}^* - \lambda\hat{k}^* - \dot{\hat{k}}^*) - (\hat{z} - \lambda\hat{k} - \dot{\hat{k}})\}] e^{-(\rho-n)t} dt,$$

where $\lambda = \mu + n + \delta$. Collecting terms,

$$D = \int_0^\infty [\{u(c^*) - u(c) - u'(c^*)(c^* - c)\} + \{q^*(\hat{z}^* - \hat{z})$$
$$- Au'(c^*)(\hat{z}^* - \hat{z})\} - q^*\{\lambda(\hat{k}^* - \hat{k}) + (\dot{\hat{k}}^* - \dot{\hat{k}})\}$$
$$+ Au'(c^*)\{f(\hat{k}^*) - f(\hat{k})\}] e^{-(\rho-n)t} dt, \tag{A4.3.3}$$

Reducing (A4.3.3) further by integrating $\int_0^\infty q^*(\dot{\hat{k}}^* - \dot{\hat{k}})e^{-(\rho-n)t} dt$ by parts. Thus,

$$\int_0^\infty q^*(\dot{\hat{k}}^* - \dot{\hat{k}})e^{-(\rho-n)t} dt = e^{-(\rho-n)t} q^*(\hat{k}^* - \hat{k}) \big|_0^\infty$$
$$- \int_0^\infty (\hat{k}^* - \hat{k})\{\dot{q}^* e^{-(\rho-n)t} - (\rho-n)q^* e^{-(\rho-n)t}\} dt.$$

Proposition 1 has demonstrated that any feasible path $\{\hat{k}\}$ is bounded above. Using (4.21), the last equation reduces to

$$\int_0^\infty q^*(\dot{\hat{k}}^* - \dot{\hat{k}})e^{-(\rho-n)t} dt$$
$$= - \int_0^\infty (\hat{k}^* - \hat{k})\{\dot{q}^* e^{-(\rho-n)t} - (\rho-n)q^* e^{-(\rho-n)t}\} dt. \tag{A4.3.4}$$

Plugging (A4.3.4) into (A4.3.3)

$$D = \int_0^\infty [\{u(c^*) - u(c) - u'(c^*)(c^* - c)\} + \{q^* - Au'(c^*)\}(\hat{z}^* - \hat{z})$$
$$- q^*\lambda(\hat{k}^* - \hat{k}) + (\dot{q}^* - (\rho-n)q^*)(\hat{k}^* - \hat{k})$$
$$+ Au'(c^*)\{f(\hat{k}^*) - f(\hat{k})\}] e^{-(\rho-n)t} dt$$
$$= \int_0^\infty [\{u(c^*) - u(c) - u'(c^*)(c^* - c)\} + \{q^* - Au'(c^*)\}(\hat{z}^* - \hat{z})$$
$$+ (\hat{k}^* - \hat{k})\{\dot{q}^* - (\rho + \lambda - n)q^* + Au'(c^*) f'(\hat{k}^*)\}$$
$$+ Au'(c^*)\{f(\hat{k}^*) - f(\hat{k}) - f'(\hat{k}^*)(\hat{k}^* - \hat{k})\}] e^{-(\rho-n)t} dt, \tag{A4.3.5}$$

adding and subtracting $Au'(c^*) f'(\hat{k}^*) - (\hat{k}^* - \hat{k})$. Note that $(q^* - Au'(c^*))\hat{z}^* = 0$ according to (A4.2.9). Further, $(q^* - Au'(c^*))\hat{z} = 0$ for reversible investment. In case of irreversible investment,

$q * -Au'(c^*) \leq 0$ and $\hat{z} \geq 0$. Hence, $(q * - Au'(c^*))(\hat{z} * - \hat{z}) \geq 0$ in all cases. Appealing to this fact along with (A4.3.2), the definition of λ, and (A4.2.19), (A4.3.5) implies

$$D > \int_0^\infty [(\hat{k} * - \hat{k})\{\hat{q} * - (\rho + \lambda - n)q *$$

$$+ Au'(c^*)f'(\hat{k}^*)\}]e^{-(\rho-n)t}dt$$

$$= \int_0^\infty [(\hat{k} * - \hat{k})\{\hat{q} * - (\rho + \delta + \mu)q *$$

$$+ Au'(c^*)f'(\hat{k}^*)\}]e^{-(\rho-n)t}dt$$

$$= \int_0^\infty (\hat{k} * - \hat{k})\{\hat{q} * - \hat{q}^*\}dt$$

$$= 0.$$

This establishes that $\{c_t^*, \hat{k}_t^*\}_0^\infty$ is a unique optimum path. We may note in passing that the last inequality will be weak if both u and f are weakly concave. Thus, we have proved the following result:[19]

Proposition A4.3.1: The conditions enumerated in *Proposition 2*, along with the strict concavity of u and f, are sufficient for the existence of a unique solution to the planner's problem.

Appendix A4.4

What Guarantees the Transversality Condition?

A steady-state path of capital accumption is defined to be one along which Y/AL, k and $\hat{c} = c/A$ are constants. If follows from (4.10) that along any steady-state path

$$\hat{c} = f(\hat{k}) - \lambda\hat{k}, \tag{A4.4.1}$$

where $\lambda = \mu + n + \delta$ as before. The value of $\hat{k}$ maximizing $\hat{c}$ in steady state is referred to as the Golden Rule (GR) value of the effective capital–labour ratio. It is the solution $\hat{k}^{**}$ to the equation

---

[19] Mangasarian (1966) proved the corresponding result for the finite-horizon problem.

$$f'(\hat{k}) = \lambda. \qquad\qquad (A4.4.2)$$

The corresponding value of $\hat{c}$ satisfying (A4.4.1) is denoted by $\hat{c}^{**}$. The per capita consumption corresponding to $\hat{c}^{**}$ is

$$c_t^{**} = A_t \hat{c}^{**} = A_t(f(\hat{k}^{**}) - \lambda \hat{k}^{**}).$$

The path of c_t^{**} will be referred to as the GR path of per capita consumption. Given any steady state pair, $(\hat{c}, \hat{k}) \neq (\hat{c}^{**}, \hat{k}^{**})$, it follows from definition that $c_t^{**} > c(t) \forall t$. The welfare associated with a steady-state path is $\int_0^\infty u(A_t \hat{c}) e^{-(\rho - n)t} dt$. As already noted in connection with Assumption T, the integral may not exist unless the assumptions on the model are strengthened further. For example, we may assume that the instantaneous utility function has the form $u(c) = (c^{1-\theta} - 1)/(1 - \theta)$, $\theta > 0$. Such a utility function has a constant elasticity of marginal utility from consumption ($= \theta$). Alternatively, it admits a constant elasticity of substitution between consumption at different points of time. When u has this form, convergence of $\int_0^\infty u(A_t \hat{c}(t)) e^{-(\rho - n)t} dt$ is guaranteed if $\rho - n > (1-\theta)\mu$.[20]

We are now ready to prove the following.

Proposition A4.4.1: For any optimal path $\{c_t^*, \hat{k}_t^*\}_0^\infty$, $\exists$ a t_0 such that $f'(\hat{k}_t^*) - \lambda$ is positive and bounded strictly away from zero $\forall t > t_0$. In other words, the optimal path of capital accumulation stays bounded away from the GR in the long run.[21]

[20] The condition, which follows from the fact that A grows at the constant rate μ, turns out to be problematic for endogenous growth theory, since μ is not exogenously given. It is frequently encountered in the literature, however. *See,* Barro (1990). Dasgupta (2001) discusses further details.

[21] Proposition (J) in Koopmans (1965) proves the stronger statement that $f'(k^*(t)) \to (\mu + \rho + \delta)$. Since, $\rho > n$, Koopmans's result implies ours. The control theory methods developed here can be used to prove Koopmans's result also in a straightforward manner. We shall not undertake that exercise here and remain satisfied with the weaker statement, given that our objective is to establish the transversality condition (A4.2.20). The stronger result is proved in Barro and Sala-i-Martin (2004) and Dasgupta (2005).

Proof: The proof holds for both reversible and irreversible investment. Further, the arguments, though stated for a Command Economy, apply, mutatis mutandis to a Private Economy also. The result will be derived in two steps. The first will demonstrate that the GR per capita consumption path $\{A_t \hat{c}^{**}\}$ associated with indefinite maintenance of $\hat{k}^{**}$ is a suboptimal policy. The second step will then show that a path for which $f'(\hat{k}_t^*) \to (\mu + n + \delta)$ is suboptimal.

Step 1: In what follows, we shall abbreviate by writing $\lambda = \mu + n + \delta$. (A4.4.1) implies that along the GR path

$$\hat{c}^{**} + \lambda \hat{k}^{**} = f(\hat{k}^{**}), \tag{A4.4.3}$$

As an alternative to the path $\{A_t \hat{c}^{**}, \hat{k}^{**}\}$, consider a path which raises per capita consumption at $t = 0$ above $A_0 \hat{c}^{**}$ by reducing $\hat{k}^{**}$ to $\hat{k}' = \hat{k}^{**} - \Delta$. It is possible to achieve this by reducing $\hat{z}$ below $\lambda \hat{k}^{**}$.[22] Thus, we have

$$\begin{aligned} f(\hat{k}^{**}) &= \hat{c}^{**} + \lambda \hat{k}' + \lambda(\hat{k}^{**} - \hat{k}') \\ &= \hat{c}^{**} + \lambda \Delta + \lambda \hat{k}'. \end{aligned}$$

Thus, the change in $\hat{c}^{**}$ is $\lambda \Delta$ and the rise in per capita consumption at $t = 0$ is $A_0 \lambda \Delta$.

The alternative path is constructed to maintain $\hat{k}$ at this constant value $\hat{k}' \; \forall t > 0$. Per capita consumption for all $t > 0$ is $A_t \hat{c}'$ along the alternative path, where $(\hat{c}', \hat{k}')$ solves (A4.4.3). Linearizing around $A_0 \hat{c}^{**}$, the gain in utility at $t = 0$ from the change is

$$\begin{aligned} \mathcal{G}(0) &= u(A_0 \hat{c}^{**} + A_0 \lambda \Delta) - u(A_0 \hat{c}^{**}) \\ &\cong u(A_0 \hat{c}^{**}) + A_0 \lambda \Delta u'(A_0 \hat{c}^{**}) - u(A_0 \hat{c}^{**}) \\ &= A_0 \lambda \Delta u'(A_0 \hat{c}^{**}). \end{aligned} \tag{A4.4.4}$$

Denote $u'(A_0 \hat{c}^{**})$ by u'^{**}.

We proceed now to compare the initial gain $A_0 \lambda \Delta u'^{**}$ with subsequent losses. The loss in utility from the change at each $t > 0$ is

$$\begin{aligned} \mathcal{L}(t) &= u(A_t \hat{c}^{**}) - u(A_t \hat{c}') \\ &= u(A_t \hat{c}^{**}) - u(A_t(f(\hat{k}') - \lambda \hat{k}')). \end{aligned}$$

---

[22] One may consume part of the capital also in the reversible investment case, but we do not follow up this possibility. The proof we construct, instead, works for both reversible as well as irreversible investment.

Linearizing around $\hat{k}^{**}$,

$$\mathcal{L}(t) \cong u(A_t\hat{c}^{**}) - u[A_t(f(\hat{k}^{**}) - \Delta f'(\hat{k}^{**}) + \frac{\Delta^2}{2} f''(\hat{k}^{**})$$

$$-\lambda\hat{k}^{**} + \lambda\Delta)]$$

$$= u(A_t\hat{c}^{**}) - u[A_t((f(\hat{k}^{**}) - \lambda\hat{k}^{**}) - \Delta(f'(\hat{k}^{**})$$

$$-\lambda) + \frac{\Delta^2}{2} f''(\hat{k}^{**})]$$

$$= u(A_t\hat{c}^{**}) - u(A_t(\hat{c}^{**}) + \frac{\Delta^2}{2} f''(\hat{k}^{**})), \text{ using (A4.4.2)},$$

$$\cong u(A_t\hat{c}^{**}) - (u(A_t(\hat{c}^{**}) + \frac{\Delta^2}{2} f''(\hat{k}^{**})u'(A_t\hat{c}^{**}))),$$

(linearizing around $A_t\hat{c}^{**}$),

$$= -\frac{\Delta^2}{2} A_t f''^{**} u'(A_t\hat{c}^{**}), \tag{A4.4.5}$$

where $f''^{**} = f''(\hat{k}^{**})$. The discounted stream of losses incurred during $(0, \infty)$ is

$$\int_0^\infty \mathcal{L}(t)e^{-(\rho-n)t}dt = \frac{\Delta^2}{2}\int_0^\infty (-f''^{**}A_t u'(A_t\hat{c}^{**})e^{-(\rho-n)t}\,dt$$
$$> 0, \tag{A.4.4.6}$$

since $f'' < 0$ by Assumption f 1. The net change in welfare to the household from the perturbation is

$$\omega = \mathcal{G}(0) - \int_0^\infty \mathcal{L}(t)e^{-(\rho-n)t}dt$$

$$= A_0\lambda\Delta u'^{**} - (\Delta^2/2)\int_0^\infty (-f''^{**}A_t u'(A_t\hat{c}^{**})e^{-(\rho-n)t}dt).$$

Let

$$\xi^* = \int_0^\infty (-f''^{**}A_t u'(A_t\hat{c}^{**})e^{-(\rho-n)t}dt),$$

so that

$$\omega = A_0\lambda\Delta u'^{**} - (\Delta^2/2)\xi^*$$

$$= \Delta\xi^*(A_0\lambda u'^{**}/\xi^* - \Delta/2).$$

Since A_0, λ, u'^{**}, and ξ^* are fixed, $\exists$ an ε such that $\Delta < \varepsilon \Rightarrow \omega > 0$. So long as the reduction in $\hat{k}$ falls short of ε, the perturbation from the path $\{A_t, \hat{c}^{**}, \hat{k}^{**}\}$ constructed above is welfare improving.

Step 2: Suppose now that the proposition is false. Then, $\exists$ an optimal path $\{\hat{c}_t^*, \hat{k}_t^*\}$ such that $|\hat{c}_t^* - \hat{c}^{**}|$ and $|\hat{k}_t^* - \hat{k}^{**}|$ are arbitrarily small for t large enough. Consider the following perturbation. At a large enough t_0, disinvest down to k' (defined in *Step 1*) and maintain $\{\hat{c}', \hat{k}'\}$ then onwards. The extra consumption generated is Δ_{t_0}, where $|\Delta_{t_0} - A_{t_0}\lambda\Delta|$ is arbitrarily small for t_0 large enough (given the definition of Δ in *Step 1*).

The per capita consumption at t_0 changes to $A_{t_0}\hat{c}_{t_0}^* + \Delta_{t_0}$ and the gain in utility from the increased consumption is $u(A_{t_0}\hat{c}_{t_0}^* + \Delta_{t_0}) - u(A_{t_0}\hat{c}_{t_0}^*) = v$ (say). For large enough t_0, the value of $v \cong u(A_{t_0}\hat{c}^{**} + A_{t_0}\lambda\Delta) - u(A_{t_0}\hat{c}^{**})$. Thus, using *Step 1* again, we may assume $v \cong A_{t_0}\lambda\Delta u'(A_{t_0}\hat{c}^{**})$.

Since $k_t^* \to \hat{k}^{**}$, it is possible to assume *wlog* that $u(c_t^*) - u(A_t\hat{c}') > 0 \;\forall t > t_0$. Thus, utility falls by $u(c_t^*) - u(A_t\hat{c}')$ at each $t > t_0$. The discounted present value of the stream of losses is $\int_{t_0}^{\infty}(u(c_t^*) - u(A_t\hat{c}'))e^{-(\rho-n)(t-t_0)}dt$. We have, by definition of GR,

$$\int_{t_0}^{\infty}(u(A_t\hat{c}^{**}) - u(A_t\hat{c}'))e^{-(\rho-n)(t-t_0)}dt$$
$$> \int_{t_0}^{\infty}(u(c_t^*) - u(A_t\hat{c}'))e^{-(\rho-n)(t-t_0)}dt,$$

or,

$$-\int_{t_0}^{\infty}(u(A_t\hat{c}^{**}) - u(A_t\hat{c}'))e^{-(\rho-n)(t-t_0)}dt$$
$$< -\int_{t_0}^{\infty}(u(c_t^*) - u(A_t\hat{c}'))e^{-(\rho-n)(t-t_0)}dt,$$

or,

$$-(\Delta^2/2)\xi_{t_0}^* < -\int_{t_0}^{\infty}(u(c_t^*) - u(A_t\hat{c}'))e^{-(\rho-n)(t-t_0)}dt,$$

where $\xi_{t_0}^*$ corresponds to ξ^* of *Step 1* with due alteration of details. Thus, the net gain is approximately equal to

$$A_{t_0}\lambda\Delta u'(A_{t_0}\hat{c}^{**}) - \int_{t_0}^{\infty}(u(c_t^*) - u(A_t\hat{c}'))e^{-(\rho-n)(t-t_0)}dt$$
$$> A_{t_0}\lambda\Delta u'(A_{t_0}\hat{c}^{**}) - (\Delta^2/2)\xi_{t_0}^* > 0$$

for an appropriately small value of Δ.

This completes the proof.

Appendix A4.5

Halkin's Counter-example

This appendix discusses a famous example due to Halkin (1974) which constructs an infinite-horizon problem for which the transversality condition is not a necessary characterization of optimality.

Before stating the details of the example, let us go back to (A4.2.15) and analyse the reason why it leads to (4.21). The inequality (A4.2.15) is a relationship between the shadow price of investment q_t^* and all subsequent shadow prices over infinite time. Note that, given the objective function and the technology, (4.21) holds because optimality imposes non-trivial restrictions on the behaviour of the capital accumulation path for all $t > t_0$. (*See* Proposition A4 above.) Halkin, on the other hand, constructs an objective function which leaves the path of accumulation unrestricted.

To get a feel for Halkin's example, consider an agent engaged in wealth accumulation. Her lifetime utility depends on the difference between the terminal (that is limiting) value of her wealth and the initial wealth she owns. Suppose that the maximum possible value of the terminal wealth is $\bar{K}$ and that her initial wealth is K_0. Then, the optimum value of her welfare is $\bar{K} - K_0$. The important characteristic of this objective function is that the agent's welfare is independent of the path followed for approaching $\bar{K}$. The marginal social product of a rise in K_0 is thus $q(0) = \partial(\bar{K} - K_0)/\partial K_0 = -1$, which is independent of the marginal social productivities of K along the way to the optimum $\bar{K}$. Consequently, the value of the shadow price at $t = 0$ does not put any restriction on future values of the shadow price. The same argument holds for the shadow price at any later point in time. In other words, $q(t) = \partial(\bar{K} - K(s))/\partial K(s) = -1 \forall s > t$. Hence, for this problem, the co-state variable does not converge to zero.

Let us now state and work out the example algebraically. The problem is stated as follows:

$$\text{Maximize} \int_0^\infty (1 - y)\, u\, dt$$

subject to

$$\dot{y} = (1 - y)u,$$

$$y(0) = 0,$$
$$u \in [0, 1].$$

Obviously, u and y are respectively the control and state variables for this problem.

Solution: Substituting the state equation in the objective function,

$$\int_0^\infty \dot{y} dt = y \big|_0^\infty$$

$$= \lim_{t \to \infty} y(t).$$

The problem thus reduces to maximizing $\lim_{t \to \infty} y(t)$. To find the upper bound of y, we solve the equation

$$\dot{y} + (y - 1) u = 0.$$

Substituting $z = y - 1$, the equation reduces to

$$\dot{z} + zu = 0.$$

The solution to this equation is

$$z(t) = be^{-\int_0^t u(v)\, dv}, \quad b = \text{constant},$$

or,

$$y(t) = 1 + be^{-\int_0^t u(v)\, dv}.$$

At $t = 0$, $y(0) = 0 = 1 + b$, or $b = -1$. Hence, the general solution is

$y(t) = 1 - e^{-\int_0^t u(v)\, dv}$.   Writing $\int_0^t u(v) dv = h(t) \geq 0$, the solution is $y(t) = 1 - e^{-h(t)}$, whence $y(t) \in [0, 1]$. Thus, the upper bound of $y(t)$ is unity and any path leading to it is a solution to the problem. There is no unique optimum path. Indeed, any constant $u \in (0, 1)$ is a solution to the problem. Suppose such a constant u^* is selected.

The Hamiltonian for the problem is

$$\mathcal{H} = (1 - y) u + \lambda(1 - y) u$$
$$= ((1 - y)(1 + \lambda)) u.$$

The FOC's are:

$$\dot{y} = u(1 - y),$$
$$\dot{\lambda} = (1 + \lambda) u,$$
$$(1 - y)(1 + \lambda) = 0.$$

Choose $\lambda^* = -1 \forall t$. Then $(u, \lambda) = (u^*, -1)$ satisfies all the optimality conditions, but $\lim_{t \to \infty} \lambda(t) \neq 0$. Note that the value of the co-state variable tallies with the one we obtained above from purely economic arguments. This completes the counter-example.

REFERENCE

AGHION P. and P. HOWITT, (1998), *Endogenous Growth Theory*, Cambridge, Masschusetts: The MIT Press.

ARROW, K.J. and M. KURZ, (1970), *Public Investment, the Rate of Return and Optimal Fiscal Policy*, Baltimore: Johns Hopkins University Press.

BARRO, R., (1990), 'Government Spending in a Simple Model of Endogenous Growth', *Journal of Political Economy*, 98, pp. S103–S125.

BARRO, R. and X. SALA-I-MARTIN, (2004), *Economic Growth*, 2nd Edition, Cambridge, Massachusetts: The MIT Press.

BELLMAN, R., (1957), *Dynamic Programming*, Princeton, New Jersey: Princeton University Press.

BOSE, S., (1970), Optimal Growth with Non-shiftable Capital, *Econometrica*, 38, pp. 128–52.

——, (1971), 'Optimal Growth and Wealth Effect: Comment', *International Economic Review*, 12, pp. 157–60.

BURMEISTER E. and R.A. DOBELL, 1970, *Mathematical Theories of Economic Growth*, New York: Macmillan.

CASS, D., (1965), 'Optimum Growth in an Aggregative Model of Capital Accumulation,' *Review of Economic Studies*, 32, pp. 233–40.

——, (1966), 'Optimum Growth in an Aggregative Model of Capital Accumulation: A Turnpike Theorem', *Econometrica*, 34, pp. 33–50.

CHIANG, A.C., (1992), *Elements of Dynamic Optimisation*, McGraw Hill.

DASGUPTA, D., (2001), Lindahl Pricing, Non-rival Infrastructure, and Endogenous Growth, *Journal of Public Economic Theory*, 3, pp. 413–30.

——, (2005), *Growth Theory: Solow and his Modern Exponents*, New Delhi: Oxford University Press.

DIXIT, A.K., (1990), *Optimisation in Economic Theory*, 2nd Edition, Oxford, UK: Oxford University Press.

DORFMAN, (1968), 'An Economic Interpretation of Optimal Control Theory', *American Economic Review*, 59, pp. 817–31.

HALKIN, H., (1974), 'Necessary Condition for Optimal Control Problems with Infinite Horizons', *Econometrica*, 42 pp. 267–72.

INTRILLIGATOR, M., (1971), *Mathematical Optimisation and Economic Theory*, Englewood Cliffs, New Jersey: Prentice-Hall.

KAMIEN, M.I. and N.L. SCHWARTZ, (2000), *Dynamic Optimisation: The Calculation of Variations and Optimal Control in Economics and Management*. 2nd Edition, Amsterdam: Elservier.

KOOPMANS, T.C., (1965), 'On the Concept of Optimal Economic Growth', in *The Econometric Approach to Development Planning*, Amsterdam: North-Holland.

MANGASARIAN, O.L., (1966), 'Sufficient Conditions for the Optimal Control of Non-linear Systems, *SIAM Journal on Control*, 4, pp. 139–52.

PONTRYAGIN, L.S., V.G. Bolthysanskü, R.V. Gankrelidze, and E.F. Mioschenko, (1962), *The Mathematical Theory of Optimal Processes*, (tr.). K.N. Triogoff; (ed.) L.W. Neustadt, New York: Wiley-Interscience.

RAMSEY, F., (1928), 'A Mathematical Theory of Saving', *Economic Journal*, 38, pp. 543–59.

SOLOW, R., (1956), 'A Contribution to the Theory of Economic Growth', *Quarterly Journal of Economics*, 32, pp. 65–94.

_____, (2000), *Growth Theory: An Exposition*, Oxford: UK, Oxford University Press.

5. Identifying the Leading Sector
Analytics of a Linear
Hayek-Inada Economy

MUKUL MAJUMDAR AND ILARIA OSSELLA-DURBAL

INTRODUCTION

The linear model of production—admittedly restrictive in its scope—
has enjoyed a privileged position as a general equilibrium system that
can provide a theoretical basis for computational and empirical work.
In this paper, we use it to discuss the problem of identifying the leading
sectors of an economy, sectors for which improvements in productivity
induce the greatest acceleration in long-run growth. The ability of
specific key sectors to lead the process of development has been an issue
of lasting importance in development economics (Ray 1998: Ch. 5). In
our earlier work (Majumdar and Ossella 1999), we found that a possible
formal treatment of the identification of leading sectors led to the study
of the sensitivity of the Perron–Frobenius root of a primitive matrix to
changes in its entries. We noted that sharp analytical results on this
mathematical problem were (and still are) elusive, and by using the 1989
input requirement matrix prepared by the Central Statistical
Organization of the Government of India, we illustrated a computational
approach. In this paper, we provide an example with a linear model of
production in which an analytical solution to the problem is possible.
We should stress right away that the special structure of the input
requirement matrix makes it unsuitable for serious empirical work.
However, the relative stability theorem reported here is not implied by
any of the available results in the theoretical literature, since the input

requirement matrix is neither strictly positive (assumed by Dasgupta and Mitra 1988) nor primitive (assumed by Ossella 1999). Although our model is 'closed' and does not allow for a 'primary' or 'non-producible' factor of production, the structure of interdependence of the sectors is similar to the Hayekian production processes studied by Inada (1968). Inada's multi-sector model allowed for 'labour', a primary factor of production, and dealt with non-linear production processes; however, he did use the 'upper-triangular structure' that is exploited in this paper. The present paper is essentially of pedagogical interest, and it aims at filling a small but awkward gap in the theoretical literature.

The structure of the paper is as follows. The second section introduces the mathematical notation. In the third section, we describe the model, as well as discuss two criteria for evaluating feasible production–consumption programmes. Specifically, we present the main results on inter-temporal efficiency and optimal growth with discounting for a closed linear model of production. We then formally define a leading sector in the fourth section and illustrate a computational approach for identifying such sectors. The fifth section introduces the special example discussed above, and the relative stability property for this production framework is proved in the last section.

NOTATION

If $x = (x_i)$ and $y = (y_i)$ are any two vectors in n-dimensional Euclidean space $\Re^n$, then $x \geq y$ implies that $x_i \geq y_i$ for all $i = 1, \ldots, n$; $x > y$ implies that $x \geq y$ and $x \neq y$; and $x >> y$ implies that $x_i > y_i$ for all $i = 1, \ldots, n$. A vector x is *non-negative* if $x \geq 0$; x is *positive* if $x > 0$; and x is *strictly positive* if $x >> 0$. Let $\Re^n_+ = \{x \in \Re^n : x \geq 0\}$ and $\Re^n_{++} = \{x \in \Re^n : x >> 0\}$. Moreover, define the sum norm ($\| \cdot \|$) in $\Re^n$ by $\| x \| = \Sigma^n_{i=1} |x_i|$ and let $e = (1, 1, \ldots, 1)$.

If $A = [a_{ij}]$ is an $n \times n$ real matrix, then A is *non-negative* ($A \geq 0$) if $a_{ij} \geq 0$, for all $i, j = 1, \ldots, n$; A is *positive* ($A > 0$) if A is non-negative and is not a zero matrix; and A is *strictly positive* ($A >> 0$) if $a_{ij} > 0$, for all $i, j = 1, \ldots, n$.

THE MODEL

We briefly recall the simple linear model of production (*see* Nikaido 1968: 6.2, pp. 88–95; Gale 1960: 9.1, pp. 294–9 for details). There are *n* goods and activities. Each activity produces one good, and each good is produced by one and only one activity. We label the activities so that the unique activity producing good *i* is the *i*-th activity. Moreover, with constant returns to scale and no possibility of input substitution, the input requirements of the activities are described by a non-negative square ($n \times n$) matrix $A = [a_{ij}]$. We interpret the activities as different sectors of an economy. Then a_{ij} is the quantity of good *i* needed to produce a unit of the *j*-th good. The *technology set* is given by

$$\Omega = \{(x, y) \in \mathfrak{R}^n_+ \times \mathfrak{R}^n_+ : Ay \leq x\},$$

where Ay are the input requirements for producing output vector *y*.

We impose the following restriction on the input requirement matrix:

(*A*.1) *A is a non-negative square matrix each of whose columns is a positive vector.*

This assumption (A.1) rules out 'free' production, in the sense that each good requires a positive amount of at least one input.

Let $\tilde{y} \in \mathfrak{R}^n_+$ be an exogenously given *initial stock* vector. A *feasible production programme* from $\tilde{y}$ is a sequence $<x(t), y(t)>$ of vectors such that

$$\tilde{y} = y(0),$$
$$0 \leq x(t) \leq y(t) \text{ for all } t \geq 0, \text{ and} \tag{5.1}$$
$$Ay\,(t+1) \leq x(t) \text{ for all } t \geq 0.$$

Associated with every feasible production programme $<x(t), y(t)>$ from $\tilde{y}$ is a *consumption programme* $<c(t)>$ where $c(t) = y(t) - x(t)$ for all $t \geq 0$. It results from (5.1), that $c(t) \geq 0$ for all $t \geq 0$.

Efficiency

We turn to alternative criteria for evaluating feasible production–consumption programmes: we begin with (inter-temporal) efficiency and then move on to optimality.

A feasible programme $<x(t), y(t)>$ from $\tilde{y}$ is *efficient* if there does not exist another feasible programme $<x'(t), y'(t)>$ from $\tilde{y}$ where $c'(t) \geq c(t)$ for all $t \geq 0$ and $c'(t) > c(t)$ for some *t*. The question of characterizing efficient programmes in terms of competitive prices in a decentralized, infinite-horizon economy was studied first by Malinvaud (1953), and his enduring contribution exposed two startling possibilities. First, even with a convex technology, an efficient infinite programme need not have a supporting system of competitive prices (a 'non-tightness' condition was introduced to prove the existence of Malinvaud prices). Secondly, inter-temporal profit maximization relative to a system of strictly positive prices need not guarantee efficiency. He introduced a 'transversality condition' that is sufficient to rule out inefficiency of competitive programmes. However, the golden rule programme in the aggregative model is an example of an efficient programme that can be supported by competitive prices and does not satisfy Malinvaud's sufficiency condition. Thus, Malinvaud's paper naturally led to the problem of providing a complete technological or price characterization of efficient programmes, and was the primary focus of subsequent studies by Koopmans, Cass, Hurwicz, Majumdar, and others particularly in the context of the decentralization of decision making (see the brief Foreword by Malinvaud as well as Chapters 1 and 2 in the collection edited by Majumdar [1993]).

It turns out that the special structure of the simple linear model of production provides a complete characterization of all efficient programme (Majumdar 1974). It is stated precisely below.

Proposition 1:

    (i)   If $< x(t), y(t) >$ is a programme from $\tilde{y}$, $\Sigma_{t=0}^{\infty} A^t c(t) \leq \tilde{y}$.

    (ii) Conversely, if $c(t) \in \Re_{+}^{n}$ for all $t \geq 0$, $\tilde{y} \in \Re_{+}^{n}$, and $\Sigma_{t=0}^{\infty} A^t c(t) \leq \tilde{y}$, there is a programme $< x'(t), y'(t) >$ from $\tilde{y}$, with $c'(t) = c(t)$ for all $t \geq 0$.

    (iii) A programme $< x(t), y(t) >$ from $\tilde{y}$ is efficient if and only if $\Sigma_{t=0}^{\infty} A^t c(t) = \tilde{y}$.

There are many efficient programmes from $\tilde{y} \gg 0$.

OPTIMAL GROWTH: THE DISCOUNTED CASE

Consider an economy that is represented by the triplet (A, w, δ), where A is the input requirement matrix; $w: \mathfrak{R}^n_+ \to \mathfrak{R}$ is the one-period return, felicity, or welfare function; and $\delta \in (0, 1)$ is a discount factor. We make a stronger assumption on the input requirement matrix, A. Specifically, we replace $(A.1)$ with the following assumption $(A'.1)$, as well as add a productivity constraint on A.

$(A'.1)$ A is a non-negative matrix which is primitive (that is, there exists a positive integer k such that $A^k \gg 0$).

$(A.2)$ A is productive (that is, there is a $z \in \mathfrak{R}^n_+$ such that $Az \ll z$).

Note that the results presented in this section were originally established under the assumption that the input requirement matrix is strictly positive (Dasgupta and Mitra 1988). Assumption $(A'.1)$, instead, allows for input requirement matrices with zero entries. This is an important point since the input requirement matrix for an economy with a large number of goods is typically not strictly positive, but can be primitive. Assumption $(A.2)$, is equivalent to the Hawkins–Simon condition in the literature on linear or Leontief systems (Nikaido 1968: 90).

In addition, we assume that the welfare function is iso-elastic (Atsumi 1969):

$(A.3)$ $w(c)=[f(c)]^{1-\alpha}$ for $c \geq 0$, where $0 < \alpha < 1$ and $f: \mathfrak{R}^n_+ \to \mathfrak{R}_+$ satisfies the following restrictions:

     (a) f is concave and continuous on $\mathfrak{R}^n_+$;

     (b) f is homogeneous of degree one;

     (c) $f(c') \geq f(c)$ when $c' \geq c$; $f(c') > f(c)$ if $c' > c$ and $f(c) > 0$;

     (d) $f(c) > 0$ if and only if $c \gg 0$.

If $<c(t)>$ is a consumption programme associated with a feasible production programme $<x(t), y(t)>$, then $w(c(t))$ is the level of utility generated from consumption at each time period t. A programme $<x^*(t), y^*(t), c^*(t)>$ from $\tilde{y}$ is *optimal* if

$$\sum_{t=0}^{\infty} \delta^t w(c^*(t)) \geq \sum_{t=0}^{\infty} \delta^t w(c(t))$$

for all programmes $<x(t), y(t), c(t)>$ from $\tilde{y}$. In order to guarantee the existence of an optimal programme it is sufficient to restrict the parameters δ and α as follows:

(*A.4*) $\delta\hat{\lambda}^{(1-\alpha)} < 1$, where $\hat{\lambda}$ is the inverse of the largest eigenvalue of A. Note that $\hat{\lambda} > 1$, due to the productivity of the input requirement matrix (Nikaido 1968).

Given Assumptions (*A'*.1)–(*A.4*), it is possible to prove that an optimal programme exists.

Proposition 2: Given an initial stock $\tilde{y} \in \Re^n_+$, if $< x(t), y(t) >$ is any programme from $\tilde{y}$, then $\Sigma^\infty_{t=0}\delta^t w(c(t)) < \infty$. Furthermore, there is an optimal programme $< x^*(t), y^*(t) >$ from $\tilde{y}$.

The proof of *Proposition 2* is identical to the proof of Proposition 1 in Dasgupta and Mitra (1988). Note that a primitive matrix is non-negative and indecomposable by definition, and thus it has a strictly positive eigenvector corresponding to its maximal eigenvalue (Debreu and Herstein 1953).

Moreover, if an optimal programme from $\tilde{y}$ exists, where $\tilde{y} \gg 0$, then it is also efficient. Such a result is not immediate, since the welfare function is not necessarily increasing in each component. The proof of *Proposition 3*, as well as of all the other propositions in this section are to be found in Ossella (1999).

Proposition 3: If $< \bar{x}(t), \bar{y}(t) >$ is an optimal programme from $\tilde{y} \in \Re^n_{++}$, then $< \bar{x}(t), \bar{y}(t) >$ is an efficient programme from $\tilde{y}$.

Observe that the characterization of efficient programmes summarized in *Proposition 1* still holds for primitive input requirement matrices. This is because a primitive matrix is indecomposable by definition. Therefore, every column of A is a positive vector, since if e^i is the i-th unit vector in $\Re^n$, then $Ae^i \neq 0$ for all $i = 1, ..., n$ (Marcus and Mink 1964: Claim 5.2.4).

Given that an optimal programme exists, what can be said about the rate at which the optimal stocks of output grow? There are, in fact, two important results that deal with the growth rate of an optimal programme within our simple linear production framework. First of all, it is possible to prove the existence of a steady-state optimal programme, an optimal programme whose output levels grow at a constant rate. A *steady-state programme* from $\tilde{y} > 0$ is a feasible programme $<x(t), y(t)>$ from $\tilde{y}$ for which

$$y(t + 1) = gy(t) \qquad \text{for all } t \geq 0,$$

where g is a positive real number. A *steady-state optimal programme* is thus a steady-state programme that is optimal. Moreover, if there exists a steady-state optimal programme from y^*, then y^* is a *steady-state optimal stock*. One can assert that given Assumptions $(A'.1)–(A.4)$, there exists a steady-state optimal stock $y^* \gg 0$ whose associated steady-state optimal programme has a growth factor of $g = (\delta\hat{\lambda})^{1/\alpha}$.

Proposition 4: There exists a $y^* \gg 0$ such that $y^*(t) = g^t y^*$ and $x^*(t) = Ay^*(t + 1)$ for all $t \geq 0$ defines a steady-state optimal programme from y^* where $g = (\delta\hat{\lambda})^{1/\alpha}$.

The growth factor presented in *Proposition 4* is for a steady-state optimal programme. It is possible, however, also to derive a 'relative stability' result regarding the long-run growth rate of optimal programmes irrespective of the initial stock $\tilde{y} \gg 0$.

In order to establish this relative stability property of optimal programmes, we introduce one last restriction of 'strict concavity' on the welfare function.

$(A.5)$ If c, c' are non-negative, c is not proportional to c', and $f(c) > 0$, $f(c') > 0$, then, for $0 < \theta < 1$, $f(\theta c + (1-\theta)c') > \theta f(c) + (1-\theta) f(c')$.

The relative stability property of optimal programmes is formally presented in *Proposition 5*.

Proposition 5: Let $< \bar{x}(t), \bar{y}(t), \bar{c}(t) >$ be an optimal programme from $\tilde{y} \gg 0$.
Given $(A'.1)$, $(A.2)$, $(A.3)$, $(A.4)$, and $(A.5)$, there is a strictly positive vector z^* such that $\lim_{t \to \infty} [\bar{y}(t) / g^t] = z^*$.

So g can be thought of as the long-run optimal growth rate associated with any economy (A, w, δ).

LEADING SECTORS

In this section we explore the sensitivity of the long-run optimal growth rate of our economy to changes in productivity. Recall that *Proposition 5*, in the previous section, states that the asymptotic growth factor, g, of an optimal programme of resource allocation depends on a technological parameter, $\hat{\lambda}$; a parameter from the welfare function, α; and the discount factor, δ. So improvements in productivity certainly affect the asymptotic growth rate, g, when the parameters α and δ are held fixed, since changes in productivity are captured by changes in the input requirement matrix A, which, in turn, alter $\hat{\lambda}$. Thus, in this context, the largest eigenvalue $(\hat{\lambda}^{-1})$ of the input requirement matrix assumes a special significance, which leads to the issue of how sensitive this eigenvalue is to changes in the entries of matrix A.

Now, reducing *any entry* of an indecomposable matrix will decrease the largest eigenvalue of that matrix (Debreu and Herstein 1953). Therefore, since primitive matrices are indecomposable by definition, it follows that reducing any element of A will increase $\hat{\lambda}$ and, consequently, g. So reducing *any* input requirement leads to an improvement of the optimal, asymptotic growth factor. Naturally, reducing the input requirements of any sector in the economy increases g. The more difficult question is to identify a specific sector in the economy for which improvements in productivity would lead to the greatest increase in the long-run optimal growth rate.[1] Indeed, are there sectors which are *leading* sectors in terms of their ability to accelerate long-run growth? We will investigate this general question by means of a computational process since sharp, analytical results on the sensitivity of g to changes in the columns of A are, unfortunately, elusive.

The improvements in productivity that we consider are as follows. Suppose that all the input requirements for only one sector (say sector j) are reduced by the same percentage. This technological change gives rise to a new input requirement matrix $A'_j = [a^1, ..., \theta a^j, ... a^n]$, where $0 < \theta < 1$ and a^j is the j-th column of A. Hence if $\theta = 0.98$, all of sector j's input requirements are reduced by 2 per cent. Furthermore, let $g'_j = (\delta \lambda'_j)^{1/\alpha}$, where λ'_j is the inverse of the largest eigenvalue of A'_j. Then g'_j is the long-run optimal growth rate associated with the economy (A'_j, w, δ).

Formally, a sector l is the *leading sector* of the original economy (A, w, δ). if

$$[g'_l / g] = \max_j [g'_j / g].$$

Therefore, identifying the leading sectors of an economy involves reducing the input requirements for each sector, one at a time, obtaining the corresponding inverse of the largest eigenvalue (λ'_j), and subsequently calculating the respective value of $[g'_j/g]$ for each of the matrices A'_j.

1 The attainment of higher economic growth is essential to achieving economic development. Even if one believes that objectives such as poverty alleviation, rather than growth, should be the focus of policy makers, there seems to be a consensus that the acceleration of the growth rate is an important ingredient of any strategy.

Note that $[g'_j / g] = [\lambda'_j / \hat{\lambda}]^{1/\alpha}$. Hence, *this ratio is independent of the discount factor of the economy but depends on the value of* α. Variations in the value of α, however, will not alter the leading sector of an economy. Suppose $\tilde{\alpha} \in (0,1)$ and $\tilde{\alpha} \neq \alpha$. Now consider the economy $(A, \tilde{w}, \delta)$, where $\tilde{w}(c) = [f(c)]^{1-\tilde{\alpha}}$. By *Proposition 5*, $\tilde{g} = (\delta\hat{\lambda})^{1/\tilde{\alpha}}$ is the long-run optimal growth factor of $(A, \tilde{w}, \delta)$. Moreover, when the input requirements for only the j-th sector are reduced, the resulting long-run optimal growth factor is $\tilde{g}'_j = (\delta\lambda'_j)^{1/\tilde{\alpha}}$. Thus the leading sector(s) of the economies (A, w, δ) and $(A, \tilde{w}, \delta)$ can be denoted, respectively, by the following sets:

$$J^* = \{j \in \{1,..., n\}: j = \text{argmax}_j [g'_j / g]\} \text{ and}$$

$$\tilde{J}^* = \{j \in \{1,...n\}: j = \text{argmax}_j [\tilde{g}'_j / \tilde{g}]\}.$$

Proposition 6:   Let (A, w, δ) and $(A, \tilde{w}, \delta)$ be any two economies where $\tilde{\alpha} \neq \alpha$. Then $J^* = \tilde{J}^*$.

Proof: For any $j^* \in J^*$, it is true that

$$[g'_{j^*} / g] \geq [g'_j / g] \qquad \text{for all } j \in \{1,...,n\},$$

or

$$[\lambda'_{j^*} / \hat{\lambda}]^{1/\alpha} \geq [\lambda'_j / \hat{\lambda}]^{1/\alpha} \quad \text{for all } j \in \{1, ...,n\}.$$

Because $f(x) = x^{(\alpha/\tilde{\alpha})}$ is a strictly increasing function for all $x > 0$, $0 < \alpha < 1$, and $0 < \tilde{\alpha} < 1$, since $1 < \hat{\lambda} < \lambda'_j$ for all $j \in \{1, ...,n\}$,

$$\{[\lambda'_{j^*} / \hat{\lambda}]^{1/\alpha}\}^{(\alpha/\tilde{\alpha})} \geq \{[\lambda'_j / \hat{\lambda}]^{1/\alpha}\}^{(\alpha/\tilde{\alpha})} \text{ for all } j \in \{1, ..., n\}.$$

So
$$[\lambda'_{j^*} / \hat{\lambda}]^{1/\tilde{\alpha}} \geq [\lambda'_j / \hat{\lambda}]^{1/\tilde{\alpha}} \text{ for all } j \in \{1,...,n\},$$
which means that $j^* \in \tilde{J}^*$, for all $j^* \in J^*$. Thus $J^* \subset \tilde{J}^*$. By the same reasoning, $\tilde{J}^* \subset J^*$. Hence $J^* = \tilde{J}^*$. QED.

It is by no means claimed that there is a unique leading sector. Moreover, it is possible to consider a *leading combination of k sectors*, sectors for which simultaneous improvements in efficiency yield the largest increase in the long-run optimal growth factor.

In Majumdar and Ossella (1999), we utilized the computational approach delineated here to identify the leading sectors of the Indian economy. Our computations were based on the Indian input requirement matrix for the year 1989, which was *primitive* (but *not* strictly positive). This empirical study suggested that, in 1989, electricity, gas, and water supply; iron and steel; and paper and paper products were the top three leading sectors for India, sectors for which an improvement in productivity generated the three largest values of $[g'_j/g]$.

ANALYTICS OF A SPECIAL EXAMPLE: THE HAYEK-INADA ECONOMY

In this section, we present a simple example of an input requirement matrix for which the problem of identifying the leading sector(s) can be settled analytically. Instead of assuming a primitive input requirement matrix, suppose that A is an upper-triangular matrix whose entries on and above the principal diagonal are all positive. In addition, let a_{11} be the largest element on the diagonal. Consequently, we replace Assumption $(A'.1)$ with the following:

(A*.1) A is a non-negative upper-triangular matrix where:
   (i) $a_{ij} > 0$ for all $i \leq j$ and $a_{ij} = 0$ for all $i > j$;
   (ii) $a_{11} > a_{ii}$ for $i = 2, 3, ..., n$.

In this case, producing one unit of good j (where $j = 1, ..., n$) requires only the use of goods $1, ..., j$ as inputs. Such interdependence between the sectors parallels the Hayekian framework presented in Inada (1968), though we do not allow for a primary factor of production such as labour. This production process, of course, has a highly special structure. Nevertheless, the assumptions of Dasgupta and Mitra (1988) $[A \gg 0]$ or Ossella (1999) $[A$ is primitive$]$ do not hold, and the qualitative results must be proved independently of these studies.

Now if A is a matrix for which $(A*.1.i)$ holds true, A has a strictly positive left-hand eigenvector, corresponding to the positive maximal eigenvalue, if and only if $(A*.1.ii)$ holds true (*Claim* 5.1 in the last section of this paper). As a result, an optimal programme exists under the new framework of Assumptions $(A*.1)$–$(A.5)$. The proof of this is identical to the proof of *Proposition 1* in Dasgupta and Mitra (1988). Furthermore, it is possible to prove a relative stability property for optimal programmes, given Assumptions $(A*.1)$–$(A.5)$. *Proposition 5** below, in fact, states that given $(A*.1)$, an optimal programme, from any strictly positive initial stock, still has an asymptotic growth factor of $g = (\delta\hat{\lambda})^{1/\alpha}$.

Proposition 5*: Let $< \bar{x}(t), \bar{y}(t), \bar{c}(t) >$ be an optimal programme from $\tilde{y} \gg 0$.

Given $(A^*.1)$, $(A.2)$, $(A.3)$, $(A.4)$, and $(A.5)$, there is a strictly positive vector z^* such that $\lim_{t \to \infty} [\bar{y}(t)/g^t] = z^*$.

The proof of this proposition is provided in the subsequent section.

Assumption $(A^*.1)$ implies that $\hat{\lambda}^{-1} = a_{11}$. This is because the eigenvalues of an upper-triangular matrix are its principal diagonal elements: $a_{11}, a_{22}, ..., a_{nn}$ (Claim 2.15.2, Marcus and Mink 1964), and $(A^*.1.ii)$ stipulates that $a_{11} > a_{ii}$ for all $i > 1$. So in this special example, the long-run optimal growth rate of the economy is $g = (\delta/a_{11})^{1/\alpha}$.

Sector 1 is, consequently, the unique leading sector of an economy (A, w, δ), for which A satisfies $(A^*.1)$.

Proposition 7: Given $(A^*.1)$, $(A.2)$, $(A.3)$, $(A.4)$, and $(A.5)$, Sector 1 is the unique leading sector of the economy (A, w, δ), for $1 > \theta > max(a_{22}, ..., a_{nn})/a_{11}$.

Proof: Recall that $g = (\delta/a_{11})^{1/\alpha}$. In addition, $g'_j = (\delta/a_{11})^{1/\alpha}$ for all $j = 2, ..., n$. This is because $(\lambda'_j)^{-1} = a_{11}$ for all $j = 2, ..., n$. Note that if $A'_j = [a'(j)_{ik}]$, then $a'(j)_{kk} = a_{kk}$ for all $k \neq j$, and $a'(j)_{jj} = \theta a_{jj}$. So when $j > 1$, $a'(j)_{11} = a_{11} > a_{kk} \geq a'(j)_{kk}$, for $k = 2, ..., n$. Moreover, the eigenvalues of an upper-triangular matrix are its principal diagonal elements (Claim 2.15.2, Marcus and Mink 1964). So, $[g'_j / g] = 1$ for all $j = 2, ..., n$. Now as long as $1 > \theta > max(a_{22}, ..., a_{nn})/a_{11}$, $(\lambda'_1)^{-1} = \theta a_{11}$. This is because $a'(1)_{11} = \theta a_{11} > (max(a_{22}, ..., a_{nn})/a_{11})a_{11} \geq a_{kk} = a'(1)_{kk}$ for all $k = 2, ..., n$. Therefore, $[g'_1 / g] = (\delta/\theta a_{11})^{1/\alpha}(\delta/a_{11})^{-1/\alpha} = (1/\theta)^{1/\alpha} > 1$, since $\theta < 1$ and $0 < \alpha < 1$. It follows that $[g'_1/g] = max_j [g'_j/g]$.

QED.

The condition $1 > \theta > max(a_{22}, ..., a_{nn})/a_{11}$ ensures that the new input requirement matrix A'_1 still satisfies Assumption $(A^*.1.ii)$, guaranteeing a unique maximal eigenvalue.

PROOFS

Several preliminary results are required to prove *Proposition 5**. These results are in fact identical to the preliminary results needed to prove

Proposition 5, and so the proof for *Proposition 5** follows the same structure as that of *Proposition 5*. Please refer to Ossella (1999) for a detailed proof of *Proposition 5*.

We will now present all the necessary preliminary results required to prove *Proposition 5**. These results are numbered in accordance with Ossella (1999) and the proofs are provided only when Assumption (A^*.1) necessitates a modification of the original proof. Again, please see Ossella (1999) for any proofs not included here.

The first two preliminary results have already been presented in this paper, within the context of a primitive input requirement matrix. Since they still hold under Assumption (A^*.1), we present them again in this section. However, we do so under the same numbering system as in Ossella (1999), in order to facilitate referencing the proofs in Ossella (1999). Result (R.1) provides a complete characterization of efficient programmes, while (R.2) specifies that optimal programmes are indeed efficient.

(R.1):   (i) If $< x(t), y(t) >$ is a programme from $\tilde{y}$, then $\Sigma_{t=0}^{\infty} A^t c(t) \leq \tilde{y}$.

     (ii) Conversely, if $c(t) \in \mathfrak{R}_+^n$ for all $t \geq 0$, $\tilde{y} \in \mathfrak{R}_+^n$, and $\Sigma_{t=0}^{\infty} A^t c(t) \leq \tilde{y}$, then there is a programme $< x'(t), y'(t) >$ from $\tilde{y}$, with $c'(t) = c(t)$ for all $t \geq 0$.

     (iii) A programme $< x(t), y(t) >$ from $\tilde{y}$ is efficient if and only if $\Sigma_{t=0}^{\infty} A^t c(t) = \tilde{y}$.

Proof: Assumption (A^*.1.i) guarantees that every column of A is a positive vector, and so the assumption of Theorem 4.1 (Majumdar 1974) is satisfied.   QED.

(R.2):   If $< \overline{x}(t), \overline{y}(t) >$ is an optimal programme from $\tilde{y} \in \mathfrak{R}_{++}^n$, then $< \overline{x}(t), \overline{y}(t) >$ is an efficient programme from $\tilde{y}$.

Proof: The proof here is identical to that in Ossella (1999) and so is omitted. However, it does appeal to *Claim* 2.1, whose proof needs to be modified, given Assumption (A^*.1). This claim and its respective proof are provided below:

Claim 2.1: Every row of A^s is a positive vector, where $s \geq 1$.

Proof: If $A^2 = [a_{ij}^{(2)}]$, then $a_{ij}^{(2)} = \Sigma_{k=1}^{n} a_{ik} a_{kj}$. Hence, $a_{ij}^{(2)} = 0$ if $j < i$ and $a_{ij}^{(2)} > 0$ if $j \geq i$. This is because, under Assumption $(A^{*}.1)$, $a_{ij} = 0$ if $j < i$ and $a_{ij} > 0$ if $j \geq i$. So A^2 is also an upper-triangular matrix. Now, for any integer $s > 2$, assume that $A^s = [a_{ij}^{(s)}]$ is an upper-triangular matrix with $a_{ij}^{(s)} = 0$ for $j < i$ and $a_{ij}^{(s)} > 0$ for $j \geq i$. Then $A^{s+1} = [A^s][A] = [a_{ij}^{(s+1)}]$, where $a_{ij}^{(s+1)} = \Sigma_{k=1}^{n} a_{ik}^{(s)} a_{kj}$. Consequently, $a_{ij}^{(s+1)} = 0$ for $j < i$ and $a_{ij}^{(s+1)} > 0$ for $j \geq i$. By induction, therefore, A^s is an upper-triangular matrix whose every row is a positive vector, for all $s \geq 1$.

Before we can present the next two preliminary results, it is first necessary to define a competitive programme. A *competitive programme* $< x(t), y(t), p(t) >$ from $\tilde{y}$, is a feasible programme $< x(t), y(t) >$ from $\tilde{y}$ and a non-negative sequence of prices $< p(t) >$ for which:

1. $\delta^t w(c(t)) - p(t) c(t) \geq \delta^t w(c) - p(t)c$
    for all $c \in \mathfrak{R}_+^n$ and $t \geq 0$,   (5.2)

2. $p(t+1) y(t+1) - p(t)x(t) \geq p(t+1)y - p(t)x$
    for all $(x, y) \in \Omega$ and $t \geq 0$.   (5.3)

It turns out that, under certain conditions, a competitive programme is optimal and, conversely, an optimal programme is competitive. See $(P.2)$ and $(P.3)$.

$(P.2)$:   If $< \bar{x}(t), \bar{y}(t), \bar{p}(t) >$ is a competitive programe from $\tilde{y} \in \mathfrak{R}_+^n$ and $\lim_{t \to \infty} \bar{p}(t)\bar{x}(t) = 0$, then $< \bar{x}(t), \bar{y}(t) >$ is an optimal programme from $\tilde{y}$.

$(P.3)$:   If $< \bar{x}(t), \bar{y}(t) >$ is an optimal programme from $\tilde{y} \in \mathfrak{R}_{++}^n$, then there is a sequence $< \bar{p}(t) >$ such that $< \bar{x}(t), \bar{y}(t), \bar{p}(t) >$ is a competitive programme with $\bar{p}(t) > 0$ for all $t \geq 0$ and $\lim_{t \to \infty} \bar{p}(t)\bar{x}(t) = 0$.

The next result, $(R.3)$, provides some useful properties of supporting prices in a closed linear model of production.

(R.3): If $(x^0, y^0) \in \Omega$, $(p^0, q^0) \in \mathfrak{R}_+^n \bullet \mathfrak{R}_+^n$, and $q^0 y^0 - p^0 x^0 \geq q^0 y - p^0 x$
for all $(x, y) \in \Omega$, then

    (i) $q^0 y^0 - p^0 x^0 = 0$,
    (ii) $q^0 - p^0 A \leq 0$,
    (iii) If $y^0 \gg 0$, $q^0 = p^0 A$,
    (iv) If $p^0 \gg 0$, $Ay^0 = x^0$.

In order to prove the existence of a steady-state optimal programme, the following three lemmas are necessary. The first lemma $(L.1)$ follows from Assumption $(A.3)$ and leads to $(L.2)$, which shows that competitive programmes are interior. Finally, $(L.3)$ establishes that scalar multiples of competitive programmes are themselves competitive.

$(L.1)$:   (a) If $p^0 \in \mathfrak{R}_+^n$, then there is a $\theta^0 > 0$ such that $w(\theta e) - p^0(\theta e) > 0$ for all $0 < \theta \leq \theta^0$.
        (b) Let p^0, $c^0 \in \mathfrak{R}_+^n$. If $w(c^0) - p^0 c^0 \geq w(c) - p^0 c$ for all $c \in \mathfrak{R}_+^n$, then $w(c^0) - p^0 c^0 > 0$, $w(c^0) > 0$, and $c^0 \gg 0$.

$(L.2)$:   If $< x(t), y(t), p(t) >$ is a competitive programme from $\tilde{y} \in \mathfrak{R}_+^n$, then

    (i) $w(c(t)) > 0$, $c(t) \gg 0$, $x(t) \gg 0$, $y(t) \gg 0$, and $p(t) \gg 0$ for all $t \geq 0$,
    (ii) $p(t + 1) = p(t)A$ and $Ay(t + 1) = x(t)$ for all $t \geq 0$.

$(L.3)$:   (a) If p^0, $c^0 \in \mathfrak{R}_+^n$, such that $w(c^0) - p^0 c^0 \geq w(c) - p^0 c$ for all $c \in \mathfrak{R}_+^n$, then for any $\beta > 0$, $w(\hat{\beta} c^0) - \beta p^0 (\hat{\beta} c^0) \geq w(c) - \beta p^0 c$ for all $c \in \mathfrak{R}_+^n$, and $\hat{\beta} = \beta^{-1/\alpha}$.
        (b) If $< x(t), y(t), p(t) >$ is a competitive programme from $\tilde{y}$ with consumption sequence $< c(t) >$, then for any $\beta > 0$, $<\beta x(t), \beta y(t), \beta^{-\alpha} p(t) >$ is a competitive programme from $\beta \tilde{y}$ with consumption sequence $<\beta c(t)>$.

Given the previous results, it is possible to prove the existence of an initial stock vector $y^* \gg 0$ from which the optimal programme is a steady-state optimal programme with growth factor $g = (\delta \hat{\lambda})^{1/\alpha}$. *Proposition 4* earlier in this paper presents the same conclusion for primitive input requirement matrices.

$(P.5)$:   There exists a $y^* \gg 0$ such that $y^*(t) = g^t y^*$ and $x^*(t) = Ay^*(t + 1)$ for all $t \geq 0$ defines a steady-state optimal programme from y^* where $g = (\delta \hat{\lambda})^{1/\alpha}$.

Proof: Let $S = \{c \in \mathfrak{R}^n_+ : \|c\| \leq [w(e)/m(\hat{p})]^{1/\alpha}\}$, where $m(\hat{p})$ $= \min_i \hat{p}_i$, and $\hat{p}$ is the strictly positive left-hand eigenvector of A corresponding to the maximal eigenvalue $(\hat{\lambda})^{-1}$.

Claim 5.1: Given Assumption $(A^*.1)$, A has a strictly positive left-hand eigenvector $(\hat{p})$ corresponding to the positive maximal eigenvalue $(\hat{\lambda})^{-1}$.

Proof: Assumption $(A^*.1.i)$ states that A is an upper-triangular matrix, and so by Marcus and Mink (1964), Claim 2.15.2, A's eigenvalues are its diagonal elements. Hence, $(A^*.1.ii)$ implies that $(\hat{\lambda})^{-1} = a_{11} > 0$.

Let $\hat{p}$ be the left eigenvector corresponding to the maximal eigenvalue $(\hat{\lambda})^{-1}$. By definition then $0 = \hat{p}\,[(\hat{\lambda})^{-1} I - A]$. That is:

$$0 = \hat{p}_1\,[(\hat{\lambda})^{-1} - a_{11}], \tag{5.4}$$

$$0 = \hat{p}_1\,(-a_{12}) + \hat{p}_2\,((\hat{\lambda})^{-1} - a_{22}),$$

$$\vdots$$

$$0 = \sum_{k=1}^{n-1} -\hat{p}_k\,a_{kn} + \hat{p}_n\,((\hat{\lambda})^{-1} - a_{nn}).$$

As a result,

$$\hat{p}_i = (a_{11} - a_{ii})^{-1}\left[\sum_{k=1}^{i-1} \hat{p}_k\,a_{ki}\right] \text{ for all } i = 2, 3, ..., n. \tag{5.5}$$

Now suppose $\hat{p}_1 = t > 0$. Then (5.4) holds because $(\hat{\lambda})^{-1} = a_{11}$. In addition, $\hat{p}_2 = (\hat{p}_1\,a_{12})/(a_{11} - a_{22}) > 0$ since, by Assumption $(A^*.1)$, $a_{11} > a_{22}$ and $a_{12} > 0$. Similarly, $\hat{p}_3 = (a_{11} - a_{33})^{-1}[\hat{p}_1\,a_{13} + \hat{p}_2\,a_{23}] > 0$ for the same reasons. It follows that $\hat{p}_k > 0$ for all $k = 1, ..., n$. This is due to (5.5), as well as the fact that $a_{11} > a_{ii}$ for all $i > 1$, and $a_{ij} > 0$ for all $j \geq i$.

Claim 5.2: If $c \in \mathfrak{R}^n_+$ but $c \notin S$, $w(c) - \hat{p}c < 0$.

Proof: $w(c) - \hat{p}c = \|c\|\,\{[w(c)/\|c\|] - [\hat{p}c/\|c\|]\} \leq \|c\|\,[\dfrac{w(c/\|c\|)}{\|c\|^\alpha} - m(\hat{p})]$

$$\leq \|c\|\,[\frac{w(e)}{\|c\|^\alpha} - m(\hat{p})] = \|c\|^{1-\alpha}\,m(\hat{p})[\frac{w(e)}{m(\hat{p})} - \|c\|^\alpha]$$

$$< 0 \text{ since } c \notin S.$$

Now $F(c) = w(c) - \hat{p}c$ is a continuous function on S, and S is a non-empty, compact set in $\Re_+^n$. Hence there exists a $c^* \in S$ such that

$$w(c^*) - \hat{p}c^* \geq w(c) - \hat{p}c \text{ for all } c \in S. \tag{5.6}$$

From $(L.1)$, there is a θ' such that $w(\theta'e) - \hat{p}(\theta'e) > 0$

$$\text{and } 0 < \theta' < (1/n)[w(e)/\|\hat{p}\|]^{1/\alpha}. \tag{5.7}$$

If $c' = \theta'e$, then $\|c'\| = n\theta' < [w(e)/\|\hat{p}\|]^{1/\alpha} \leq [w(e)/m(\hat{p})]^{1/\alpha}$. Hence $c' \in S$ and from (5.6), $w(c^*) - \hat{p}c^* \geq w(c') - \hat{p}c' > 0$ by (5.7). So $w(c^*) > \hat{p}c^* > 0$, and from $(A.3.d)$ $c^* >> 0$. Now for $c \notin S$, $w(c) - \hat{p}c < 0$. Thus,

$$w(c^*) - \hat{p}c^* \geq w(c) - \hat{p}c \text{ for all } c \in \Re_+^n. \tag{5.8}$$

Let $g = (\delta\hat{\lambda})^{1/\alpha}$, and by $(A.4)$ $\delta < (1/\hat{\lambda})^{1-\alpha}$. So

$$g < [(1/\hat{\lambda})^{1-\alpha}\hat{\lambda}]^{1/\alpha} = [\hat{\lambda}^\alpha]^{1/\alpha} = \hat{\lambda}. \tag{5.9}$$

Hence $(I - gA)^{-1}$ exists and is non-negative, by Nikaido (1968), Theorem 7.1(ii). This is because, $(1/\hat{\lambda}) < (1/g)$, so $[(1/g)I - A]^{-1}$ exists and $[(1/g)I - A]^{-1} = g[I - gA]^{-1}$. Now let

$$y^* = [I - gA]^{-1} c^*. \tag{5.10}$$

Also let $< x^*(t), y^*(t) >$ be such that $y^*(0) = y^*$, $y^*(t+1) = gy^*(t)$ and $x^*(t) = A y^*(t+1)$ for all $t \geq 0$. So,

$$y^*(t) - x^*(t) = y^*(t) - A y^*(t+1) = g^t y^* - A g^{t+1} y^*$$
$$= g^t [I - gA] y^* = g^t c^* >> 0.$$

Therefore, $< x^*(t), y^*(t) >$ is a steady-state programme from y^* with consumption sequence $c^*(t) = g^t c^*$.

Claim 5.3: Given Assumption $(A^*.1)$, $y^* >> 0$.

Proof: Let $B = [I - gA]^{-1}$, so $B = [\text{determinant } (I - gA)]^{-1}$ adjoint $(I - gA)$. Since $[I - gA]$ is an upper-triangular matrix, it follows that determinant $(I - gA) = \Pi_{k=1}^n (1 - ga_{kk})$. In addition, let $D = $ adjoint $(I - gA)$ and $E(i,j) = $ the determinant of $(I - gA)$ without its j-th row and i-th column. Then, by the definition of the adjoint of a matrix, $d_{ij} = (-1)^{i+j} * E(i, j)$. Since $(I - gA)$, without its i-th row and column, is also an upper-triangular matrix, it follows that $d_{ii} = \Pi_{k \neq i}(1 - ga_{kk})$. Hence, for all $i = 1, \ldots, n$, $b_{ii} = \left[\Pi_{k=1}^{n}(1 - ga_{kk}) \right]^{-1}$ $\left[\Pi_{k \neq i}(1 - ga_{kk}) \right] = (1 - ga_{ii})^{-1}$. Now for all $i = 1, \ldots, n$, $y^{*}_{i} = \Sigma_{k=1}^{n} b_{ik} c_{k}^{*} \geq b_{ii} c_{i}^{*} = c_{i}^{*} /(1 - ga_{ii})$.

This is because $b_{ik} \geq 0$ for all i and k, given that $[I - gA]^{-1}$ is non-negative. Moreover, (5.9) implies that $1/ g > 1/\hat{\lambda} \geq a_{ii}$ for all i. Therefore $y^{*}_{i} > 0$ for $i = 1, \ldots, n$, since $1 > ga_{ii}$ and $c_{i}^{*} > 0$, for all i.

It results that, $x(0)^{*} \gg 0$ since $x(0)^{*} = Ay^{*}(1) = gA y^{*}$, $g > 0$, $y^{*} \gg 0$, and $a_{ii} > 0$ for all $i = 1, \ldots, n$ [Assumption $(A^{*}.1)$].

Claim 5.4: $< x^{*}(t), y^{*}(t) >$ is a steady-state optimal programme.

Proof: Let $p^{*}(t) = \hat{p}/\hat{\lambda}^{t}$ for all $t \geq 0$. By (5.8) and (L.3.a):

$$w(g^{t}c^{*}) - (g^{t})^{-\alpha} \hat{p}(g^{t}c^{*}) \geq w(c) - (g^{t})^{-\alpha} \hat{p}c \text{ for all } c \in \Re_{+}^{n}$$
$$\text{and } t \geq 0. \tag{5.11}$$

Recall that $g = (\delta\hat{\lambda})^{1/\alpha}$, $g^{t}c^{*} = c^{*}(t)$, and $p^{*}(t) = \hat{p}/\hat{\lambda}^{t}$. So (5.11) becomes

$$\delta^{t}w(c^{*}(t)) - p^{*}(t) c^{*}(t) \geq \delta^{t}w(c) - p^{*}(t)c$$
$$\text{for all } c \in \Re_{+}^{n} \text{ and } t \geq 0. \tag{5.12}$$

Now $p^{*}(t + 1) - p^{*}(t)A = \hat{\lambda}^{-(t+1)} (\hat{p} - \hat{\lambda}\hat{p}A) = 0$, so

$$p^{*}(t + 1)y - p^{*}(t)x \leq p^{*}(t+1)y - p^{*}(t)Ay = 0$$
$$\text{for all } (x, y) \in \Omega \text{ and } t \geq 0$$
$$= p^{*}(t + 1)y^{*}(t + 1) - p^{*}(t)A y^{*}(t + 1)$$
$$= p^{*}(t + 1)y^{*}(t + 1) - p^{*}(t)x^{*}(t). \tag{5.13}$$

Hence by (5.12) and (5.13), $< x^{*}(t), y^{*}(t) >$ is a competitive programme.

Moreover, $p^{*}(t)y^{*}(t) = (\hat{p}/\hat{\lambda}^{t})g^{t} y^{*} = \hat{p}y^{*}(g/\hat{\lambda})^{t}$ and $(g/\hat{\lambda}) < 1$. So, $\lim_{t \to \infty} p^{*}(t)y^{*}(t) = 0$, and by (P.2), $< x^{*}(t), y^{*}(t) >$ is optimal from y^{*}. In fact, $< x^{*}(t), y^{*}(t) >$ is a steady-state optimal programme.   QED.

Three additional lemmas are still needed to prove *Proposition 5**. In particular, $(L.5)$ establishes the strict concavity of the welfare function on $\mathfrak{R}^n_{++}$, while $(L.6)$ addresses the convergence of a consumption sequence.

$(L.4)$: If $< x(t), y(t), p(t) >$ is a competitive programme from $\tilde{y} = \mathfrak{R}^n_+$, then

  (i) $w(c(t)/g^t) - \hat{\lambda}^t p(t)(c(t)/g^t) \geq w(c) - \hat{\lambda}^t p(t)c$ for all $c \in \mathfrak{R}^n_+$ and $t \geq 0$,

  (ii) $w(c(t)/g^t) - \hat{\lambda}^t p(t)(c(t)/g^t) > 0$ for all $t \geq 0$.

$(L.5)$: Under $(A'.3)$ and $(A.5)$, if $c^0, c' \in \mathfrak{R}^n_+$, with $c^0 \neq c'$, $w(c^0) > 0$, $w(c') > 0$, and $0 < \theta < 1$, then $w(\theta c^0 + (1 - \theta)c') > \theta w(c^0) + (1 - \theta)w(c')$.

$(L.6)$: Under $(A'.3)$ and $(A.5)$, if $< p^s >$ and $< c^s >$ are sequences in $\mathfrak{R}^n_+$; if $\bar{p}, \bar{c} \in \mathfrak{R}^n_+$; and if

  (i) $\lim_{s \to \infty} p^s = \bar{p}$,

  (ii) $w(c^s) - p^s c^s \geq w(c) - p^s c$ for all $c \in \mathfrak{R}^n_+$ and for all $s \geq 0$,

  (iii) $w(\bar{c}) - \bar{p}\bar{c} \geq w(c) - \bar{p}c$ for all $c \in \mathfrak{R}^n_+$,

  then $\lim_{s \to \infty} \iota^s - \bar{\iota}$.

Finally, the relative stability property for optimal programmes, under Assumptions $(A^*.1)$–$(A.5)$, can be proved by appealing to $(L.6)$.

Proof of Proposition 5*: Since $< \bar{x}(t), \bar{y}(t) >$ is an optimal programme from $\tilde{y} \gg 0$, then by $(P.3)$, there exists a positive sequence $< \bar{p}(t) >$ such that $< \bar{x}(t), \bar{y}(t), \bar{p}(t) >$ is a competitive programme. Applying $(L.2)$, $[\bar{x}(t), \bar{y}(t), \bar{p}(t)] \gg 0$ for all $t \geq 0$, $w(\bar{c}(t)) > 0$ for all $t \geq 0$, and $0 = \bar{p}(t + 1) - \bar{p}(t)A$ for all $t \geq 0$. So

$$\hat{\lambda}^t \bar{p}(t) = \bar{p}(0) \, \hat{\lambda}^t \, A^t \quad \text{for all } t \geq 0. \tag{5.14}$$

It is possible to prove that $\lim_{t \to \infty} \hat{\lambda}^t \bar{p}(t)$ exists. However, in order to do so, it is first necessary to introduce the diagonal matrix $P = [p_{ij}]$, where $p_{ii} = \hat{p}_i$ for $i = 1, ..., n$ and $p_{ij} = 0$ for all $i \neq j$. Recall from the proof of $(P.5)$ that $\hat{p}$ is the strictly positive left-hand eigenvector of A corresponding to the maximal eigenvalue $(\hat{\lambda})^{-1}$. In addition, let $\Pi = \hat{\lambda}PAP^{-1}$.

Claim 6.1: The matrix Π^T is a fully regular stochastic matrix.

Proof: If $\Pi = [\pi_{ij}]$, then $\pi_{ij} = \hat{\lambda}(\hat{p}_i / \hat{p}_j)\,a_{ij} \geq 0$ for all $i, j = 1, ..., n$. Moreover, if $\Pi^T = [\pi_{ij}^T]$, then $\pi_{ij}^T = \pi_{ji}$ for all $i, j = 1, ..., n$.

It follows that for any i, $\sum_{j=1}^n \pi_{ij}^T = \sum_{j=1}^n \pi_{ji} = \sum_{j=1}^n [\hat{\lambda}(\hat{p}_j / \hat{p}_i)\,a_{ji}]$

$= (\hat{\lambda} / \hat{p}_i)\,\sum_{j=1}^n \hat{p}_j\,a_{ji} = (\hat{\lambda} / \hat{p}_i)(\hat{p}_i / \hat{\lambda}) = 1.$

Thus Π^T is a stochastic matrix.

Now, by Assumption $(A^*.1)$, $a_{ij} = 0$ for all $i > j$ and so $\pi_{ij}^T = 0$ for all $j > i$. Therefore, Π^T is a lower-triangular matrix and its eigenvalues are its diagonal elements: $\hat{\lambda}a_{11}$, $\hat{\lambda}a_{22}, ..., \hat{\lambda}a_{nn}$. In fact, $\hat{\lambda}a_{11} = 1$ (*Claim* 5.1) and, by Assumption $(A^*.1.\text{ii})$, $\hat{\lambda}a_{ii} < 1$ for all $i > 1$. So Π^T is a fully regular stochastic matrix (Gantmacher 1959, Vol. 2: 88).

Claim 6.1 together with Gantmacher (1959), Vol. 2, Theorem 11.2 implies that

$$\lim_{q \to \infty} [\Pi^T]^q = \bar{\Pi}, \text{ where } \bar{\Pi} = [\bar{\pi}_{ij}] \text{ is such that } \bar{\pi}_{ij}$$

$$\bar{\pi}_{ij} = \bar{\pi}_{*j} \geq 0 \text{ for } j = 1, ..., n \text{ and } \sum_{j=1}^n \bar{\pi}_{*j} = 1. \qquad (5.15)$$

That is, the limit of $[\Pi^T]^q$ exists, and is equal to a matrix whose rows sum to one and for which all elements of the j-th column are equal to the same non-negative number $\bar{\pi}_{*j}$.

Claim 6.2: If $\lim_{q \to \infty} [\Pi^T]^q = \bar{\Pi}$, then $\lim_{q \to \infty} [\Pi]^q = \bar{\Pi}^T$.

Proof: Let $[\Pi^T]^q = D^q = [d_{ij}^{(q)}]$. Now if $\lim_{q \to \infty} [\Pi^T]^q = \bar{\Pi}$, then $\bar{\pi}_{ij} = \lim_{q \to \infty} d_{ij}^{(q)}$ for all $i, j = 1, ..., n$ (Gantmacher 1959, Vol. 1: 33, n. 3). Thus, for every $\varepsilon > 0$, there exists an integer $Q(\varepsilon)$ such that $|d_{ij}^{(q)} - \overline{\pi}_{ij}| < \varepsilon$ for all $q \geq Q(\varepsilon)$. In addition, for all $q > 0$, $[\Pi^q]^T = [\Pi^T]^q$ and so $\pi_{ji}^{(q)} = d_{ij}^{(q)}$ for all i, j, and q. Hence for all i, $j = 1, \ldots, n$,

$$|\pi_{ij}^{(q)} - \overline{\pi}_{ji}| = |\pi_{ij}^{(q)} - d_{ji}^{(q)} + d_{ji}^{(q)} - \overline{\pi}_{ji}|$$

$$\leq |\pi_{ij}^{(q)} - d_{ji}^{(q)}| \left[+ |d_{ji}^{(q)} - \overline{\pi}_{ji}| \right] = |d_{ji}^{(q)} - \overline{\pi}_{ji}|.$$

Consequently, for every $\varepsilon > 0$, there exists an integer $Q(\varepsilon)$ such that $|\pi_{ij}^{(q)} - \overline{\pi}_{ji}| < \varepsilon$ for all $q \geq Q(\varepsilon)$, which implies that for all $i, j = 1, \ldots, n$, $\overline{\pi}_{ji} = \lim_{q \to \infty} \pi_{ij}^{(q)}$.

Recall that $\Pi = \hat{\lambda} PAP^{-1}$. So $P^{-1} \Pi P = P^{-1}[\hat{\lambda} PAP^{-1}]P = \hat{\lambda} A$ and $(\hat{\lambda} A)^t = (P^{-1} \Pi P)^t = P^{-1} \Pi^t P$. Now let $\Pi^t = [\pi_{ij}^{(t)}]$. Consequently, if $\overline{p}(0) \hat{\lambda}^t A^t = C^t = [c_j^{(t)}]$ for all $t > 0$, then, $c_j^{(t)} = \hat{p}_j [\Sigma_{k=1}^n \overline{p}_k(0) \pi_{kj}^{(t)} / \hat{p}_k]$ for all $j = 1, \ldots, n$ and $t > 0$. It follows from *Claim 6.2* and (5.15) that, for all $j = 1, \ldots, n$,

$$\lim_{t \to \infty} c_j^{(t)} = \hat{p}_j [\Sigma_{k=1}^n \overline{p}_k(0) \overline{\pi}_{jk} / \hat{p}_k] = \hat{p}_j [\Sigma_{k=1}^n \overline{p}_k(0) \overline{\pi}_{*k} / \hat{p}_k]$$

$$= \hat{p}_j [\overline{p}(0) z], \text{ where } z = \begin{bmatrix} \overline{\pi}_{*1} / \hat{p}_1 \\ \overline{\pi}_{*2} / \hat{p}_2 \\ \vdots \\ \overline{\pi}_{*n} / \hat{p}_n \end{bmatrix}.$$

Hence, the reasoning above, together with (5.14), yields:

$$\lim_{t \to \infty} \hat{\lambda}^t \overline{p}(t) = \lim_{t \to \infty} \overline{p}(0) \hat{\lambda}^t A^t = \lim_{t \to \infty} C^t = [\overline{p}(0) z] \hat{p}. \quad (5.16)$$

Denote $\mu = [\overline{p}(0) z]^{-1/\alpha}$ and let $y'(t) = \mu y^*(t) = \mu g^t y^*$; $x'(t) = \mu x^*(t) = \mu A g^{t+1} y^*$; $p'(t) = \mu^{-\alpha} p^*(t)$; $c'(t) = \mu c^*(t)$, where $< x^*(t)$, $y^*(t) >$ is the steady-state optimal programme, and $c^*(t)$ is the steady-state optimal consumption with price $p^*(t)$ from (P.5). In (P.5) it was proved that $< x^*(t), y^*(t), p^*(t) >$ is a competitive programme. In addition $\mu > 0$, since $\overline{p}(0) >> 0$ by (L.2), $\hat{p} >> 0$, $\overline{\pi}_{*j} \geq 0$ for

$j = 1, \ldots, n$, and $\sum_{j=1}^{n} \overline{\pi}_{*j} = 1$.

It ensues from $(L.3.b)$ that $< x'(t),\ y'(t),\ p'(t) >$ is a competitive programme. So from (5.2):

$$w(c'(0)) - p'(0)c'(0) \geq w(c) - p'(0)c \text{ for all } c \in \mathfrak{R}_+^n. \qquad (5.17)$$

Now, by definition, $p'(0) = \mu^{-\alpha} p*(0) = [\overline{p}(0)z]\hat{p}$ $[(P.5)]$. So from (5.16),

$$\lim_{t \to \infty} \hat{\lambda}^t \overline{p}(t) = p'(0). \qquad (5.18)$$

Moreover, given that $< \overline{x}(t),\ \overline{y}(t), \overline{p}(t) >$ is a competitive programme, and appealing to $(L.4.i)$:

$$w[\overline{c}(t)/g^t] - \hat{\lambda}^t \overline{p}(t)[\overline{c}(t)/g^t] \geq w(c) - \hat{\lambda}^t \overline{p}(t)c \text{ for all}$$
$$c \in \mathfrak{R}_+^n \text{ and } t \geq 0. \qquad (5.19)$$

Thus by (5.17), (5.18), (5.19), and $(L.6)$

$$\lim_{t \to \infty} [\overline{c}(t)/g^t] = c'(0). \qquad (5.20)$$

For $s \geq 0$, it is true that $< \overline{x}(t+s),\ \overline{y}(t+s) >$ is an optimal programme from $\overline{y}(s)$, by the 'principle of optimality'. Furthermore, by $(R.2)$, $< \overline{x}(t+s),\ \overline{y}(t+s) >$ is efficient from $\overline{y}(s)$, for $s \geq 0$. Therefore, from $(R.1)$: for all $s \geq 0$, $\overline{y}(s) = \Sigma_{t=0}^{\infty} A^t \overline{c}(t+s) = \Sigma_{t=0}^{\infty} g^t A^t [\overline{c}(t+s)/g^t]$, and

$$[\overline{y}(s)/g^s] = \sum_{t=0}^{\infty} g^t A^t [\overline{c}(t+s)/g^{t+s}].$$

By construction, $y'(0)$

$$= \mu y* = \mu[I - gA]^{-1} c* = [I - gA]^{-1} c'(0) = \Sigma_{t=0}^{\infty} g^t A^t c'(0).$$

Note that $[I - gA]^{-1} = \Sigma_{t=0}^{\infty} g^t A^t$ follows from Nikaido (1968), Theorem 6.4(i), because $[(1/g)I - A]^{-1}$ exists (*see* proof of $(P.5)$), and $[I - gA]^{-1}$

$$= [g[(1/g)I - A]]^{-1} = (1/g)[(1/g)I - A]^{-1} = (1/g)g \sum_{t=0}^{\infty} g^t A.$$

So for $s \geq 0$,

$$[\overline{y}(s)/g^s] - y'(0) = \sum_{t=0}^{\infty} g^t A^t [\overline{c}(t+s)/g^{t+s}) - c'(0)].$$

From the definition of convergence and ,(5.20), it is true that for any $\varepsilon > 0$, there exists a positive integer N^* such that for $N \geq N^*$,

$$\| \bar{c}(N)/g^N) - c'(0) \| < \varepsilon.$$

Thus, $[\bar{y}(s)/g^s] - y'(0) \leq \varepsilon \Sigma_{t=0}^{\infty} g^t A^t e = \varepsilon [I - gA]^{-1} e$ for all $s \geq N^*$.

Also, $[\bar{y}(s)/g^s] - y'(0) \geq -\varepsilon \Sigma_{t=0}^{\infty} g^t A^t e = -\varepsilon [I - gA]^{-1} e$ for all $s \geq N^*$

Therefore, $\| [\bar{y}(s)/g^s] - y'(0) \| \leq \varepsilon \| [I - gA]^{-1} e \|$ for all $s \geq N^*$,

proving that $\lim_{s \to \infty} [\bar{y}(s)/g^s] = \mu y^* = z^* >> 0$. QED.

REFERENCES

ATSUMI, H., (1969), 'The Efficient Capital Program for a Maintainable Utility Level', *Review of Economic Studies*, 36, pp. 263–87.

DASGUPTA, S. and T. MITRA, (1988), 'Intertemporal Optimality in a Closed Linear Model of Production', *Journal of Economic Theory*, 45, pp. 288–315.

DEBREU, G. and I. N. HERSTEIN, (1953), 'Nonnegative Square Matrices,' *Econometrica*, 21, pp. 597–607.

GALE, D., (1960), *The Theory of Linear Economic Models*, New York: McGraw-Hill.

GANTMACHER, F. R., (1959), *The Theory of Matrices*, Vols 1 and 2, New York: Chelsea Publishing Company.

INADA, K., (1968), 'On the Stability of the Golden Rule Path in the Hayekian Production Process', *Review of Economic Studies*, 35, pp. 335–45.

MAJUMDAR, M., (1974), 'Efficient Programs in Infinite Dimensional Spaces: A Complete Characterization', *Journal of Economic Theory*, 7, pp. 355–69.

MAJUMDAR, M., 1993, *Decentralization in Infinite Horizon Economies*, Boulder: Westview Press.

MAJUMDAR, M. and I. OSSELLA, (1999) 'Identifying Leading Sectors that Accelerate the Optimal Growth Rate: A Computational Approach', in G. Ranis and L. Raut (eds), *Trade, Growth, and Development: Essays in Honor of Professor T.N. Srinivasan*, Amsterdam: Elsevier, pp. 273–89.

MALINVAUD, E., (1953), 'Capital Accumulation and Efficient Allocation of Resources', *Econometrica*, 21, pp. 233–68.

MARCUS, M. and H. MINK, 1964, *A Survey of Matrix Theory and Matrix Inequalities*, New York: Dover Publications, Inc.

NIKAIDO, H., (1968), *Convex Structures and Economic Theory*, New York: Academic Press.

OSSELLA, I., (1999), 'A Turnpike Property of Optimal Programs for a Class of Simple Linear Models of Production', *Economic Theory*, 14, pp. 597–607.

RAY, D., (1998), *Development Economics*, Princeton: Princeton University Press.

6. Income Distribution and Structural Change in Dual Economy

Anthony B. Atkinson

INTRODUCTION

Dual economy models, developed notably by Lewis (1954), Jorgenson (1961) and Fei and Ranis (1964), characterize the process of development in terms of transferring employment from the traditional to the advanced sector of the economy. The dual economy model has major attractions. Like the associated two-sector growth model of Uzawa (1961), it is an example of general equilibrium in action, allowing one to trace the interaction between the two sectors and their evolution over time. The two sectors can be distinguished in different ways. They can be agriculture and manufacturing, rural and urban, advanced and backward, or consumption goods and capital goods, but in each case they allow us to investigate the allocation of factors between sectors, the role of differential factor prices, and the determination of relative prices for goods. Unlike the one-sector Solow–Swan growth model, the dual economy model allows examination of the process of development by which an advanced manufacturing sector increasingly replaces a backward agricultural sector. It is a model of *non*-steady-state growth.

As such, dual economy provides a natural theoretical basis for the Kuznets curve, the relationship showing income inequality first rising and then falling as an economy industrializes. Compared with the income distribution in the one-sector neoclassical growth model (Stiglitz 1969), the dual economy model allows for a richer set of outcomes, associated with structural change. As it was put by Kuznets, 'the income distribution of the total population, in the simplest model, may ... be viewed as a combination of the income distributions of the rural and urban populations' (1955: 7). It is indeed the mechanism of structural change on which most attention has focussed; and it is well known that, under certain circumstances, it can generate an inverse U-shape for the Gini coefficient of income inequality (Robinson 1976). Kuznets did however also refer to a second important mechanism causing widening inequality: the concentration of savings in the upper income brackets. This has received less attention, although it relates to other explanations of income inequality, such as the classical savings theories (Kaldor 1955–6). Again, dual economy models, where capital accumulation drives the growth of the advanced sector, provide a natural starting point for an investigation of this link between growth and personal income distribution.

Dualism and income distribution seem an appropriate subject for the present volume, given Sanjit's early contribution to our understanding of dual economy models. To quote Avinash Dixit: 'The need for a general equilibrium analysis of the dual economy was first emphasized by Bose (1968)' (1971: 384). The aim of the paper is to give an exposition of the relationship between individual income distribution and structural change in the dual economy. It asks how the link with the underlying theoretical model can help us understand the vast empirical literature on the Kuznets curve and in particular the recent studies using a panel of countries. What can observations on, say, the Gini coefficients for a series of years in a range of countries tell us about the underlying process?

The paper is based on the dual economy model of Jorgenson (1961). The first section sets out the key assumptions and describes the evolution of the macroeconomy. In the second section, I consider the implications for the personal income distribution, building on the work of a number of previous authors, including Anand and Kanbur (1985 and 1993) and Fields (1979 and 1980). In particular, I adopt the approach of Bourguignon (1990), and Brandolini (1992), who have shown how we can link macroeconomic variables to the Lorenz curve and Gini coefficient that are the main tools used in empirical studies of the personal income distribution. The main conclusions are summarized at the end of the paper.

A SIMPLE DUAL ECONOMY MODEL

The economy considered here has two sectors (agriculture and industry) and three classes of income recipient (farmers, industrial workers, and capitalists). It is therefore of some inherent complexity. In view of this, I make no apology for adopting one of the simplest possible dual economy models—that of Jorgenson (1961)—and for stripping out some of the richer features of his model (those concerned with endogenous population growth). The Jorgenson model is based on strong assumptions, particularly with regard to the demand side. More general versions of the dual economy have been studied by Bose (1968), Zarembka (1970), Marino (1975), Amano (1980), and others. The Jorgenson model has however two important merits for the present paper. The first is that it permits an explicit solution for the momentary equilibrium of the economy, which we can then use to examine the personal income distribution. The second is that the model allows us to incorporate the two elements highlighted by Kuznets (1955): structural change and concentration of capital.

The economy, which is assumed to be closed to foreign trade, produces two goods. In the agricultural sector, denoted by a subscript a, food output Y_a is produced by labour, L_a, and a fixed quantity of land, according to a Cobb–Douglas production function with labour exponent α, where technical progress takes place at the exogenous rate γ:

$$Y_a = e^{\gamma t} A L_a^{\alpha}. \tag{6.1}$$

Total output is divided equally between all those employed in the sector (there are no landlords), so that each worker receives the output y_a per head:

$$y_a = Y_a/L_a. \tag{6.2}$$

The relative price of agricultural output, relative to manufactures (taken as the numeraire), is denoted by q. In the industrial sector, denoted by a subscript b, labour L_b and capital K produce manufacturing output Y_b according to a Cobb–Douglas production function with labour exponent β and labour-augmenting technical progress at rate δ:

$$Y_b = \beta [L_b e^{\delta t}]^{\beta} K^{(1-\beta)}. \tag{6.3}$$

Industry is operated by perfectly competitive profit-maximizing firms, who hire labour such that the industrial wage, w, is equal to the value marginal product of labour:

$$w = e^{\beta \delta t} B \beta (K/L_b)^{(1-\beta)} = \beta Y_b / L_b. \tag{6.4}$$

Following Jorgenson, I assume that the wage differential between agriculture and industry necessary to cause movement between the two sectors is proportionate to the industrial sector wage, so that

$$q y_a = \mu w. \tag{6.5}$$

The assumption that μ is less than 1 generates inter-sectoral inequality. Profits accrue to the class of owners of capital, who are assumed to be an infinitesimal, fixed fraction of the total population. Total population is assumed here to grow at an exogenous rate n, and everyone is assumed to be employed (there is no unemployment and zero non-participation):

$$L_a + L_b = L_0 \, e^{nt}. \tag{6.6}$$

On the demand side, Jorgenson assumes that, once a certain level of prosperity is reached, food consumption per head is a constant, denoted here by f (i.e., the income elasticity falls to zero and there is no price responsiveness). We can deduce from (6.1) that

$$L_a = e^{-(\gamma-n)/\alpha t}[f L_0 / A]^{1/\alpha} \equiv c^{1/\alpha} L_0 \, e^{-(\gamma-n)/\alpha t}. \tag{6.7}$$

At time 0, $c = f L_0 /(A L_0^\alpha)$, which is the ratio of total food demand to total production if everyone were employed in agriculture. $(1 - c)$ is therefore a measure of the initial marketable surplus, and it is assumed that c is strictly less than unity. Finally, Jorgenson assumes that all profits are invested in capital accumulation and that there is no saving by workers or farmers. The rate of increase of capital is therefore (ignoring depreciation):

$$dK / dt = (1-\beta) Y_b. \tag{6.8}$$

From (6.1)–(6.8) describe both the current general equilibrium and the dynamic evolution of the dual economy. The simplifying assumption about the demand side means that the momentary equilibrium can be solved sequentially. At any time t, the allocation of labour to the agricultural sector is given by (6.7). If we assume that technical progress in food production is fast enough to outpace population growth (γ is greater than n), the labour force falls exponentially to zero. From (6.6), the labour force in industry grows such that

$$L_b = L_0 [e^{nt} - c^{1/\alpha} e^{-(\gamma-n)/\alpha t}] \equiv \lambda(t) L_0 \, e^{nt}, \tag{6.9}$$

where the share of the industrial sector in total employment is defined as λ. The rate of change of λ over time is given by

$$d\lambda/dt = (n+(\gamma-n)/\alpha)\,(1-\lambda) \equiv \theta(1-\lambda), \qquad (6.10)$$

where θ is positive. The value of L_b allows the industrial wage at any time to be determined from (6.4), since the capital stock is a state variable. Hence from (6.2) and (6.5), the terms of trade between agriculture and industry can be determined. For a given output per head in agriculture, at any date, once L_a is given, an increase in the demand for industrial labour caused by there being a larger capital stock, by bidding up the industrial wage w, leads to a corresponding rise in the price of agricultural produce.

Total national income, valued using industrial goods as a numeraire, is given by [using (6.4) and (6.5)]

$$Y = qY_a + Y_b = \mu w \, L_a + (1/\beta)w \, L_b, \qquad (6.11)$$

so that national income per head of the population, y, is a function of w and the share of the industrial sector in employment, λ:

$$y = w[(1-\lambda)\mu + \lambda/\beta]. \qquad (6.12)$$

It can be seen that the rise in λ causes y to rise relative to w (since $1/\beta$ is greater than μ). The share, Π, of profits in national income is given by

$$\Pi = (1-\beta)/[1 + \beta\mu(1-\lambda)/\lambda]. \qquad (6.13)$$

The profits share rises towards $(1-\beta)$ as λ rises towards 1.

Over time, the equilibrium is affected by the accumulation of capital and by technical progress. Technical progress in agriculture releases labour to be employed in industry. The proportionate rate of growth of industrial employment is equal to

$$(1/L_b)\,dL_b/dt = \theta(1-\lambda)/\lambda + n. \qquad (6.14)$$

If nothing else changed, this would require a fall in the industrial wage and a fall in the terms of trade, q. But capital accumulation in the B sector raises the demand for industrial labour, and technical progress makes labour in industry more productive. In order to allow for the latter effect, let us define k as the capital/effective labour ratio ($k \equiv K/(L_b e^{\delta t})$), so that the factor prices w and r (the rate of return on capital) can be rewritten, using (6.4), as

$$w = e^{\delta t} B\beta k^{1-\beta},$$ (6.15a)

$$r = B(1-\beta)k^{-\beta}.$$ (6.15b)

Profits are rK, so that the rate of growth of capital is [from (6.8)]

$$(1/K)dK/dt = (1-\beta)Bk^{-\beta}.$$ (6.16)

The evolution of k over time is given by [using (6.14)]

$$(1/k)dk/dt = (1-\beta)Bk^{-\beta} - \theta(1-\lambda)/\lambda - (n+\delta)$$ (6.17)

As λ rises from $(1-c)$ at time 0 towards 1, the second term falls from $\theta c/(1-c)$ towards zero. The asymptotic value of k, denoted by k^*, is given by

$$(1-\beta)Bk^{*-\beta} = (n+\delta),$$ (6.18)

that is, the asymptotic rate of return is $r^* = n + \delta$.

The dynamics of this dual economy are governed by (6.10) and (6.17). The evolution of the economy in terms of the state variables, k and λ, is plotted in Figure 6.1. As shown by Dixit (1970) and Marino (1975), (A) either the economy may converge along a path where the capital-effective labour ratio is always rising, or (B) the ratio may first decline and then rise to reach k^* asymptotically. The initial position depends on the marketable surplus and on the inherited capital stock in industry. A country with a relatively large marketable surplus, but

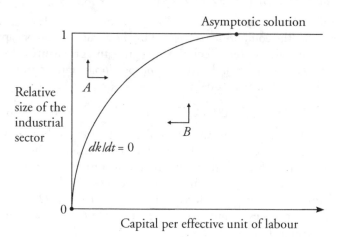

Figure 6.1: Dynamic Paths for Dual Economy

little capital, starts above the line $dk/dt = 0$, and k rises throughout. A country with relatively little spare food, but more inherited capital, starts below the line $dk/dt = 0$ and sees k first fall before rising. Ultimately, the industrial sector comes to dominate the economy. The asymptotic long-run equilibrium corresponds to that of the one-sector model (Jorgenson 1961: 329). But even though the ultimate state is the same, countries follow different paths depending on their initial marketable surplus and inherited capital stock.

For the distribution of personal income, the key variables are the wage rate, the proportion of workers in the industrial sector, the share of profits, and mean per capita income, y. In the next section, I consider how these combine to determine the personal distribution of income and its evolution over time. We know that asymptotically, the economy approaches a situation where everyone is employed in the industrial sector and the only inequality is that between workers and capitalists. But what happens along the path?

DISTRIBUTION IN THE DUAL ECONOMY AND THE KUZNETS CURVE

The Kuznets curve is concerned with the *relative* distribution of income. In his citation of empirical evidence, and in his numerical illustration, Kuznets (1955) refers to the proportionate shares of different income groups. These are different from measures of the absolute standard of living, as with the World Bank $1 a day poverty line. The proportion of the population living below a specified absolute level could well be falling even though relative income inequality is rising. This difference should be borne in mind throughout this section, since I focus on the relative distribution. The conclusions could well be different if we were to take an absolute approach.

I begin with the Lorenz curve, showing the proportion of income received cumulatively by the bottom x per cent of the distribution. This curve has the advantage of depicting the whole distribution, rather than seeking to summarize the distribution in a single index, such as the Gini coefficient. The Lorenz curve for the dual economy is drawn by Bourguignon (1990), and a version is shown in Figure 6.2. The lowest income group are, by assumption, the farmers, whose income relative to the mean is [using (6.12)].

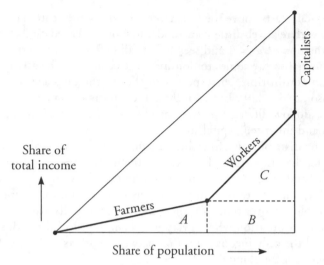

Figure 6.2: Lorenz Curve for Dual Economy

$$\mu w / y = \mu / [\mu(1-\lambda)+ \lambda / \beta]. \tag{6.19}$$

This is the slope of the first segment of the Lorenz curve, and it covers a proportion $(1-\lambda)$ of the population. The next segment has slope w/y, and takes us up to the capitalist class. Here, as noted earlier, I simplify by assuming that the capitalist class is of negligible size in relation to the total population, so that the final point on the Lorenz curve is on the vertical axis. (This assumption also avoids any ambiguity as to whether or not capitalists are better or worse off than workers or farmers.) The vertical distance from the final point to the corner measures the share of profits in national income, given by (6.13).

From this description of the Lorenz curve, we can see that the relative distribution is governed purely by λ, and not by k. The amount of marketable surplus determines, with the specific assumptions made here, the size of the industrial sector, and hence the location and slopes of the Lorenz curve. The level of capital per effective labour does not affect it. A rise in k determines the level of total output and hence is relevant to determining the rate of absolute poverty [from (6.15) we can see that w is an increasing function of k]. But it does not affect the relative distribution.

How does the Lorenz curve shift with λ? From (6.13), we can see that the top point of the Lorenz curve shifts downward over time as the

share of profits rises. This rise occurs not because of an increasing profit
share within industry but because industrial output is a progressively
larger share of total income. For example, with $\beta = 2/3$, $\mu = 3/4$, an
initial value of $\lambda = 1/3$ would mean that the initial profit share is half
its final value. As far as the rest of the Lorenz curve is concerned, we
know that the interior point is moving to the left, as the agricultural
sector contracts. Moreover, we have seen from (6.12) that, as the
industrial sector grows, y rises relative to w and μw. Real wages may be
rising in each sector, but mean income is rising faster on account of the
structural change. The slopes of the two linear segments therefore fall.

The Lorenz curve therefore shifts outwards at both top and bottom.[1]
Does it cross? If there were no profit income, the upper part of the
Lorenz curve would end at the same point, and its slope would be less,
so that the shifted Lorenz curve would have to intersect. Both the rich
(industrial workers) and the poor (farmers) would find that they were
worse off relative to the rising average. The gainers would be those
making the transition between sectors. Where there is profit income,
whether or not there is an intersection depends on λ. It can be shown
that there will be an intersection where

$$\lambda > (1-\beta)/(1/\mu - \beta). \tag{6.20}$$

In this sense, there is a Kuznets inverse-U. In the initial stages, the
Lorenz curve moves unambiguously outwards; after a certain point the
Lorenz curve intersects.

Where the Lorenz curves intersect, different summary measures of
inequality can give different answers. The summary measure to be used
for empirical analysis is therefore a matter for careful choice. Most
commonly employed is the Gini coefficient. In the present case, the
Gini coefficient, G, can be calculated using the fact that it is equal to
the ratio of the area between the diagonal and the Lorenz curve to the
whole triangle. This leads to[2]

$$G = [1-\beta(\lambda+\mu(1-\lambda))]/[1+\beta\mu(1-\lambda)/\lambda]. \tag{6.21}$$

G is a non-linear function of λ. It is zero for $\lambda = 0$ and equal to

[1] Where the capitalist class is a finite proportion of the total population, there
are three line segments — *see* Bourguignon (1990) and Bardhan and Udry (1990:
Chapter 15)—and we have to keep track of the changing income of the capitalist
class relative to the mean.
[2] $1 - G$ is equal to twice the area (A+B+C) in Figure 6.2.

$(1 - \beta)$ for $\lambda = 1$. This is illustrated for different values of β in Figure 6.3. As we have seen, the initial value of λ depends on the extent of marketable surplus. An economy well endowed with food will have a larger initial industrial sector and have a shorter period of rising relative income inequality.

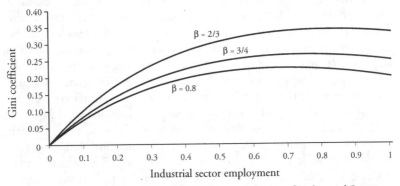

Figure 6.3: Evolution of Gini Coefficient with Size of Industrial Sector

The first conclusion that we can draw is the obvious but often neglected one: the Gini coefficient (or other summary measure) is directly governed by the level of development, as represented by the size of the industrial sector, and depends only indirectly on the level of national income or on time. Clearly, the level of national income varies with λ, but the relation between national income and the size of the industrial sector depends on such factors as the level of productivity in the industrial sector (B affects w and hence y). Two countries may have the same values for β and μ, the two parameters that enter (6.21), but have a different relation between y and λ. Looking across countries, a country with more capital per effective labour has a higher national income corresponding to the same value of λ. Mapped into y space, the two countries have different Kuznets curves. In the same way, the two countries may have a different rate of change of λ over time [from (6.10)] it may be seen that the speed of sectoral change depends on the rate of technical progress in agriculture). Empirical studies that use national income per head or time as explanatory variables are implicitly assuming that countries are identical in all respects that affect the mapping between λ and these variables. This is recognized in a number of theoretical contributions, such as Robinson (1976), but less commonly taken into account in econometric estimation.

The second conclusion concerns the functional form. For a country with given, constant values of the parameters, (6.21) gives the functional relation between G and λ. This is clearly non-linear and we may seek a transformation. Nielsen (1994) used for this purpose the difference between the population share and the income share of the agricultural sector. As he notes, this is the value of the Gini coefficient when the only source of inequality is the sectoral income difference. Setting $\beta = 1$ in (6.21) we obtain

$$G_0 = \lambda(1-\lambda)(1-\mu)/[\lambda + \mu(1-\lambda)]. \tag{6.22}$$

The dual economy model described here allows us to see how this variable can be introduced into a model with other sources of inequality. Rearranging (6.21) we can write

$$G = G_0(1-\Pi) + \Pi. \tag{6.23}$$

(The same conclusion can be reached by 'scaling down' the Lorenz curve for farmers and workers on their own and adding the completely unequal distribution among capitalists.) When β is not equal to 1, G_0 does not have the interpretation as a 'sector dualism' variable. Equation (6.23) does however allow us to highlight the role of the share of profits (Π). The Gini coefficient can be expected to vary across countries on account of differences in β.

An alternative approach is to define $z \equiv y/(Y_b/L_b)$, where this is the ratio of total output per head to output per head in the industrial sector. z is less than 1, but approaches 1 asymptotically. Using the fact that

$$z = \lambda + \beta(1-\lambda)\mu, \tag{6.24}$$

we can write

$$G = 1 + 2\beta\eta\mu - \eta z - \beta\mu(1+ \beta\eta\mu)/z, \tag{6.25}$$

where

$$\eta \equiv \beta(1-\mu)/(1-\beta\mu)^2 \tag{6.26}$$

Here (6.25) shows G as a function of z and $1/z$. This is the same functional form as that suggested by Anand and Kanbur (1993) with regard to mean income, y. As they stress, the form depends on the choice of inequality index and vice versa: 'the right index must be used with the right functional form for estimation purposes' (1993: 39). Also (6.25) is different from the quadratic specification often adopted in equations for the Gini coefficient. It should also be noted that use of

z is different from using national income per head, since it is a measure of income relative to the potential maximum when the economy has been fully transformed. The potential maximum is rising over time as a result of technical progress. A country may be enjoying rising income per head but standing still in terms of development.

Moreover (6.25) may be regarded as a 'reduced form' expression, in that we have solved out the different elements. It should however be noted that the coefficients of z and $1/z$ depend on β and μ. While it may be reasonable to assume that these are constant over time, it does not reasonable to assume that they are identical across countries. It may not appear therefore be enough to treat country differences as fixed effects entering the constant term. Countries with different β, for example, would have different coefficients for z and $1/z$.

One lesson that one can draw is that there is a choice of strategy for specifying the models to be estimated. One approach is to work with a variable coefficient 'reduced form' relating the Gini coefficient (or other summary measure) to the level of development. An alternative approach is to seek to explain the different elements and then combine them as in (6.23). The latter approach can be extended, for example, to allow for within-sector inequality,[3] but in the form here we have incorporated two of the major elements identified by Kuznets: structural change and the concentration of capital.

CONCLUDING COMMENTS

At a time when economics is becoming increasingly compartmentalized, it is important to show how one can join up different elements. Here I have taken a simple general equilibrium model and tried to show how it can be related to the equations that are estimated in empirical studies of income inequality in panels of countries. Making this link is not just a search for completeness. It helps define the explanatory variables, emphasizing that the key determinant is the level of development, not national income or time. It provides guidance, as Anand and Kanbur (1993) earlier pointed out, about the choice of functional form. It allows us to see the distinction between 'structural' and 'reduced form' approaches. It serves as a caution about using panels of countries

---

[3] Where the distributions in the two sectors do not overlap, the expression for the Gini coefficient can be readily modified—*see* Anand and Kanbur (1993).

without regard to how the coefficients may vary across countries and over time. It shows how we can bring together in one model the two key factors identified by Kuznets. Everyone is aware of the role of structural change, but less attention has been paid to the concentration of capital and the role of profits.

The dual economy model used here ignores many important interactions. The reader will have noted that the terms of trade, much discussed in the literature, have been left at the side of the stage. The assumption about the demand for food drives the development of the model in too strong a way. The migration process is not based on an explicit individual calculus. It is therefore only a starting point for studying the distribution of income.

REFERENCES

AMANO, M., (1980), 'A Neoclassical Model of the Dual Economy with Capital Accumulation in Agriculture', *Review of Economic Studies*, 47, pp. 933–44.

ANAND, S. and KANBUR, S.M.R., (1985), 'Poverty Under the Kuznets Process', *Economic Journal*, 95, pp. 42–50.

——, (1993), 'The Kuznets Process and the Inequality-Development Relationship', *Journal of Development Economics*, 40, pp. 25–52.

BARDHAN, P. and UDRY, C., (1999), *Development Microeconomics*, Oxford: Oxford University Press.

BOSE, S., (1968), 'Wage, Price and Investment in the Dual Economy', Brandeis University, manuscript.

BOURGUIGNON, F., (1990), 'Growth and Inequality in the Dual Model of Development: The Role of Demand Factors', *Review of Economic Studies*, 57, pp. 215–28.

BRANDOLINI, A., (1993), 'Nonlinear Dynamics, Entitlement Rules, and the Cyclical Behaviour of the Personal Income Distribution', CEPR Discussion Paper No. 84, London School of Economics.

DIXIT, A.K., (1970), 'Growth Patterns in a Dual Economy', *Oxford Economic Papers*, 22, pp. 229–34.

——, (1971), 'Short-run Equilibrium and Shadow Prices in the Dual Economy', *Oxford Economic Papers*, 23, pp. 384–400.

FEI, J.C.H. and G., RANIS, (1964) *Development of the Labor Surplus Economy*, Homewood, Illinois: Richard D. Irwin.

FIELDS, G.S., (1979), 'A Welfare Economic Approach to Growth and Distribution in the Dual Economy', *Quarterly Journal of Economics*, 93, pp. 325–53.

_____, (1980), *Poverty, Inequality and Development*, Cambridge, UK: Cambridge University Press.

JORGENSON, D., (1961), 'The Development of a Dual Economy', *Economic Journal*, 71, pp. 309–34.

KALDOR, N., (1955–6), 'Alternative Theories of Distribution', *Review of Economic Studies*, 23, pp. 83–100.

KUZNETS, S., (1955), 'Economic Growth and Income Inequality', *American Economic Review*, 45, pp. 1–28.

LEWIS, W.A., (1954), 'Economic Development with Unlimited Supplies of Labour', *Manchester School*, 22, pp. 139–91.

MARINO, A.M., (1975), 'On the Neoclassical Version of the Dual Economy', *Review of Economic Studies*, 42, pp. 435–43.

NIELSEN, F., (1994), 'Income Inequality and Industrial Development: Dualism Revisited', *American Sociological Review*, 59, pp. 654–77.

ROBINSON, S., (1976), 'A Note on the U Hypothesis Relating Income Inequality and Economic Development', *American Economic Review*, 66, pp. 437–40.

STIGLITZ, J.E., (1969), 'Distribution of Income and Wealth Among Individuals', *Econometrica*, 37, pp. 382–97.

UZAWA, H., (1961), 'On a Two-Sector Model of Economic Growth', *Review of Economic Studies*, 29, pp. 40–7.

ZAREMBKA, P., (1970), 'Marketable Surplus and Growth in the Dual Economy', *Journal of Economic Theory*, 2, pp. 107–21.

7. Information and Price Dynamics

Evidence from Selected Potato Markets in West Bengal

ABHIRUP SARKAR AND *SANDIP MITRA*

INTRODUCTION

Do large sellers, on an average, get a better price for their products than small sellers in backward agricultural markets? And if they do, what is a plausible explanation? The present paper is concerned with these questions, more with the second than with the first. The answer to the first question has to be primarily empirical. One has to check, in the context of specific markets, whether small sellers are really getting lower prices than their larger counterparts. The present paper reports our study of selected potato markets in the Indian state of West Bengal. Our study confirms that indeed small sellers get a lower price on an average in the markets that we have studied. The second question, on the other hand, begs a theoretical answer. The theoretical explanation, of course, may be further supported by empirical facts. Consequently, the paper offers a theoretical explanation as to why the average price received by a large seller may be higher than that received by a small seller. It then

The paper is based on a two-year survey of selected potato markets in West Bengal. The study was funded by a research grant from the Indian Statistical Institute and has benefited immensely from the encouragement and advice of Professor Sanjit Bose. We dedicate this paper to Professor Bose without implicating him for the errors and omissions that remain.

looks at the empirical evidence from our survey of selected potato markets in West Bengal to support the theoretical argument.

Indeed, if the small and the large sellers sell in the same markets, they cannot possibly get different prices. So, in order to get different prices, they must be selling in different markets. The question is: why are they selling in different markets? One explanation can be given in terms of the differential power of stockholding of the small and the large sellers (Bhaduri 1983). The explanation runs as follows: the small sellers are usually cash-constrained and are therefore compelled to sell their stocks just after the harvest. In other words, due to their immediate need for cash, the small sellers are unable to participate in markets which are far away *in time* from the harvest. This compulsion to sell early increases the supply and depresses the price just after the harvest. This, in turn, induces the large sellers, who are not so much cash-constrained, to sell late when prices are relatively higher. Thus it is argued that the small and the large sellers sell in different inter-temporal markets and hence get different prices.

There is, indeed, quite a bit of truth in this explanation. But unfortunately, it cannot explain the different prices received by the large and the small sellers in *all* markets. For example, the potato markets that we study reveal that the small sellers do not necessarily hold on to their stocks for a shorter period than the large sellers. We, therefore, need an alternative explanation.

The explanation, in our opinion, lies in the very nature of agricultural production and consumption. Agricultural production, by its very nature, is discrete, while consumption of agricultural goods is continuous. Hence storage is an important activity in most agricultural markets. But storage, by definition, is for the future and the future is, in general, uncertain. We argue that the large sellers can handle this uncertainty better than the small sellers. They can do so because they possess more and better information about production and demand conditions than their smaller counterparts.

To develop our ideas, we first present a theoretical model of a storage-dependent agricultural commodity. We have two types of sellers in the model: uninformed small sellers and informed large sellers. The small sellers' sales, being based on imperfect information like rumours, gossips, etc., are fluctuating. These fluctuating sales, in turn, lead to fluctuating prices. We show that the informed large sellers get higher revenue from the fluctuating prices by selling less (or even buying) when prices are low and selling more when prices are high. Indeed, the higher the fluctuations in sales by the small sellers, the higher is the revenue earned by the large sellers. On the other hand, these higher fluctuations lead to lower revenue for the small sellers themselves. Obviously, higher revenue for the large sellers basically means that they receive a higher price, on an average.

With the theoretical results in the background, we look at the functioning of selected potato markets in West Bengal, a major potato-producing state of India. We choose potato markets of West Bengal as the object of our study because potato is a highly storage-dependent product. Moreover, West Bengal is a major producer of potato in the Indian market contributing about 33 per cent of the total produce of the country. Therefore, a study of the West Bengal potato market gives a fairly good idea about the Indian market as well. Our study consists of a two-crop-year survey we conducted for the production years 1998–9 and 1999–2000 in the potato-producing district of Hoogly in West Bengal. Our empirical findings are the following. First, we find that the average price received by a seller over a particular year goes up as we move from the smallest potato-producing class (producing potatoes on 0–2 bighas[1] of land) to larger and larger classes, the largest class consisting of producers producing potatoes on 10 bighas or more. Second, we define an index of stockholding over any harvest year and find, in terms of the index, that it is the smaller producers who tend to hold on to their stocks for a longer period than the larger producers. Thus, at least in West Bengal potato markets, longer holding of stocks cannot explain why the larger sellers receive higher prices. Next, we explain why small sellers, in spite of holding on to their output for a longer period of time on an average, get a lower price. We show that the large sellers gather more information about the demand and production sides of the market and this helps them to fetch a better price. The paper is organized in the following way. In the following section we develop the theoretical model which serves as the background of our empirical analysis. The third section contains the empirical findings of the paper. The last section concludes.

THE THEORETICAL FRAMEWORK

We consider the market for a single agricultural good. Output is seasonal and is obtained at discrete points in time. These discrete points are

[1] 1 bigha = 0.331 acre

identified with the harvest. The time interval, which lies between two consecutive harvests, is denoted by [0, T]. We focus our attention on this time interval. Though production is discrete, consumption is continuous. To meet continuous consumption, output has to be stored from one harvest to another. Thus, storage is a very important activity in the present model.

There are three types of agents operating in the market: large sellers, small sellers, and consumers. Both large and small sellers own some stocks at the initial time point 0. The problem of each seller is to decide upon the optimal sequence of sales from these stocks over the interval [0, T] so as to maximize profits. There are two differences between the large and the small sellers. First, a large seller is able to affect the market price through his sales decision. Thus each large seller enjoys oligopolistic market power. Each small seller, on the other hand, is a price taker. Second, the large and the small sellers differ with respect to the information they possess. In particular, we assume that the large sellers have complete knowledge about *aggregate production* while the small sellers' knowledge about aggregate production is incomplete, being based on rumours, gossips, and the like.

We may think of a small seller choosing his optimal sales path at any point in time by maximizing expected future profits subject to the information he has at that point in time. Since the information set typically varies from one small seller to another, the sales will also typically vary. Moreover, a small seller may change his optimal sales path if his information set changes. Finally, a small seller may also be fund-constrained to some extent, which induces him to choose a particular path. In other words, exogenously given information sets and exogenously given fund constraints primarily determine the sales paths of small sellers. Accordingly, we treat inter-temporal market sales by the small sellers taken as a whole as *exogenously given*. Finally, we assume that there are a large number of small sellers and n large sellers in the market.

As compared to the sellers, the consumers are passive in this model. They do not, by assumption, hold any stock for future consumption. They buy and consume at the same instant. At any point in time they have a demand curve which is assumed to be linear and uniform across time. The inverse demand function takes the form

$$p(t) = a - q(t), \tag{7.1}$$

where $p(t)$ is the price of the good and $q(t)$ is the quantity demanded at time t. Let $y(t)$ be market sales (market purchase, if $y(t)$ is negative) by the large sellers and $z(t)$ be market sales (market purchase if $z(t)$ is negative) by the small sellers at time t. Throughout the analysis we take $\{z(t)\}$, the sequence of sales (and purchases) by the small sellers as exogenously given. Demand–supply equality at time point t implies that $q(t) = y(t) + z(t)$. Consequently (7.1) may be written as

$$p(t) = a - \{y(t) + z(t)\}. \tag{7.1a}$$

The large sellers take (7.1a) as given while maximizing their profits.

A large seller maximizes his inter-temporal profits by choosing his sequence of sales (and purchases) *given* the sequence of sales of the small sellers, the sequence of sales of the other large sellers, and the demand equation (7.1a). Formally, a large seller's problem is to

$$\max \int_0^T p(t) y_i(t) dt - k_i$$

subject to $X_i(0) = X_i$, $X_i(T) = 0$,
where $y_i(t) = -\dot{X}_i(t)$. $\tag{7.2}$

In the above maximization problem, $X_i(T)$ denotes stocks held by the i-th large seller at time t. His initial stocks are X_i and his terminal stocks are zero. Sales at any t are denoted by $y_i(t)$ which is equal to the fall in stocks at t. If $y_i(t)$ is negative, it is interpreted as purchase. k_i denotes the fixed cost of storage of the i-th large seller. Since these fixed costs are not going to play any role in the subsequent analysis, we assume that $k_i = 0 \forall i$. For simplicity, we also assume that the initial stock X_i is the same for all i. Each large trader chooses his sequence of sales (or purchases) $\{y_i(t)\}$ to maximize profits. We assume that a large seller knows the *total* amount of output produced by the small sellers in a harvest year. Obviously, this total output is given by $\int_0^T z(t)] dt$. We also assume that a large seller knows the total number of large sellers operating in the market, that is, the value of n. We will show below that just these two pieces of information are sufficient to keep him on his optimal path. The first-order conditions, given by the Euler equations are

$$\dot{m}_i(t) = 0 \quad \text{for } i = 1, 2, ..., n. \tag{7.3}$$

Using the demand equation (7.1a) we can solve (7.3) simultaneously for all i to obtain

$$\dot{y}_i(t) = -\frac{\dot{z}(t)}{n+1}, \tag{7.4}$$

$$\dot{y}(t) = -\dot{z}(t)\frac{n}{n+1},\tag{7.5}$$

and $$\dot{p}(t) = -\frac{\dot{z}(t)}{n+1}.\tag{7.6}$$

A few comments on the maximization and the consequent solutions are now in order. First, a large seller chooses his sequence of sales and purchases $\{y_i(t)\}$ to maximize (7.2). We confine our attention to the case where the path of purchase and sales is *pre-committed*. In other words, the i-th large seller chooses his optimal path at time 0 and sticks to this path for the entire interval of time. We could alternatively assume that the seller is able to revise his optimal path at any point in time in future. This, however, would not change the solutions (Sarkar 1993 for a formal argument).

Second, as is clear from (7.4)–(7.5), the rate of change in optimal sales and purchases of the i-th large seller is independent of the sales or purchases of the other large sellers. The rate of change depends only on the rate of change in the market arrival of stocks from the small sellers and the *number* of large sellers in the market. The latter variable n is inversely related to the degree of monopoly in the market.

Third, from (7.6) it follows that the extent of price fluctuations (as represented by the rate of change in price at any t) depends only on the extent of fluctuation in market arrival from the small sellers and the degree of monopoly. In particular, for any given fluctuation in market arrival, the higher the value of n, that is, the lower the degree of monopoly in the market, the lower is the extent of price fluctuations. We shall have more to say on this point after we compute the equilibrium paths.

The time paths of $\{y_i(t)\}$, $\{y(t)\}$, $\{p(t)\}$ may be derived from (7.4), (7.5) and (7.6) along with the initial conditions. These time paths are

$$y_i(t) = \frac{1}{n+1}[\bar{z} - z(t)] + \bar{y}_i,\tag{7.7}$$

$$y(t) = \frac{n}{n+1}[\bar{z} - z(t)] + \bar{y},\tag{7.8}$$

and $$p(t) = a - \frac{n}{n+1}\bar{z} - \frac{1}{n+1}z(t) - \bar{y},\tag{7.9}$$

where $\bar{y}_i = \dfrac{1}{T}\displaystyle\int_0^T y_i(t)dt, \quad \bar{y} = \dfrac{1}{T}\displaystyle\int_0^T y(t)dt, \quad \bar{z} = \dfrac{1}{T}\displaystyle\int_0^T z(t)dt.$ Clearly, $\bar{y}_i, \bar{y}, \bar{z}$ are *average* sales. It is clear that given the time path of sales $z(t)$ by the small sellers, the other time paths are known from (7.7)–(7.9). A few comments on the equilibrium time paths are now in order.

First, consider the optimal strategy of a large seller as given by (7.7). A large seller sells the average amount $\bar{y}_i$ from his own stocks at each time t; in addition, he sells an extra amount if at any t the market arrival $z(t)$ falls short of the average market arrival $\bar{z}$. This is captured by the first term in the right-hand side of (7.7). If, on the other hand, the actual market arrival at t is greater than the average, he withholds some stocks and sells less than $\bar{y}_i$. In the extreme case, when the actual market arrival exceeds the average market arrival by a very large amount, $y_i(t)$ becomes *negative* and, in this case, the large seller *buys* from the market. Clearly, through his purchase and sales over time, a large seller tends to smooth out inter-temporal prices.

Secondly, to follow their optimal sequence of sales and purchases, the large sellers have to know only the average market arrival $\bar{z}$ or equivalently, the total market arrival H from the small sellers. The market arrival at any time t can, of course, be observed by a large seller at time t. In particular, a large seller has to know neither the future sequence $\{z(t)\}$ of market arrival coming from the small sellers nor the sequence of sales of other large sellers in order to follow his optimal path of sales and purchases. All we need to assume is that a large seller knows the *total* amount of production of the small sellers and the *number* of large sellers operating in the market.

Thirdly, the degree of withholding or over-releasing of stocks by the large sellers in response to the difference between actual and average market arrival depends on the degree of monopoly which is inversely related to n. The higher the value of n, that is, the lower the degree of monopoly, the higher is the total response of the large sellers. This is clear from (7.8) where, in the right-hand side, $n/(n+1)$ is increasing in n. In the extreme case, when $n \to \infty$, this total response is the highest and is equal to unity. In this case, whatever be the fluctuations in $\{z(t)\}$, $\{y(t)\}$ adjusts in such a way that at each point in time the average amount, that is, $\bar{z} + \bar{y}$, is sold in the market and $p(t) = \bar{p}, \forall t$. Here we define $\bar{p} = a - \bar{z} - \bar{y}$. Thus, as the number of large sellers grows very large, there is *perfect arbitrage* leading to perfect smoothing of inter-temporal prices. The extent of arbitrage goes down and the price path exhibits fluctuations as the degree of monopoly increases.

Let us now look at the value of sales of the large and small sellers. Let the variance of market arrival from the small sellers be denoted by $\sigma_z^2 = \frac{1}{T}\int_0^T [z(t) - \bar{z}]^2\, dt$. Let the value of sales of the large sellers and the small sellers be denoted by V_L and V_S respectively. Straightforward calculations using (7.7)–(7.9) yield

$$V_L = \int_0^T p(t)y(t)dt = \frac{T n \sigma_z^2}{(n+1)^2} + \bar{p}\, T\, \bar{y}, \qquad (7.10)$$

$$\text{and } V_S = \int_0^T p(t)z(t)dt = \bar{p}\, T\, \bar{z} - \frac{T \sigma_z^2}{(n+1)}. \qquad (7.11)$$

It is clear from (7.10) and (7.11) that the value of sales of the large sellers is increasing in the variance of market arrival from the small sellers. On the other hand, the value of sales of the small sellers is decreasing in this variance. It is reasonable to assume that if the small sellers depend more on rumours and unreliable second-hand information to decide the time profile of market sales, the variance in market arrival from the small sellers will go up. This is due to the fact that rumours have an inherent random element embedded in them. In other words, we are trying to argue that the more the lack of information on the part of the small sellers, the higher is the variance in their market sales. This higher variance, in turn, increases the profits of the large sellers and reduces the profits of the small sellers.

It is also clear from (7.10) and (7.11) that p_L, p_S, the average price received by the large and the small sellers respectively, are given by

$$p_L = \frac{V_L}{T\bar{y}} = \bar{p} + \frac{n\sigma_z^2}{\bar{y}(n+1)^2}, \qquad (7.12)$$

$$\text{and } p_S = \frac{V_S}{T\bar{z}} = \bar{p} - \frac{\sigma_z^2}{\bar{z}(n+1)}. \qquad (7.13)$$

Clearly, $p_L > p_S$ and it is obvious from the above model that the large sellers receive a better price due to the combined effect of their oligopolistic power and their informational advantage.

THE EMPIRICAL EVIDENCE

The empirical evidence that we are going to report in this section is obtained from our survey of potato producers of 14 villages in the district of Hoogly in West Bengal. From a population size of 5325 potato-producing households we chose a sample of 385 (*see* table for the distribution of population according size class). These households were classified according to the size of their landholdings and were surveyed consecutively for two production years 1998–9 and 1999–2000.

Sample Distribution Across Different Size Classes

	Size class (bighas)					Total
	0–2	2.01–4	4.01–6	6.01–10	10	
Sample size	107	95	47	93	43	385

One peculiar feature of the potato market is that along with the wholesale and retail markets there is an active *bond market*. It is necessary to explain, at the outset, what a potato bond market is all about. Potato is a storage-dependent product. The output, which is obtained in late January/February, cannot be kept in the open for more than three months. It has to be kept in cold stores. When a producer puts his produce in a cold store, he gets a receipt, which when produced at a later date, allows him to withdraw his potatoes from the cold store. Now, this receipt is freely bought and sold in the open market and is called a *potato bond*. Free transactions in bonds allow the producers to sell the bonds instead of the actual output to the traders. The traders, in turn, release the potato from the cold store against the bond they buy to take it to the wholesale or retail markets. The market reflects a constant differential between the price of potato in the wholesale market and the price of bonds. This difference is roughly equal to the storage and handling costs at the time of releasing potato from the cold store. In short, the bond market helps the producers transact with the traders without actually handling the potatoes.

The bond markets are usually operative in the neighbourhood of cold stores. Moreover, there is usually a time-dependent difference between the wholesale price and the bond price of potato. Due to arbitrage, this difference is equal to the storage cost and depreciation. Over time, as potato gets dehydrated and loses weight while remaining in the cold store, the value of a bag of potato in the cold store goes down and hence the difference between the wholesale price and the bond price goes up over time. However, this difference is completely predictable. As a result, one can get a fairly good idea of the movement of wholesale prices from the movement of bond prices. Apart from our household survey, we have collected price data of potato bonds from the cold stores.

The movement of post-storage weekly bond price for the years 1998–9 and 1999–2000 are given in Figures 7.1 and 7.2. We report *average* prices over a number of markets around a number of cold stores. For each year, we start with the third week of May and go up to the last week of December. These extreme time points are indicated by week 1 and week 32 respectively on the horizontal axis of Figures 7.1 and 7.2 and the intermediate weeks are defined accordingly. It may be mentioned that each year the cold stores open around the third week of May and close around the last week of December. This explains the choice of weeks in the figures. Obviously, during the interval lying between week 1 and week 32, potato can be withdrawn from the stores at any point in time.

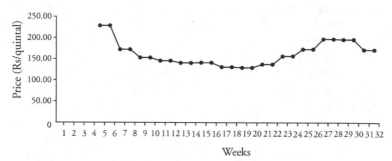

Figure 7.1: Movement of Post-storage Weekly Bond Price Across Various
Potato Markets (1999)

Note: Weeks 1–4 are not explicitly showing up in figure because no transactions in
bonds were recorded in the first four weeks.

The important thing to notice about Figures 7.1 and 7.2 is that there is no overall trend of bond prices to go up over time and there is quite a bit of fluctuation in bond prices. In fact, as is evident from the figures, bond prices have followed a *random walk*. Thus even if a producer waits for a sufficiently long time to sell his bonds, there is no guarantee that he will get a better price. In other words, short-term fluctuations are important in determining exactly what price a producer would get. A short-run upward trend in the price creates expectations that price will go down in the near future. This urges a lot of producers to unload their stocks which in turn depresses the prices. A fall in the price, once more, leads to a rise in the future expected price, leading sellers to sell less stocks for a while which again jacks up the current price. In this way, a short-run cyclical movement of prices is created. These cycles are repeated with unequal amplitude over time.

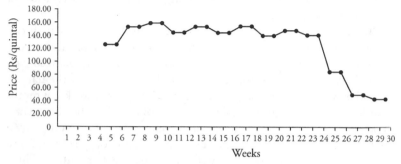

Figure 7.2: Movement of Post-storage Weekly Bond Price Across Various Potato Markets (2000)

Note: Weeks 1–4 are not explicitly showing up in figure because no transactions in bonds were recorded in the first four weeks.

How do small and large sellers gain from these fluctuations? To see this, consider Table 7.1 which gives the average price received by producers of different classes in the two years. Now, typically, a producer distributes his total sales over the harvesting year and gets different prices at different points in time. The total revenue he gets is the sum of the prices he gets at different points in time multiplied by the corresponding quantities he sells. The average price is simply the total revenue divided by the total quantity he sells for the entire year. The average, for each size class, of these average prices is represented in Table 7.1. If we look at the average of these prices over the two years

Table 7.1: Average Price in Rupees Received Per Quintal Across Different Size Classes

Profit		Size class (bighas)				
		0 – 2	2.01–4	4.01–6	6.01–10	> 10
Price (per qunital): P	1st round	211.09	207.50	209.41	226.64	227.70
	2nd round	162.98	180.75	182.18	179.24	175.41
	Average	187.04	194.13	195.80	202.94	201.56

under study, it becomes clear that larger producers tend to receive a better price than their smaller counterparts.

The price paths given in Figures 7.1 and 7.2 suggest that in the potato market there is no clear gain to be obtained by holding on to the stocks for longer periods. This is due to the fact that the price paths do not exhibit any clearly increasing trend. It is still of some interest to find out which category of producers is holding on to their stocks for a longer time in the potato market.

To accomplish our end, first we have to find an index which can measure the extent of holding of stocks over time by a producer. Let t refer to a typical week and let $q(t)$ refer to the amount of potato sold by a particular producer in week t. Denote the beginning of the harvest period by week 0. Therefore, if the producer sells $q(t)$ at week t, it means that he has held the quantity of potato $q(t)$ for t weeks. Thus his *average* holding of stocks is given by a weighted average of the time points when he has sold his stocks, the weights being the fraction of total potato sold at the particular time point. Therefore, we construct an index I which represents the average holding of stocks over time and which is mathematically represented as

$$I = \sum_{t=1}^{T} \frac{tq(t)}{\sum_{t=1}^{T} q(t)}. \tag{7.14}$$

In the above formula, each t is weighted by $q(t)/\Sigma q(t)$ and if in any week sales are zero, the weight on that particular t is also zero.

We have calculated the value of the index I for each individual producer and averaged them over the different size classes. We have started with the Bengali month of Baishakh (which starts in the middle of April) and the first week of Baishakh is taken as $t = 1$. We have looked at *bond sales* for each individual producer for 36 weeks. T, the terminal week, is the last week of the Bengali month *Poush* (which ends in the middle of January). This is basically the period over which potato is kept in the cold stores and gradually withdrawn from there. It may be noted that if potato were sold *uniformly* over the 36 weeks, that is, if $q(t) = \Sigma q(t)/T \, \forall t$, the value of the index I would be equal to 18.5. It is with this benchmark value that the calculated values of I are to be compared.

The calculated values of *I* for different size classes are represented in Table 7.2. It is clear from Table 7.2 that for both rounds, the smallest size class has the *highest* value of the index. On the other hand, the average values of the index over the two rounds are the *lowest* for the highest two size classes. We have already seen from Table 7.1 that the average price received is the lowest for the lowest size class and the highest for the two highest size classes. Thus our study suggests that for the potato market it is simply not true that holding stocks for a longer period allows a producer to sell at a higher price.

Table 7.2: Index of Bond-selling Across Various Size Classes

Size class (Bighas)		0–2	2.01–4	4.01–6	6.01–10	>10
Class index	1st round	19.12	18.33	17.69	17.81	18.92
	2nd round	23.10	22.20	22.63	21.52	20.90
	Average	21.11	20.27	20.16	19.67	19.91
No. above average	1st round	28.00	38.00	20.00	47.00	22.00
(w.r.t. class index)	2nd round	30.00	30.00	29.00	43.00	17.00
	Average	29.00	34.00	24.50	45.00	19.50
No. below average	1st round	30.00	40.00	23.00	44.00	20.00
(w.r.t. class index)	2nd round	20.00	30.00	26.00	35.00	15.00
	Average	25.00	35.00	24.50	39.50	17.50
Total bond seller (312 out of 385 or 81.04 per cent)	1st round	58 (18.59%)	78 (25%)	43 (13.78%)	91 (29.17%)	42 (13.46%)
Total bond seller (275 out 385 or 71.46 per cent)	2nd round	50 (18.18%)	60 (21.82%)	55 (20%)	78 (28.36%)	32 (11.64%)
Average bond sellers (294 or 76.23 per cent)	Average	54 (18.38%)	69 (23.41%)	49 (16.89%)	84.5 (28.73%)	37 (12.55%)
Average for all class	1st round	18.31				
	2nd round	22.11				
	Averaage	20.21				

However, from the third and the fourth rows of Table 7.2 it becomes clear that there may be wide variations in the value of the index of bond-holding within each class. Therefore, for each individual producer, we have plotted the value of the index of bond-selling against the average price received. These plots for round 1 and round 2 are represented in Figures 7.3 and 7.4 respectively. Clearly, there is no relationship between the average time of bond-holding and the average price received at the aggregate level. Thus, variations in the time of holding of stocks cannot explain the variations in average price received across individual producers[2].

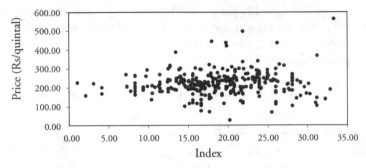

Figure 7.3: Index of Stockholding and the Average Bond Price Received by Producers (1999)

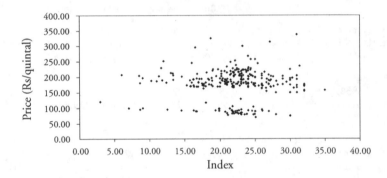

Figure 7.4: Index of Stockholding and Average Bond Price Received by Producers (2000)

However, the fundamental question as to why large producers, on an average, command a better price still remains unanswered. We wish to answer this question in terms of differential information between the small and the large producers. Note that potato prices change on a day-to-day basis. With prices fluctuating so rapidly, short-run

---

[2] One important reason why smaller sellers hold on to their stocks for a longer period is that their stakes are small. Since they hold small amount of bonds, they have a tendency to wait longer for a better price.

information about the global situation can definitely help a seller to command a better price. This information includes knowledge about possible supply bottlenecks in the near future, arising out of, say, a likely transport strike or the closure of a road or bridge as well as temporary changes in demand due to, for example, an unanticipated announcement by the government about the opening up of an export market. Knowledge about longer-run global situations is also important. For example, it is important to know for a producer in West Bengal how much potato has been produced in a particular year in the other important potato-producing states like UP, Punjab, or Bihar. The large sellers gather this information more quickly than the small sellers do.

The anecdotal evidence that we have got from our survey may be of some help. In 1999, due to bad weather, production was low in the potato-producing areas where we conducted our survey. The small farmers, therefore, expected a high price in the future and hence held a lot of bonds. Gradually, however, it became clear that prices were not going to rise very sharply. The reason was a bumper crop in UP and Bihar. But the information about the level of production in UP and Bihar did not reach the small sellers immediately. As a result, the small sellers held on to their bonds and eventually suffered losses. The big sellers, on the other hand, had early information about global production. They, therefore, held a small amount of bonds and did not suffer as much losses as their smaller counterparts.

It is by no means easy to quantify the information possessed by a seller. But it is certainly true that the more frequently a seller visits the market, the more information he collects about the future behaviour of the market price. In Table 7.3, we report the average number of times producers of different size classes have visited the market. Clearly, the larger producers have made more frequent market visits on an average than the smaller ones. In fact, for both rounds, the number of visits has gone up with the size of land devoted to potatoes and hence with production. On the other hand, if we look at the average price[3] received over the two rounds, it increases with the class size. This indicates that gathering information through frequent market visits has a role to play in commanding a better market price.

Through our survey we have also collected some qualitative data

[3] The average prices reported in Table 7.3 are slightly different from those reported in Table 7.1. The reason is that while in Table 7.1 the prices are those of actual potato in the wholesale market, in Table 7.3, the prices are those of potato bonds.

Table 7.3: Index, Market Visits, and Price Received by Bond-holder

Size/Class (bighas)		Index	No. of times	Average price
0–2	1st yr.	19.12	1.37	211.09
	2nd yr.	23.10	1.28	176.47
	Average	21.11	1.33	193.78
2.01–4	1sr yr.	18.33	2.30	207.50
	2nd yr.	22.20	2.08	181.71
	Average	20.27	2.19	194.60
4.01–6	1st yr.	17.69	2.64	209.41
	2nd yr.	22.63	2.62	175.56
	Average	20.16	2.63	192.48
6.01–10	1st yr.	17.81	3.10	226.64
	2nd yr.	21.52	3.77	186.40
	Average	19.67	3.43	206.52
>10	1st yr.	18.92	3.98	227.70
	2nd yr.	20.90	5.44	187.95
	Average	19.91	4.71	207.82

which might shed some light on the problem of differential information across different size classes. We specifically asked the respondents whether they had information on: (i) local production, (ii) production in other important-potato producing states, for example, in Punjab and Uttar Pradesh, (iii) the amount of potato that went into the local cold stores after the harvest, (iv) the amount of potato that went into the distant cold stores after the harvest, (v) demand in outside markets, and (vi) opening up of new markets. The survey also asked the respondents whether their actions were influenced by the action of others and whether rumour had any role to play when they took their decisions of buying and selling. Each respondent said yes or no to the questions related to gathering of information. The results are summarized in Table 7.4.

It is to be noted that a much higher fraction of the largest size class responded positively to the question of gathering private information on global production, global demand, and the rate at which potato was released from cold stores than those belonging to the smaller size classes. Thus the behaviour of the large sellers was grounded on a more solid informational base. On the other hand, the smaller producers depended a lot more on rumours. Their actions had also been influenced to a larger extent by what others had been doing. Since rumours are often baseless,

Table 7.4: Information Assimilation Across Various
Size Classes of Producers

Type of information	Size class (bighas)					
	0–2 p.c. of	2–4 p.c. of	4–6 p.c. of	6–10 p.c. of	>10 p.c. of	All average
Local production	17.76	20.00	21.28	22.58	41.86	24.69
Punjab–UP production	13.08	14.74	14.89	17.20	30.23	18.03
Seed inputs cost	42.06	44.21	44.68	52.69	62.79	49.29
Loading in local stores	44.86	53.68	57.45	50.54	58.14	52.93
Loading in distant stores	22.43	18.95	40.43	26.88	46.51	31.04
Loading in competitor state (UP)	5.61	4.21	8.51	15.05	25.58	11.79
Demands in outside markets	18.69	13.68	29.79	20.43	41.86	24.89
Release from stores of other states	3.74	4.21	6.38	9.68	9.30	6.66
Opening of new market	6.54	9.47	2.13	10.75	6.98	7.17
Others' influence	10.28	22.11	17.02	21.51	9.30	16.04
Influence of gossip	86.23	5.26	95.74	14.00	6.80	41.61
Dependence on govt information	4.67	2.11	4.26	4.30	4.65	4.00
Dependence on panchayat	7.48	3.16	95.74	92.47	7.02	41.17
Dependence on newspaper reports	61.68	70.53	78.72	76.34	67.44	70.94
Dependence on cooperative	8.41	5.26	6.38	7.53	11.63	7.84
Dependence on other sources	3.25	29.47	25.53	41.94	39.53	27.95

we conclude that the smaller sellers' sales behaviour were to a great extent arbitrary and added to price fluctuations. Our theory, developed in the second section, as well as the empirical findings, suggest that the gainers from this differential information were the large sellers and the losers were the smaller sellers themselves.

CONCLUDING REMARKS

The paper tried to provide an explanation as to why large sellers, on an average, get a better price for their produce than small sellers. The standard explanation is in terms of differential power of stockholding among the various classes of sellers. We empirically show that this standard explanation is not valid in all agricultural markets. In particular, in the potato markets we have studied, it is the small sellers who tend to hold on to their stocks for a longer time than the large sellers and yet tend to get a lower price on an average. We provide an alternative explanation in terms of differential information. We argue that it is not the power to sell late, but the power to know exactly when to sell which gives the large sellers the relative advantage.

Our argument has important policy implication. If the small sellers were disadvantaged due to their fund constraints, the obvious policy implication would be to provide more credit, at reasonably low rates of interest, to these sellers for holding inventories. Our analysis suggests that such a policy cannot improve the position of the small sellers in potato markets. The right policy would be to provide more *information* to the small sellers. This can be done through government agencies, cooperatives as well as through local public bodies.

REFERENCES

BHADURI, A., (1983), *Economic Structure of Backward Agriculture*, New York: Macmillan.

MITRA, S. and A. SARKAR, (2003), 'Relative Profitability from Production and Trade—A Study of Selected Potato Markets in West Bengal', *Economic and Political Weekly*, Nov. 1–7, Vol. XXXVIII, No. 44, pp. 4694–99

NARASIMHAN, V., (1986), 'An Essay on the Formation and Dynamics of the Marketed Surplus and Price of Food Grains', PhD thesis, Indian Statistical Institute, Kolkata.

NEWBERY, D. and J. STIGLITZ, (1981), *The Theory of Commodity Price Stabilization*, Oxford: Clarendon Press.

SARKAR, A., (1993), 'On the Formation of Agricultural Prices', *Journal of Development Economics*, 41, pp. 1–17.

——, (1997), 'On the Relationship between Price and Output Seasonality in Backward Agriculture', *Indian Economic Review*, 32(1), pp. 105–15.

8. The Robustness of Closed Orbits in a Class of Dynamic Economic Models

Anjan Mukherji

INTRODUCTION

While formulating dynamic models in economics, cyclical phenomenon around equilibrium have merited close attention. This paper is addressed towards such cyclical behaviour around equilibrium for a class of models and looks into the question of how robust this behaviour is.

More explicitly, we consider a class of predator–prey models (Lotka–Volterra equations). It is by now well known that such models are not structurally stable; that is, perturbation in the coefficients may change the qualitative properties of the equilibria (Gandolfo 1997 and Hirsch and Smale 1974 for example). However, the nature of these changes do not appear to have been clearly investigated. It turns out that the Hopf Bifurcation Theorem may be an appropriate tool to use for this purpose. The paper begins with a standard predator–prey model and introduces a suitable parameter and shows how global stability arises for appropriate values of this parameter; in a sense, we add to the class of models analysed by Hsu and Huang (1995) for which global stability results were also obtained. We next consider a well–known example in economics, (Goodwin 1967) and show what happens in this context. It turns out that global stability may be obtained for a range of parameter values; and for the remaining complementary range, the solutions are

The paper is affectionately dedicated, with some trepidation, to Professor Sanjit Bose on his retirement from the Indian Statistical Institute, Kolkata.

unbounded. Thus the chances of robust periodic behaviour appear non–existent.

PRELIMINARIES: HOPF BIFURCATION

An interesting area of research is the theory of bifurcations; the main point of enquiry is whether the qualitative properties of a system of differential equations change when any of the parameters, which may define the laws of motion, alter. More explicitly, consider

$$\dot{x} = F(x, \mu), \quad x \in R^n, \mu \in R. \tag{8.1}$$

First of all, let $n = 1$. Assume that for $\mu = 0$, the above system has an equilibrium $x^* = 0$, that is, $F(0, 0) = 0$. It is known that if the multiplier

$$\lambda^0 = \frac{\partial F(0, 0)}{\partial x}$$

is negative, the equilibrium $(0, 0)$ is locally asymptotically stable. Note that at an equilibrium (x^0, μ^0) if $\lambda (x^0, \mu^0) \neq 0$, then by the implicit function theorem, in a neighbourhood of μ^0, we may express x^0 solving $F(x^0, \mu^0) = 0$, as a differentiable function $x(\mu)$ with $x^0 = x(\mu^0)$; $x(\mu)$ is called *a branch of equilibrium*. If at a particular $(\tilde{x}, \tilde{\mu})$ several branches come together, then $(\tilde{x}, \tilde{\mu})$ is called a *bifurcation point*. At a bifurcation point, we have necessarily, $\lambda(\tilde{x}, \tilde{\mu}) = 0$. The types of bifurcation are classified according to the signs of the other partial derivatives; for example, *fold bifurcation*, when on one side of $\tilde{\mu}$, there is no equilibrium, while on the other side, there are two equilibria; or we may have a *trans–crtical bifurcation*, where on one side of $\tilde{\mu}$, the equilibrium $x(\mu)$ is stable and on the other side, this becomes unstable and another stable equilibrium branch emerges. Finally, we may have *pitchfork bifurcation*, where on one side of $\tilde{\mu}$, $x(\mu)$ is stable and on the other side, two additional branches of stable equilibria emerge. When $n > 1$, we may still have bifurcations of the type described above; except, we must note that the multipliers become the eigenvalues (characteristic roots of the Jacobian of $F(.)$ at the bifurcation point); and out of the n eigenvalues, a single eigenvalue is zero and so on.

However when $n \neq 1$, a possibility which emerges is that characteristic roots (multipliers) are pure imaginary numbers; since these appear in pairs, we must have $n = 2$ at least. This brings us to what is called the *Hopf Bifurcation*. It is best to state a version of what is known as the Hopf Bifurcation Theorem (Lorenz 1993: 96, for example):

Proposition 1: Suppose that the system (8.1) has an equilibrium $(\tilde{x}, \tilde{\mu})$ at which the following conditions hold:

(i) The Jacobian of $F(., \tilde{\mu})$ evaluated at $\tilde{x}$ has a pair of pure imaginary eigenvalues $(\lambda(\tilde{\mu}), \overline{\lambda(\tilde{\mu})})$ and no other eigenvalues with zero real parts; and

(ii) $\dfrac{d(\operatorname{Re}\lambda(\mu))}{d\mu}\Big|_{\mu=\tilde{\mu}} > 0.$

Then there exist periodic solutions bifurcating from $x(\tilde{\mu})$ at $\mu = \tilde{\mu}.$

Notice that the theorem tells us about the existence of periodic solutions only; no information is contained about either their number or their stability. To establish stability, we need to transform the system (8.1), say for $n = 2$, by a change of coordinates into the following:

$$\begin{pmatrix} \dot{x} \\ \dot{y} \end{pmatrix} = \begin{pmatrix} \mu & -\omega \\ \omega & \mu \end{pmatrix} \cdot \begin{pmatrix} x \\ y \end{pmatrix} + \begin{pmatrix} f(x, y) \\ g(x, y) \end{pmatrix}. \tag{8.2}$$

The matrix of linear terms in x and y on the RHS is in the normal form; and the fixed point of the original system (8.1) has been shifted to the origin and the terms have been sorted into the linear terms and non–linear terms $f(x, y)$, $g(x, y)$, Note that the eigenvalues of the Jacobian evaluated at the fixed point are $\mu \pm i\omega$; the real part of the complex root is a positive function of the bifurcation parameter. And we know that we have a Hopf bifurcation; to determine the stability of the periodic solutions, the non–linear terms play a role. The expression

$$a = \frac{1}{16}\left(f_{xxx} + f_{xyy} + g_{xxy} + g_{yyy} \right)$$

$$+ \frac{1}{16\omega}\left(f_{xy}\left(f_{xx} + f_{yy} \right) - g_{xy}\left(g_{xx} + g_{yy} \right) - f_{xx}g_{xx} + f_{yy}g_{yy} \right)$$

is computed and if found positive (negative) the emerging limit cycles are stable (unstable, respectively). *See* also Kind (1999), for the relevance of the Hopf Bifurcation Theorem to economics. For demonstrating the existence of cyclical orbits, the Hopf Bifurcation Theorem is very useful; an early application of this result appears in Benhabib and Nishimura (1979). But as should be clear, checking the stability or robustness of periodic orbits, obtained via the Hopf Bifurcation Theorem, is a messy affair.

LOTKA-VOLTERRA SYSTEM OF EQUATIONS

Consider an environment made up of two species of life forms, one of which preys on the other: the prey and the predator. Let the population of the prey be designated by x and that of the predator by y. The basic assumption is that in the absence of the predator, the population of the prey *grows* at a constant proportional rate a; and on the other hand, in the absence of the prey, the population of the predator *decays* at a constant proportional rate b (here both a and b are assumed positive). In the presence of both the prey and predator, adjustments to this basic story have to be made and we have

$$\dot{x} = x\,(a - \alpha y) \text{ and } \dot{y} = y(\beta x - b), \tag{8.3}$$

where α, β are also assumed to be positive and are to be interpreted as the effect of the presence of one population on the other.

There are two equilibria for the above system of equations: ($x = 0$, $y = 0$) Trivial Equilibrium or (TE) and ($x = b/\beta$, $y = a/\alpha$) Non–Trivial Equilibrium or (NTE).

We are interested in what happens to the solution, $z(t) = (x(t), y(t))$ to the system (8.3) beginning from an initial configuration $z^0 = (x^0, y^0)$; we shall represent this solution by $z(t, z^0)$.

Stability: Local and Global

We note, first of all, the following local stability properties of the equilibria mentioned above:

Claim 1:   For the system (8.3), TE is a saddle point while NTE is a centre.

Proof: The Jacobian of the RHS of the system (8.3) is given by:

$$\begin{pmatrix} a - \alpha y & -\alpha x \\ y\beta & \beta x - b \end{pmatrix}.$$

It is then straightforward to check that at TE the characteristic roots are: $(a, -b)$; while at NTE, the characteristic roots are purely imaginary: $(i\sqrt{a}.\,b, -i\sqrt{a}.\,b)$. The claim follows. Next, we note that

Claim 2: With any $z^0 = (x^0, y^0) > (0, 0)$ as initial point, the solution to the system (8.3) is a closed orbit around NTE.

Proof: From the system (8.3), we observe that:

$$\frac{dy}{dx} = \frac{y(\beta x - b)}{x(a - \alpha y)}$$

and hence, performing the integration is straightforward and it yields:

$$\beta x - b \log x = K + (a \log y - \alpha y),$$

where K is some constant to be determined from initial conditions. It should be clear from this that the solution $(x(t), y(t))$ beginning from an arbitrary initial point is a closed curve around the non–trivial equilibrium; there are many such curves depending on the initial point. To put the matter somewhat differently, (Hirsch and Smale 1974: 262, Theorem 1) consider:

$$V(t) = \{\beta x(t) - b \log x(t)\} + \{\alpha y(t) - a \log y(t)\}$$

and consider the derivative V along the solution $(x(t), y(t))$ to the system (8.3) and check that

$$\dot{V} = (\beta x - b)\frac{\dot{x}}{x} + (\alpha y - a)\frac{\dot{y}}{y} = 0.$$

Thus the function V remains constant along the solution to the system (8.3); the value of this constant is defined by the initial point. This also defines the level curve along which the solution moves.

This claim may be seen from the following diagram.

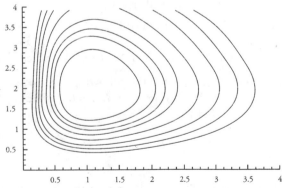

Figure 8.1: The Predator–Prey Model ($\alpha, \beta, b = 1, a = 2$)

The above has been used to explain why the population of some species constantly keep chasing one another and never settle down to any fixed values. We investigate next what happens when we change the basic story a little bit.

A Generalization

Suppose we say that when left to itself, in the absence of the predator, the population of the prey behaves according to a more complicated relationship:

$$\dot{x} = x\,(a + \gamma x);$$

that is, the rate of growth of the population of the prey $\dot{x}/x$ depends on the size of the population x. In case the parameter γ is negative, we have the well–known *logistic* equation. The logistic equation allows the population to achieve a maximum, beyond which decay sets in. This may be rationalized by means of an appeal to the environment which can only sustain a given amount of the species. In case the parameter γ happens to be positive, it is being said that the larger the population of x, the greater is its rate of growth. What we are interested in analysing is the effect of introducing such a term and we shall examine what happens for small values of the parameter.

The presence of the predator affects the population of the prey in the same manner as described earlier and keeping the behaviour of the predator population unaltered, we have the following:

$$\dot{x} = x(a + \gamma x - \alpha y) \text{ and } \dot{y} = y(\beta x - b). \tag{8.4}$$

Notice that by putting the value of γ to zero we revert back to the earlier system.

Due to the presence of the term γ, it may be noted that

Claim 3:   The system (8.4) has the following three equilibria:
$(x = 0, y = 0)$ (TE), $(x = -a/\gamma,\ y = 0)$ (MPE) and $(x = b/\beta,\ y = \delta)$ (NTE)

where $\delta = \dfrac{a\beta + \gamma b}{\beta \alpha}$.

We assume δ to be positive. In other words, if γ is negative, we have yet another restriction, $0 > \gamma > -a\beta/b$; since we are interested in showing what happens for small values of the parameter γ, this restriction is not a problem for our analysis. Also note that the equilibrium MPE (Maximum Prey Equilibrium) is meaningful only when γ is negative; in such a situation, we have now a position of equilibrium where the prey attains its maximum population size and the predators die out; due to this reason, we shall discuss the nature of MPE only when $\gamma < 0$. Finally, in the NTE, although the size of the prey is the same as in the earlier case (when $\gamma = 0$), the size of the predator population is *reduced* (*increased*) depending on the sign of the parameter γ.

We turn next to the stability properties of these equilibria; first, as before, we consider the local stability of equilibria.

Claim 4: For the system (8.4), TE is a saddle point; MPE is a saddle point while for $\gamma <(>)0$, NTE is locally asymptotically stable (unstable).

Proof: The Jacobian of the RHS of the system (8.4) is given by:

$$\begin{pmatrix} a + 2\gamma x - \alpha y & -\alpha x \\ y\beta & \beta x - b \end{pmatrix}.$$

Consequently, one may conclude that the characteristic roots at TE are $(a, -b)$ and hence TE is a saddle point; similarly, the characteristic roots at MPE are: $(-a, -\delta\alpha\beta/\gamma)$ and hence MPE is a saddle point for $\gamma < 0$; and finally at NTE, the characteristic roots are:

$$\frac{b\gamma \pm \sqrt{b}\sqrt{(-4a\beta^2 - 4b\beta\gamma + b\gamma^2)}}{2\beta}$$

and hence for all $\gamma < 0$, NTE is locally asymptotically stable.

We remark here that the stability property of the NTE (and MPE) is thus shown to depend crucially on the sign of the term γ: if $\gamma = 0$, the relevant equilibrium is a centre as we have seen in the last section; and as we now see that for γ small, the characteristic roots are still imaginary; their real parts are non–zero and they are positive whenever $\gamma > 0$ while the real parts are negative whenever $\gamma < 0$. Thus with the sign of this parameter, we have locally, either a spiralling into the equilibrium or a spiralling away from the equilibrium.

For global stability, we have the following:

Claim 5: Any solution to (8.4) with $z^0 = (x^0, y^0) > (0, 0)$ as initial point converges to the NTE whenever $\gamma < 0$.

Proof: Let us write the solution to (8.4) with $z^0 = (x^0, y^0) > (0,0)$ as initial point as $z(t, z^0)$ or as $z(t)$ in short; consider

$$W(z(t)) = \{\beta x(t) - b \log x(t)\} + \{\alpha y(t) - (a + \frac{\gamma b}{\beta}) \log y(t)\}.$$

Check that $W(t) > 0$ and

$$\dot{W} = (\beta x - b)\frac{\dot{x}}{x} + \left(\alpha y - \left(a + \frac{\gamma b}{\beta}\right)\right)\frac{\dot{y}}{y} = (\beta x - b)^2 \cdot \frac{\gamma}{\beta}.$$

Note that the above expression, whenever $\gamma < 0$, is strictly negative unless $x = b/\beta$. Thus, for the case $\gamma < 0$, $W(t)$ is monotone non–increasing and bounded below. Hence $\lim_{t \to \infty} W(t)$ exists and is equal to $\overline{W}$, say.

Note that this also shows that the solution $z(t, z^0)$ remains bounded and hence limit points exist; let $\overline{z} = (\overline{x}, \overline{y})$ be one such. Thus there is a subsequence t_s such that

$$\lim_{s \to \infty} z(t_s, z^0) = \overline{z}.$$

Consider next, the solution to the system (8.4) with $\overline{z}$ as initial point: $z(t, \overline{z}) = \overline{z(t)}$; now note that

$$W(\overline{z(t)}) = W(z(t, \lim_{s \to \infty} z(t_s, z^0))) = W\left(\lim_{s \to \infty} z(t + t_s, z^0)\right)$$

$$= \left(\lim_{s \to \infty} W(z(t + t_s, z^0))\right) = \overline{W};$$

consequently, $\dot{W}(\overline{z(t)}) = 0$ for all t; hence $z(t, \overline{z}) = (\overline{x(t)}, \overline{y(t)})$ is such that $\overline{x(t)} = b/\beta$ for all t; thus $\dot{\overline{x}}(t) = 0$ for all t; hence $\overline{y(t)} = \delta$ for all t. Thus $\overline{z}$ must be the NTE; since this is true for an arbitrary limit point $\overline{z}$, the claim follows.

To clarify the situation further, Figure 8.2 should be compared with Figure 8.1 presented earlier.

Global stability for some other forms of predator-prey models have been discussed in Hsu and Huang (1995); the form of the predator–prey equation considered here does not seem to be covered by their result. In this connection, preliminary remarks by Hirsch and Smale (1974: 265) may also be of interest. To distinguish our result from these, note that the solution to (8.4), when $\gamma < 0$, starting from any $(x^0, y^0) >$

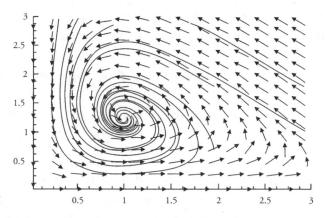

Figure 8.2: The Predator–Prey Model (α, β, b, a as above, $\gamma = -0.5$)

$(0, 0)$ converges to the NTE. What about cyclical behaviour then ? Our claim clearly demonstrates that cycles cannot exist for $\gamma < 0$. Note that cycles, if they exist, must necessarily be for the case $\gamma \geq 0$. That such cycles exist is guaranteed by:

Claim 6: The system (8.4) has an equilibrium $(x(0), y(0)) = (b/\beta, a/\alpha; \gamma = 0)$ at which both the conditions for the Hopf Bifurcation Theorem are satisfied and as a consequence, there exist periodic solutions bifurcating from $(x(\gamma), y(\gamma))$ at $\gamma = 0$.

Proof: That the conditions hold can be checked from the proof of (8.4). Recall that the characteristic roots at the NTE are given by

$$\left(\frac{b\gamma \pm \sqrt{b}\sqrt{(-4a\beta^2 - 4b\beta\gamma + b\gamma^2)}}{2\beta} \right).$$

Note that at $\gamma = 0$, the roots are purely imaginary; and secondly note that

$$\left. \frac{d(\mathrm{Re}\,\lambda(\gamma))}{d\gamma} \right|_{\gamma=0} = \frac{b}{2\beta} > 0\,;$$

thus both the conditions hold and the conclusions hold.

Thus, for the type of predator–prey model considered, cyclical behaviour requires $\gamma \geq 0$. Moreover, we show below, that when $\gamma > 0$, the *only* solution to (8.4) which is *bounded* is the one with the NTE as initial point and thus the only periodic solutions possible are the ones with period unity.

Claim 7: For the system (8.4), suppose $\gamma > 0$; any solution with z^0 $=(x^0, y^0) \neq (b/\beta, \delta)$ is unbounded.

Proof: Suppose to the contrary, for some $z^0 = (x^0, y^0) \neq (b/\beta, \delta)$, the solution $z(t, z^0)$ is bounded; then consider the function $W(z(t))$ introduced in the proof of *Claim 5* and note that the function $W(z(t))$ is monotonic non–decreasing ($\gamma > 0$); further, $W(z(t))$ being bounded too (since the solution is bounded), must converge and hence $\lim_{t \to \infty} W(t)$ exists and is $\overline{W}$, say. Following the proof of the *Claim 5*, one may conclude that the limit point must be $(b/\beta, \delta)$, that is, $\overline{W} = W (b/\beta, \delta) = W^*$, say. But since $W(x, y)$ is minimized at $(b/\beta, \delta)$ and hence, $W(x, y) \geq W^*$ for all $(x, y) \neq (b/\beta, \delta)$ and $W(t)$ is non–decreasing, we must have $W(t) = W^*$ for all t but then $z^0 = (x^0, y^0) = (b/\beta, \delta)$ —a contradiction. Hence the claim.

Thus the only possibility of periodic behaviour is when $\gamma = 0$.

THE GOODWIN MODEL OF GROWTH

As an application, we consider the very well–known model of growth put forward in Goodwin (1967). The model is a stark one and contains the following notations and assumptions:

First the list of assumptions:

   (i) steady disembodied technical progress;
  (ii) steady growth in labour force;
 (iii) only two factors of production: labour and capital;
  (iv) all quantities are real and net;
   (v) all wages are consumed and all profits are saved;
  (vi) a constant capital–output ratio; and
 (vii) a real wage rate which rises in the neighbourhood of full employment.

The notations are as follows:

q is output; k is capital ; w is wage rate; $a = a_o e^{\alpha t}$ is labour productivity growth, α is a positive constant; the constant capital–output ratio is σ; u the share of workers in total product $= w/a$; naturally the share of the capitalists is $1 - w/a$; investment $k = (1 - w/a) q$; l employment, is then q/a; labour n at time t is given by $n_0 e^{\beta t}$ where β is a positive constant. The employment ratio is given by $v = l/n$. Finally, the assumption (vii) is captured by the equation:

$$\frac{\dot{w}}{w} = f(v) = -\gamma + \rho v. \tag{8.5}$$

In this set–up, Goodwin pointed out, the following: first of all,

$$\frac{\dot{l}}{l} = (1 - \frac{w}{a})\frac{1}{\sigma} - \alpha,$$

so that

$$\frac{\dot{v}}{v} = \frac{1-u}{\sigma} - (\alpha + \beta); \tag{8.6}$$

and further using the assumption contained in (8.5) we have:

$$\frac{\dot{u}}{u} = -(\gamma + \alpha) + \rho v \tag{8.7}$$

It should be clear that the system of equations made up of (8.6) and (8.7) constitute a Lotka–Volterra system of the type we analysed above. Consequently, for any arbitrary initial point $(v^0, u^0) > (0, 0)$, the above system of equations generates a closed orbit around the NTE $\left(\frac{\alpha+\gamma}{\rho}, 1 - (\alpha + \beta)\sigma\right)$. The situation depicted in Figure 8.1 applies and so does the analysis.

The model presented above generated great interest since it describes a scenario where two ratios u, v (respectively, the share of workers and the employment ratio) are chasing one another along a closed orbit. To see what this has to say about Goodwin's model, we need to note a few things first:

$$u = \frac{w}{a}: \text{share of workers}; \quad 1 - u: \text{share of capitalists}.$$

Thus the rate of profit is given by $\frac{1-u}{\sigma}$ which, given the assumptions made above is also the rate of growth (that is, $\dot{q}/q$). Referring to Figure 8.1, where we now treat the variables u, v to be represented on the two axes, it should be clear that along any solution to the Goodwin equations, the variables u, v will fluctuate between limits say $u_{min} \leq u \leq u_{max}$ and $v_{min} \leq v \leq v_{max.}$ In the words of Goodwin, one may note the following: '... when profit is at its greatest ($u = u_{min}$), employment is average ($v_{min} < v < v_{max}$) and the high growth rate pushes employment up to its maximum ($v = v_{max}$), which squeezes the profits to its average level ($u_{min} < u < u_{max}$). The deceleration of growth lowers employment.... The improved profitability carries the seed of its own destruction by engendering a too vigorous expansion of output and employment...' (Goodwin 1967: 57–8). According to Goodwin, this is what Marx's idea of 'contradictions of capitalism' was all about.

To study how robust the above construction is, one needs to reconsider the specifications of the model. There are many ways of considering perturbation of the Goodwin equations; an easy method would be to look at (8.7). Consider the specification of the function (8.5); this represents a sort of wage bargaining and it is being specified that this is dependant on v alone; this is the usual Phillips curve argument, of course; it would not be too implausible (perhaps, arbitrary though) to require that the RHS of (8.5) depends on the variable u too, (for instance, Lorenz 1993: 70); as a result we have:

$$\frac{\dot{u}}{u} = -(\gamma + \alpha) + \rho v + \theta u. \tag{8.8}$$

Since our main purpose is to analyse the effect of small perturbations, we follow up the consequences of having such a formulation; it should also be pointed out that for the present, we do not specify the sign of the term θ; but our purpose is to assume that this term is *small in magnitude*; note that $\theta = 0$ takes us back to the model of Goodwin. Consider then the system made up of (8.6) and (8.8). For this system, we have then:

Claim 8:   For the system made up of (8.6) and (8.8) the following are the possible equilibria:

$(u = 0, v = 0)$: (TE1); $(u = b/\theta, v = 0)$: (TE2);

and $\left(u = \sigma a, v = \dfrac{b - \sigma a\theta}{\rho} \right)$: (NTE).

And computing the Jacobian and checking characteristic roots, the local properties of the equilibria are as follows:

Claim 9: The characteristic roots of the Jacobian of the RHS of the system made up of (8.6) and (8.8) are as below:

(TE1): $(a, -b)$: hence a saddle point;

(TE2): $\left(b, a - \dfrac{b}{\theta\sigma} \right)$: thus the nature depends on the sign of θ: unstable when $\theta < 0$; a saddle point when $\theta > 0$ and small;

(NTE): $\dfrac{1}{2}\left\{ a\theta\sigma \pm \sqrt{a}\sqrt{(-4b + 4a\theta + a\theta^2\sigma^2)} \right\}$,

which is locally asymptotically stable when $\theta < 0$.

Once again by using methods similar to the ones employed earlier, we may show:

Claim 10: Any solution $(u(t), v(t))$ for the system made up of (8.6) and (8.8) beginning from any $(u_0, v_0) > (0, 0)$ converges to the equilibrium (NTE) when $\theta < 0$.

Proof: Consider the function

$$W(t) = \left(\frac{1}{\sigma} u(t) - A \log u(t) \right) + (\rho v(t) - (\gamma + \alpha - A\sigma\theta) \log v(t)),$$

where $A = \dfrac{1}{\sigma} - (\alpha + \beta)$, and note that along the solution to the system under consideration, we have:

$$\dot{W}(t) = \theta\sigma \left(\frac{u}{\sigma} - A \right)^2$$

and hence the claim follows.

Finally note that $\theta = 0$ does provide a point of Hopf Bifurcation to the system made up of (8.6) and (8.8). This follows by considering the NTE and the characteristic roots at $\theta = 0$ and checking the behaviour of the real part of the characteristic roots as θ varies, all exactly as before. What of the existence of cyclical behaviour?. The Hopf Bifurcation Theorem assures us that there should be one for $\theta \geq 0$; once more as before, it may be shown that for $\theta > 0$, solution paths emanating from disequilibrium points all become unbounded and consequently, for cyclical behaviour in this model, $\theta = 0$ is not only *sufficient* but *necessary* as well.

CONCLUDING REMARKS

We studied here a class of motion on the plane described by the Lotka–Volterra equation and considered their application to a well–known model in economics, Goodwin (1967). To place our analysis in a proper perspective, it should be pointed out that it is perhaps well understood that the Lotka–Volterra equations are structurally unstable (Gandolfo 1997; Hirsch and Smale 1974); in fact the possibility that the so–called *conservative character* of the Lotka–Volterra system may be destroyed by introducing diminishing returns was demonstrated in Samuelson (1972 a, b), where some local properties of the altered system were established; more recently, the possibilities of global stability in a class of predator–prey models have been analysed in Hsu and Huang (1995), for example.

Note first of all that the class of predator–prey models considered here do not appear to be covered by the contribution in Hsu and Huang (1995). And the possibility of a Hopf Bifurcation in such models does not seem to have been noted. Together with the global stability result for a range of parameter values, the existence of a Hopf Bifurcation point indicates the range of parameter values for which periodic orbits are not possible. Consequently, the possibility of existence of cycles is shown to depend crucially on the parameters themselves. And it therefore follows that, the question of how meaningful the cyclical phenomenon is may be reduced to a question of how meaningful is the range of parameter values for which such phenomenon may exist.

We need to mention that the Hopf Bifurcation Theorem may not have been expected to add any new insight so far as the motion on the plane is considered, since the well–known Poincare–Bendixon Theorem serves to locate cycles in dimension 2. In Benhabib and Nishimura (1979), for example, the Hopf Bifurcation was appropriately exploited to show the existence of cyclical behaviour in a multi–sector model of optimal growth. For the case at hand, however, location of the ranges where cycles exist has been made possible by the twin considerations of the global stability result together with the existence of a Hopf Bifurcation point. There is no necessity of trying to locate a positively invariant region to apply the Poincare–Bendixon Theorem; for an excellent example of such an analysis, *see* Hirsch and Smale (1974: 264–5).

The application to the model of Goodwin reveals the problems which must be faced while trying to model cyclical behaviour in economic models. The studies concerning the modification of the Goodwin Model, reported in Gandolfo (1997) and Lorenz (1993), all relate to the change from a conservative system to a dissipative one. A crucial element is added by the presence of a Hopf Bifurcation point together with *global stability* on one side of the parameter range and unboundedness on the other. It can be concluded then that the entire description of cyclical behaviour (what was referred to as the contradictions of capitalism) crucially hinges on $\theta = 0$ or for the rate of growth of wages being independent of the share of workers. And the issue then is whether this is acceptable.

Finally, in any dynamic economic model, there are several aspects in the specification of the laws of change: one is the functional form; for example, whether processes are linear or non–linear; and if non–linear, what terms are present. In economics, the problem has been that these specifications can never be made with any degree of exactitude. It is because of this reason that the exercise carried out above assumes significance. What we specifically showed was that there was a degenerate Hopf Bifurcation point; and it was only at this point that cyclical behaviour was being exhibited; consequently, behaviour described by these models lack robustness. And we need alternative formulations if we need to provide robust explanations for such phenomenon.

REFERENCES

BENHABIB J. and K. NISHIMURA, (1979), 'The Hopf Bifurcation and the Existence of Closed Orbits in Multisector Models of Optimal Economic Growth', *Journal of Economic Theory*, 21, pp. 421–44.

GANDOLFO, G., (1997), *Economic Dynamics* Study Edition, Berlin: Springer Verlag.

GOODWIN, R. M., (1967), 'A Growth Cycle', in C.H. Feinstein, (ed.), *Socialism, Capitalism and Economic Growth Essays Presented to Maurice Dobb*, London: Cambridge University Press, pp. 54–58.

HIRSCH, M.W. and S. SMALE, (1974), *Differential Equations, Dynamical Systems and Linear Algebra*, New York: Academic Press.

HSU, S.B. and T.W. HUANG, (1995), 'Global Stability for a Class of Predator–Prey Systems', *SIAM Journal of Applied Mathematics*, 55, pp. 763–83.

KIND, C., (1999), 'Remarks on the Economic Interpretation of Hopf Bifurcations', *Economic Letters*, 62, pp. 147–54.

LORENZ, H. W., (1993), *Nonlinear Dynamical Economics and Chaotic Motion*, Second Revised and Enlarged Edition, Berlin: Springer Verlag.

SAMUELSON, P. A., (1972a), 'Generalized Predator–Prey Oscillations in Ecological and Economical Equilibrium', in R.C. Merton (ed.), *The Collected Scientific Papers of Paul A. Samuelson* Volume III, pp. 487–90, Cambridge, Massachusetts: MIT Press.

———, (1972b), 'A Universal Cycle', in R.C. Merton (ed.), *The Collected Scientific Papers of Paul A. Samuelson*, Volume III, pp. 473–86, Cambridge Massachusetts: MIT Press.

Part II: Public Policy and Economic Theory

9. Incentive Contracts for Faith-based Organizations to Deliver Social Services

AVINASH DIXIT

INTRODUCTION

When I was a newcomer to economics, Sanjit Bose was one of the fellow-students from whom I learned a great deal. My dissertation research closely followed his, using optimal growth theory to examine some issues of development planning. Therefore, it is an honour and pleasure for me to contribute to this volume. However, our research interests later diverged, and I would have been at a loss to choose a fitting topic were it not for Sanjit's defining characteristic. He is a Bengali intellectual, and therefore, seriously interested in everything. So I can just chose something from my current work and be confident that it will fit; that is what I have done.

Many governments enlist and support faith-based organizations to provide various social services. The argument in favour of this policy is that such organizations can be efficient providers of such services, not only because they are closer to the recipients of the services than are official civil servants and, therefore, have better information about the needs, but also because they experience some direct benefit from these actions and will, therefore, perform them for smaller salaries and/ or weaker incentive payments.

I thank Karla Hoff and Sajal Lahiri for useful comments on a preliminary version, and the National Science Foundation for financial support.

These policies are controversial. Some have questioned the validity of the claims of efficiency of faith-based organizations. But the main counter-argument is that the actions of these organizations have by-products, for example, promotions of their religious beliefs, which society may regard as improper for the government to support.

One of the Bush administration's first actions on taking office in January 2001 was to establish an office for faith-based initiatives; it promptly generated heated controversy. So did the Blair government's programme of government funding for faith-based schools.[1] India, being a secular democracy with different large and organized religions, must confront similar dilemmas.

In this paper I initiate some theoretical analysis of the issues. The framework is that of a principal–agent model. The government is the principal. It engages an agent to perform actions that will contribute to an outcome which the government values, but have a second outcome which is undesired by the government. The government designs an optimal incentive scheme. I examine the properties of this scheme, and the comparative statics of the outcomes and their valuations with respect to the parameters of the agent's productivity and preferences. I conclude with some further thoughts suggested by the model, and ideas for future research.

THE MODEL

My model is based on Baker (2000, 2002). These papers advance the principal–agent literature by recognizing that agents typically take numerous actions, and these have imperfectly correlated impacts on the payoff to the principal and the observable performance measure on which the agent's remuneration must be based. I adapt this to the case of a faith-based agency taking several actions that serve the social purpose and its own private agenda.

The agent takes a large number n of action, denoted by x_j, where $j = 1, 2,..., n$. These are not directly observable. They produce two outcomes y_1 and y_2 according to the functions

---

1   Two recent articles in *The Economist*, 'Compassionate Conservatism Takes a Bow', 1 February 2001, and 'Tony and the Little Children', 8 December 2001, offer good accounts of these policy proposals and the controversies they generated.

$$y_i = \sum_{j=1}^{n} f_{ij} x_j + \varepsilon_i \text{ for } i = 1, 2, \tag{9.1}$$

where the f_{ij} are constants (not necessarily positive) and the ε_i are random shocks with zero expectation. The interpretation is that y_1 is the direct product desired by the principal and y_2 is a by-product. For example, faith-based schools have to teach a standard curriculum, and this education is represented by y_1 in the model. But they offer additional religious instruction, and conduct their activities in a way that inculcates a general culture of religion in their students; this is captured in the y_2.

The principal (government) observes y_1 but not y_2; or at least is precluded from making the payment to the agent conditional on y_2. This can be interpreted as the requirement of a secular constitution. The payment function is assumed to be linear:[2]

$$w(y_1) = s + b y_1, \tag{9.2}$$

where s is the fixed payment or salary, and b the marginal bonus or incentive payment coefficient. The principal chooses these parameters subject to the agent's incentive and participation constraints.

The agent's pay-off function is

$$U = E[w(y_1) + a_1 y_1 + a_2 y_2] - \frac{1}{2} \sum_j (x_j)^2. \tag{9.3}$$

His outside opportunity utility is u_0. Thus a_1 and a_2 are the agent's direct valuations of the two kinds of outputs.

The principal's pay-off is

$$\Pi = E[p_1 y_1 + p_2 y_2 - w(y_1)]. \tag{9.4}$$

The principal's valuation p_2 of the by-product can be negative.[3]

---

[2] Linear schemes can be justified because they are simple and usable in reality, or by appeal to some dynamics of actions and random shocks, as in Holmström and Milgrom (1987, 1991).

[3] I am assuming both parties to be risk-neutral in their pay-offs. This is a departure from much of the early principal–agent literature. But Baker (2000) convincingly argues that in reality the imperfect correlation between the principal's objective and the available observable performance measures is more important than the issue of sharing risk between the principal and the agent. Similarly, in my context, the relationship between the principal's objective and the by-products is more important.

ANALYSIS

Given the principal's payment scheme, the agent chooses the efforts x_j to maximize

$$s + \sum_j [(a_1 + b)f_{1j} + a_2 f_{2j}]x_j - \frac{1}{2}\sum_j (x_j)^2 .$$

The first-order condition is

$$x_j = (a_1 + b)f_{1j} + a_2 f_{2j} \quad \text{for } j = 1, 2 \; n. \tag{9.5}$$

Substituting into the expression for utility, the agent's participation constraint is

$$s + \frac{1}{2} \sum_j [(a_1 + b)f_{1j} + a_2 f_{2j}]^2 \geq u_0. \tag{9.6}$$

The principal chooses s and b to maximize his pay-off Π subject to the incentive and participation constraints (9.5) and (9.6). Substituting out the constraints, we can express Π as a function of b alone:

$$\Pi = \sum_j [(p_1 - b)f_{1j} + p_2 f_{2j}][(a_1 + b)f_{1j} + a_2 f_{2j}]$$

$$+ \frac{1}{2} \sum_j [(a_1 + b)f_{1j} + a_2 f_{2j}]^2 - u_0.$$

To simplify this, introduce the notation

$$\Omega_{hi} = \sum_j f_{hj} f_{ij}, \text{ for } h, i = 1, 2. \tag{9.7}$$

Note that Ω_{11} and Ω_{22} are always positive, whereas the sign of Ω_{12} tells us whether the marginal effects of the agent's actions on the two types of outputs are positively or negatively correlated across actions. A positive sign means that the agent's actions that promote the primary activity on the average also promote the by-product; this is the pertinent case in the faith-based organization application.

Then the expression for the principal's pay-off becomes

$$\Pi = (p_1 - b)(a_1 + b)\Omega_{11} + [(p_1 - b)a_2 + p_2(a_1 + b)]\Omega_{12} + p_2 a_2 \Omega_{22}$$

$$+ \frac{1}{2}(a_1 + b)^2 \Omega_{11} + (a_1 + b)a_2 \Omega_{12} + \frac{1}{2}(a_2)^2 \Omega_{22} - u_0. \tag{9.8}$$

The first-order condition for b to maximize this is

$$\frac{\partial \Pi}{\partial b} = [(p_1 - b) - (a_1 + b)]\Omega_{11} + (p_2 - a_2)\Omega_{12} + (a_1 + b)\Omega_{11} + a_2\Omega_{12}$$

$$= (p_1 - b)\Omega_{11} + p_2\Omega_{12} = 0. \qquad (9.9)$$

Therefore, the principal's optimal choice of the marginal reward coefficient is given by

$$b = p_1 + p_2\,\Omega_{12}/\Omega_{11}. \qquad (9.10)$$

Thus the marginal reward coefficient equals the principal's own valuation of the primary output plus an indirect provision for the principal's valuation of the by-product. The salary component of the agent's remuneration can be found using the participation constraint (9.6) and the abbreviation (9.7) as

$$s = u_0 - \frac{1}{2}[(a_1 + b)^2\Omega_{11} + 2(a_1 + b)a_2\Omega_{12} + (a_2)^2\Omega_{22}], \quad (9.11)$$

where the optimal b given by (9.10) is to be used. All the other entities in the optimal solution can also be found—the agent's actions from (9.5) and the principal's pay-off from (9.8).

Now we can examine how the solution is affected by the by-product. For this, we carry out comparative statics of the solution with respect to the agent's preference parameter a_2 and the productivity parameters f_{2j}. For this, first note that

$$\frac{\partial\Omega_{12}}{\partial f_{2j}} = f_{1j}, \; \frac{\delta\Omega_{22}}{\delta f_{2j}} = 2f_{2j} \; \text{for } j = 1, 2,..., n \qquad (9.12)$$

The mathematics thus far has required no restrictions on the various parameters. When interpreting it, however, I do so only for the application of immediate interest, namely, faith-based organizations, and impose appropriate restrictions. Specifically, I make the following assumptions. (1) The agent values the by-product and may also value the one the principal desires, so $a_2 > 0$ and $a_1 \geq 0$. (2) The principal values the first product and dislikes the by-product, so $p_1 > 0$ and $p_2 < 0$. (3) All of the agent's actions promote his main objective, namely the by-product. Thus $f_{2j} \geq 0$ for all j, but some of the f_{1j} may be negative. (4) The agent's actions have positively correlated effects on the two products, that is, $\Omega_{12} > 0$, because the principal would not hire an agent whose actions were overall detrimental to the principal's objective.

First consider the bonus coefficient b. With $p_2 < 0$ and $\Omega_{12} > 0$, the second term in the expression in (9.10) is negative, that is, the principal weakens his marginal incentive payment because the agent's actions have the undesirable by-product. This is obvious. What is not so obvious is that the expression is independent of the agent's direct valuations of the two outputs a_1 and a_2. The principal can indeed exploit such intrinsic valuation, but does so entirely by adjusting the base salary s through the participation constraint. The productivity coefficients for the by-product do affect the bonus coefficient:

$$\frac{\partial b}{\partial f_{2j}} = \frac{p_2 f_{1j}}{\Omega_{11}}. \tag{9.13}$$

To understand the intuition for this, consider the case where $f_{1j} < 0$, so action j is undesirable from the principal's point of view. But if f_{2j} increases, the agent will do more of j, holding other things constant. Specifically, (4.5) shows that $\partial x_j / \partial f_{2j} = a_2 > 0$ when b is held constant. To mitigate this effect, the principal wants to make the agent pay more attention to the effect on y_1, and he does this by increasing b. That is what (9.13) shows: with $p_2 < 0$ and $f_{1j} < 0$, we have $\partial b / \partial f_{2j} > 0$.

Now we can find the effect of f_{2j} on the levels of the actions:

$$\frac{\partial x_j}{\partial f_{2j}} = f_{1j} \frac{\partial b}{\partial f_{2j}} + a_2 = \frac{p_2 (f_{1j})^2}{\Omega_{11}} + a_2. \tag{9.14}$$

The second term on the right-hand side is the partial effect of f_{2j} on x_j, holding b constant. With $p_2 < 0$, the first term on the RHS is the indirect effect via the principal's response of changing b, and it is negative. So the total effect of f_{2j} on x_j is always less than the direct effect. This result is independent of the sign of f_{1j}. If $f_{1j} < 0$ the principal raises b, and if $f_{1j} > 0$ the principal lowers b, so the sign of the change in b multiplied by f_{1j} is always negative.

For $j \neq k$,

$$\frac{\partial x_j}{\partial f_{2k}} = f_{1j} \frac{\partial b}{\partial f_{2k}} = \frac{p_2 f_{1j} f_{1k}}{\Omega 11}. \tag{9.15}$$

Since $p_2 < 0$, this is positive if f_{1j} and f_{1k} have opposite signs. The intuition for this is easy to construct along the same lines as above.

Finally, we can find the 'bottom line' effects on the principal's pay-off.

Since the principal chooses b to maximize Π, the envelope theorem says that the total derivatives of Π with respect to various parameters equal the corresponding partial derivatives holding b constant, evaluated at the optimum b. Thus

$$\frac{\partial \Pi}{\partial a_2} = (p_1 - b)\Omega_{12} + p_2 \Omega_{22} + (a_1 + b)\Omega_{12} + a_2 \Omega_{22}$$

$$= (a_1 + p_1)\Omega_{12} + (a_2 + p_2)\Omega_{22}.$$

This can be negative only if $a_2 + p_2$ is negative and sufficiently large in numerical value. Thus, if the principal dislikes the by-product sufficiently more strongly than the agent likes it, the agent's intrinsic motivation for action can hurt the principal.

Similar calculations show

$$\frac{\partial \Pi}{\partial f_{2j}} = (a_1 + p_1)(a_2 + p_2)f_{1j} + (p_2)^2 f_{1j} \frac{\Omega_{12}}{\Omega_{22}} + a_2(2p_2 + a_2)f_{2j}. \quad (9.16)$$

The first term on the right-hand side is negative if $a_2 + p_2 < 0$ or $f_{1j} < 0$ but not both; the second term is negative if and only if $f_{1j} < 0$; the third term is negative if $p_2 < -\frac{1}{2} a_2$. The conditions pertaining to negative p_2 are milder than they were when we considered the effect of a_2 on Π.

What if all the productivity coefficients f_{2j} increase in the same proportion λ? Using (9.16) and applying the chain rule, we have

$$\frac{\partial \Pi}{\partial \lambda} \sum_{j=1}^{n} f_{2j} \frac{\partial \Pi}{\partial f_{2j}}$$

$$= (a_1 + p_1)(a_2 + p_2)\Omega_{12} + (p_2)^2 \frac{(\Omega_{12})^2}{\Omega_{22}} + a_2(2p_2 + a_2)\Omega_{22}.$$

The first term on the RHS is negative if $p_2 < -a_2$, and the third term is negative if $p_2 < -\frac{1}{2}a_2$. The second term is always positive. Thus the agent's neutral productivity increase in the by-product can hurt the principal if he dislikes the by-product sufficiently strongly.

CONCLUDING COMMENTS

This model captures some of the arguments concerning the use of faith-based agencies in providing the services desired by a secular government. Although it simplifies some issues and ignores others, it produces some interesting results. In particular, we have seen that a secular government that dislikes the by-product sufficiently strongly may get a lower pay-off if it employs an agent who is very efficient in creating the by-product. This argues in favour of using those agencies that are relatively inefficient at promoting their own agendas.

In the political debate there is no single principal; instead the parties to the arguments make different assumptions about the p_1 and p_2 the government *should* use. As one would expect, those who most value separation of church and state and regard any direct or indirect state aid to promotion of religious beliefs as constitutionally inappropriate have a high negative p_2; they are the ones most opposed to this initiative. The religious right has a positive p_2; they should support the use of such organizations and argue that it is a good way for the government to promote its primary objectives for the socially worthwhile activities.

However, such policy proposals in the US and the UK have been opposed even by some religious groups. This may be because these groups fear a loss of their independence if they receive money from the government, or because each does not like the prospect that other rival religious groups would be supported. In my model the agent's participation constraint is binding; thus he is not getting any rent from this relationship and may be swayed by such other considerations outside the model even if they are relatively unimportant per se. I can easily modify the model to include a term in the agent's utility to capture the loss of independence. Then the principal will have to increase the agent's salary to offset this, which will lower the principal's pay-off from the relationship. It is also possible to have several agents, each of whom gets negative utility from the presence of others. Then the principal has to give each some rent to overcome this. Unlike usual agency models where the presence of multiple agents enables the principal to exploit competition among them and get a higher pay-off for himself, here the existence of multiple agents can lower the principal's pay-off.

Finally, the analysis assumes that the principal knows the agent's utility function (especially the motivation coefficient a_1), but in reality this may be the agent's private information. Then it is optimal for the agent to play hard to get, so the principal's scheme has to share some rent with the agent to induce him to reveal his information. This may be another reason for the apparent opposition of the religious groups. It also suggests further theoretical possibilities. I have considered only the moral hazard (unobservable action) aspect of the agency, but the adverse selection aspect (pre-contract information asymmetry about type) is also present in reality and worth theoretical analysis.

REFERENCES

BAKER, G.P., (2000), 'The Use of Performance Measures in Incentive Contracting', *American Economic Review*, 90(2), Papers and Proceedings, pp. 415–20.

——, (2002), 'Distortion and Risk in Optimal Incentive Contracts', *Journal of Human Resources*, 37 (4), Fall, pp. 728–51.

HOLMSTRÖM, B. and P. MILGROM, (1987), 'Aggregation and Linearity in the Provision of Intertemporal Incentives' *Econometrica*, 55(2), March, pp. 303–28.

——, (1991), 'Multi-task Principal–Agent Analysis: Incentive Contracts, Asset Ownership, and Job Design, *Journal of Law, Economics, and Organization*, 7 (Special Issue), pp. 24–52.

10. Education Expenditure and School Participation

A Theoretical and Empirical Analysis

Sajal Lahiri and Kevin Sylwester

INTRODUCTION

It is an unfortunate fact that tens of millions of children in the developing world do not attend school and work full-time.[1] Apart from poverty which has been identified as one of the main reasons for this phenomenon,[2] the low quality of education has also been mentioned as another important reason.[3] However, improving the quality of education involves significant investments and the financing of such investments needs to be properly thought through and investigated. Given the reluctance of the international community to put their money where

[1] *See* Ashagrie (1993), Grootaert and Kanbur (1995), ILO (1996), and Basu (1999) for a sense of the magnitude and nature of the problem. In recent years there has been a resurgence of interest, at both the empirical and theoretical levels, in explaining the existence of child labour. Some theoretical contributions are Basu and Van (1998), Basu (2000, 2002) Baland and Robinson (2000), Dessy (2000), Jafarey and Lahiri (2000, 2002), Ranjan (1999). Econometric studies include Addison et al. (1997), Bhalotra (1999), Cockburn (2000), Ilahi (1999), Ravallion and Woodon (2000), and Ray (1999, 2000). For two extensive surveys of the literature *see* Basu (1999) and Jafarey and Lahiri (2001).

[2] *See*, Bhalotra (1999) and Ray (1999) for empirical evidence.

[3] The case for more investment in education quality has been made, amongst others, by The PROBE Team (1999), Drèze and Gandhi-Kingdon (2001) and Ray (2000).

their mouth is,[4] the governments of the poor countries will need to obtain resources for such investments from domestic sources, and this may have consequences for the real side of the economy and thus also long-run job opportunities and poverty. For example, investing in education would raise the level of human capital. However, if such investments are financed by income taxation it is likely to have an adverse effect on investments in physical capital and thus on job opportunities in the future.

In this paper, we examine the interaction between investment in human capital (quality of education) and investments in physical capital, and its implications for the incidence of school participation in a two-period aggregative general equilibrium model. There are two groups of families: rich and poor. The rich send all their children to school, the poor send only a fraction of their children while the remaining poor children work as child labourers. The children who go to school in period 1 earn a higher wage in period 2 than those who do not. The wage premium for education depends on the quality of education, which is in turn determined by the amount of public resources invested in education. The proportion of poor children that go to school in period 1 is determined endogenously by their families. Investment in physical capital is made endogenously by the rich. We assume that investment in education is financed by taxing the rich.

The theoretical model is spelt out in the following section. In the third section we shall examine the effect of an increase in the tax rate on the level of investments (both physical and human) and the school participation rate. In the fourth and fifth sections we empirically estimate the theoretical relationships obtained in the third section using cross-country data. Finally, some concluding remarks are made.

[4] Although it was agreed by all parties at the United Nations (after the publication of the Pearson Commission Report) that the developed countries should provide 1 per cent of the their national income as aid, the actual amount of aid has fallen far short of this figure, except for four or five countries. For example, in 1998 foreign aid as a percentage of national income was 0.10 for the USA, 0.27 for the UK, 0.26 for Germany, and 0.28 for Japan (www.worldbank.org/data/wdi2000/pdfs/tab6_8.pdf).

THE MODEL

There are two types of households: rich and poor, indexed by r and p respectively. Total number of (identical) households in each type are M^r and M^p. For simplicity we assume that each household has one adult and N^i ($i = r, p$) number of children. There are two time periods, indexed by $t = 1, 2$. In period 1, there are two factors of production: unskilled labour and capital. In period 2, there is an additional third factor of production: skilled labour. The rich households earn all their income exclusively from rents on capital, and the poor households from wage income. The poor household heads are unskilled labourers in both periods. The children from poor households are born unskilled, and a proportion of them, e, go to school in period 1 and become skilled workers in period 2. The rest of the children from poor households work in period 1 as unskilled labourers and remain so in period 2. All the children from rich households go to school in period 1 and become capitalists in period 2.

An arbitrary number of goods are produced in the country which is assumed to be a small open economy so that the commodity price vector, P, is exogenous. We assume constant returns to scale and perfect competition in both product and factor markets so that the production side of the economy in the two periods is represented respectively by the two revenue functions $R^1(P, L_u, \bar{K})$ and $R^2(P, L_u + \theta(z) L_s, \bar{K} + M^r I)$, where L_u is the amount of unskilled labour in the two periods, L_s is skilled labour in period 2, $\bar{K}$ is the initial capital stock, I is the amount of investment made in period 1 by each rich household, and $\theta(z)$ is the skill parameter which depends positively on the amount of resources invested in education, with $(\theta(z) - 1) R_2^2$ being the skill premium.

The partial derivative of a revenue function with respect to the endowment of a factor gives the price of that factor. Moreover, the matrix of second-order partial derivatives with respect to the endowments is negative semi-definite.[5] We shall also assume that more endowment of one of the factors does not reduce the price of the other factor. These properties and assumptions are stated formally as:

$$R_j^i > 0,\ R_{jj}^i < 0,\ R_{jk}^i > 0,\ i = 1, 2;\ j = 1, 2;\ k(\neq j) = 1, 2.$$

[5] For this and other properties of the expenditure function *see*, Dixit and Norman (1980).

Given the assumptions made above, we have

$$L_u = M^P(1+(1-e)N^P),\qquad(10.1)$$

$$L_s = eM^P N^P.\qquad(10.2)$$

On the consumption side, the expenditure function for each rich household is given by $E^r(P, u^r)$, where u^r is the level of utility of each rich household. As for poor households, each parent's preferences are represented by a utility function, u^p, over the inter-temporal consumption vector C and a measure of the aggregate educational level of children. In particular,

$$u^P = v^P(C) + N^P g(e),\ g' > 0,\ g'' < 0.$$

The assumption of separability is assumed for analytical simplicity. Consumption goods are assumed to be non-rivalrous within the household, but rivalrous across households. This allows us to abstract from the intra-household distribution of resources. The sub-utility function u^p is increasing and concave in its arguments. The sub-utility function g is also increasing and concave. The inclusion of education in the utility function is cosistent both with the assumption that parents receive utility from seeing their children educated and that they receive disutility from subjecting their children to labour. The concavity of g with respect to education reflects decreasing marginal utility of education and/or increasing marginal disutility of child labour. The above direct utility function for the poor households gives rise to the inter-temporal expenditure function $E^p(P, u^p - N^p g(e))$ for each poor household. It is well known that $E_2^i (>0)$ is the reciprocal of the marginal utility of income for group i, and the assumption of diminishing marginal utility of income implies that $E_{22}^i > 0$ for each i, $i = r, p$. Formally,

$$E_2^i > 0,\ E_{22}^i > 0,\ i = r, p.$$

We assume that the resources invested by the government on education, z, is financed by taxing the income of rich households at rate t. Thus, the budget constraints for the two types of households and the government are given by

$$M^r(E^r(P, u^r) + I) = (1-t)\left[R_3^1 \bar{K} + \frac{(\bar{K} + M^r I)R_3^2}{1+r}\right],\qquad(10.3)$$

$$M^p\, E^p\, (P,\, u^p - N^p\, g(e)) = R_2^1\, L_u + \frac{(L_u + \theta(z)\, L_s)\, R_2^2}{1+r}, \qquad (10.4)$$

$$z = t\left[R_3^1\, \bar{K} + \frac{(\bar{K} + M^r I)\, R_3^2}{1+r} \right], \qquad (10.5)$$

where r is the interest rate and R_j^i is the partial derivative of R^i with respect to the j-th argument. We assume perfect international capital markets so that r is exogenous.

The level of investment, I, is determined by each rich household by maximizing the welfare u^r, taking the factor and commodity prices, and the level of public expenditure z as given. From (10.3), setting $\partial u^r / \partial I = 0$, we obtain the first-order condition as:

$$(1-t)R_3^2 = 1+r. \qquad (10.6)$$

This equation simply states that the net rate of return to investment is equal to the opportunity cost of such investment.

Similarly, a poor household determines the level of school participation, e, by maximizing its welfare, u^p, taking the factor and commodity prices as given. From (10.1), (10.2) and (10.4), setting $\partial u^p / \partial e = 0$, we obtain the first-order condition as:

$$R_2^1 = E_2^p\, g'(e) + \frac{(\theta(z)-1)R_2^2}{1+r}. \qquad (10.7)$$

The left-hand side (LHS) of the equation is the opportunity cost of sending the marginal child to school: an increase in e results in a loss of income at $t = 1$, due to the foregone wages of an unskilled child worker R_2^1., The RHS gives marginal benefits. E_2^p is the inverse of the marginal utility of income: it represents the extra income needed to increase utility by one unit. An increase in e leads to a marginal increase in $g(e)$, resulting in a gain equal to $E_2^p g'(e)$ in units of income. It also leads to a direct increase in income at $t = 2$ by the amount of the skill premium $(\theta(z)-1)R_2^2$, which is then discounted back to $t = 1$ via the discount rate.

This completes the description of the model which has seven equations in (10.1)–(10.7) and seven unknowns: L_s, L_u, e, I, u^r, u^p, and z.

TAX AND SCHOOL ENROLMENT

In this section we shall examine how a change in the tax rate t affects the equilibrium. Differentiating (10.1)–(10.7), we obtain:

$$M^r E_2^r \, du^r = -\left[R_3^1 \bar{K} + \frac{(\bar{K} + M^r I) R_3^2}{1+r} \right] dt + \frac{(1-t) M^r (\bar{K} + M^r I) R_{33}^2}{I+r} \, dI$$

$$+ \frac{(1-t)(\bar{K} + M^r I) R_{32}^2 \, e \, M^p N^p \theta'}{1+r} \, dz$$

$$+ (1-t) M^p N^p \left[-\bar{K} R_{32}^1 + \frac{(\bar{K} + M^r I) R_{32}^2 (\theta-1)}{1+r} \right] de \tag{10.8}$$

$$R_{33}^2 \, M^r \, dI = \frac{R_3^2}{1-t} \, dt - R_{32}^2 \, M^p N^p \, (\theta-1) de - R_{32}^2 \, e \, M^p N^p \theta' dz, \tag{10.9}$$

$$\Delta de = g' E_{22}^p \, du^p + \beta_1 \, dz + \frac{(\theta-1) R_{23}^2 M^r}{1+r} \, dI, \tag{10.10}$$

$$\Delta_1 \, dz = \frac{(1+r)z}{t} \, dt + \beta_2 \, dI + \beta_3 de, \tag{10.11}$$

$$(1+r) M^p E_2^p \, du^p = \beta_4 \, de + \beta_5 \, dz + (L_u + \theta L_s) M^r R_{23}^2 \, dI, \tag{10.12}$$

where

$$\Delta = -R_{22}^1 \, M^p N^p - E_2^p g'' + (g')^2 E_{22}^p N^p - \frac{(\theta-1)^2 R_{22}^2 \, M^p N^p}{1+r} > 0,$$

$$\Delta_1 = (1+r) \left[1 - \frac{te \, M^p N^p \theta' R_{32}^2 (\bar{K} + M^r I)}{1+r} \right],$$

$$\beta_1 = \frac{\theta' R_2^2 + (\theta-1) R_{22}^2 \, e \, M^p N^p \theta'}{1+r},$$

$$\beta_2 = t M^r \left[R_3^2 + (\bar{K} + M^r I) R_{33}^2 \right],$$

$$\beta_3 = t \, M^p N^p \left[(\bar{K} + M^r I) R_{32}^2 (\theta-1) - (1+r) \bar{K} R_{32}^1 \right],$$

$$\beta_4 = M^p N^p [-(1+r) L_u R_{22}^1 + (L_u + \theta L_s)(\theta-1) R_{22}^2],$$

$$\beta_5 = L_s \theta' [R_2^2 + (L_u + \theta L_s) R_{22}^2].$$

The above equations can be explained as follows. An increase in t reduces the disposable income of the rich for a given level of income. This effect is given by the first term on the RHS of (10.8). An increase in $I(z)$ reduces (increases) the rental rate of capital and therefore lowers (raises) the income of the rich.[6] This effect is captured by the second (third) term in (10.8). The education participation variable e has two opposing effects on the welfare of the rich. First, an increase in e reduces labour supply in period 1 and this reduces the rental rate of capital in period 1 and therefore the income of the rich. Second, a higher e increases the size of effective labour in period 2 and raises the rental rate of capital in period 2.

As for investment (10.9), an increase in the tax rate t reduces the net return on investment and therefore the level of it. The first term on the RHS of (10.9) captures this negative effect. An increase in either e or z increases the effective amount of labour in period 2 and therefore raises the return to, and thus the level of, investment. These effects are given in the remaining two terms in (10.9).

The tax rate t has no direct effect on the education participation rate e, but it has three indirect effects via changes in utility level of the poor u^p, tax revenue z, and the level of investment I as can be seen from the RHS of (10.10). An increase in u^p reduces the marginal utility of income of the poor and therefore the poor families give more importance to the non-pecuniary benefit from education, raising the school participation rate. An increase in z has two opposing effects. First, it raises the skill premium $(\theta - 1)$ and therefore the school participation rate e. However, it also increases the supply of effective labour and therefore reduces the wage rate in period 2. It can be shown that the net effect is positive if and only if $\varepsilon_{22}^2 (\theta - 1) L_s / (L_u + \theta L_s) < 1$ where $\varepsilon_{22}^2 (\equiv -(\partial R_2^2 / \partial (L_u + \theta L_s))((L_u + \theta L_s) / R_2^2))$ is the elasticity of the period 2 wage rate with respect to the supply of effective labour in that period. This condition is likely to be satisfied if the proportion of skilled labour to the total labour force is very small. Finally, an increase in I raises the wage rate in period 2 and therefore e.

An increase in t raises tax revenue for a given level of income of the rich and therefore education expenditure z (*see* the first term on the

---

[6] Note that we assume that $R_{jk}^i > 0$ for $j \neq k$. R_{jj}^i on the other hand is always negative. Also note that since the level of I is chosen optimally by the rich, most of the direct effects of I on the welfare of the rich are neutralized because of the envelope theorem.

right-hand side of (10.11)).[7] An increase in I however has two opposite effects as can be seen from the second term in (10.11). First, for a given value of the rental rate of capital, it increases the tax base and thus the tax revenue. Second, because of diminishing returns, an increase in I reduces the rental rate of capital and therefore the tax base and revenue. It can be shown that the net effect is positive if and only if $\varepsilon_{33}^2 < 1$ where $\varepsilon_{33}^2 (\equiv -(\partial R_3^2 / \partial(\bar{K} + M^r I))((\bar{K} + M^r I)/R_3^2))$ is the elasticity of the rental rate of capital with respect to the stock of capital in period 2. An increase in e also has two opposing effects on tax revenue. First, an increase in e reduces the size of the labour force in period 1 and this reduces the rental rate of capital in that period. This has a negative impact on tax revenue. Second, a rise in e increases the effective size of the labour force in the second period and this has the opposite (positive) effect on tax revenue. If the cross-elasticities—namely the elasticity of the wage rate with respect to the capital stock in the two periods, that is, $\varepsilon_{23}^1 (\equiv (\partial R_2^1 / \partial \bar{K})(\bar{K} / R_2^1))$ and $\varepsilon_{23}^2 (\equiv (\partial R_2^2 / \partial(\bar{K} + M^r I))((\bar{K} + M^r I)/R_3^2))$—are the same, it can be shown that the net effect of an increase in e on z is negative.

Finally, we examine the effects on the per capita utility level of the poor, u^p, from (10.12). Since the tax is imposed on the rich, it has no direct effect on the utility level of the poor. Furthermore, due to the envelope property, many of the direct effects of an increase in e on u^p are absent. Since an increase in e reduces labour supply in period 1 and increases labour supply in period 2, it raises the wage rate in period 1 and lowers the wage in period 2. These two opposite effects of e on u^p are given in the first term on the RHS of (10.12). Using (10.7) it can be shown that if $\varepsilon_{22}^2 = \varepsilon_{22}^1$ where $\varepsilon_{22}^1 (\equiv -(\partial R_2^1 / \partial L_u)(L_u / R_2^1))$ is the elasticity of the period 1 wage rate with respect to the supply of effective labour in that period, the net effect of an increase in e on u^p is in fact positive. An increase in z has two opposing effects. First, it raises the skill premium $(\theta - 1)$ and therefore the income of the poor in period 2. However, it also increases the supply of effective labour and therefore reduces the wage rate in period 2. It can be shown that the net effect is positive if and only if $\varepsilon_{22}^2 < 1$. An increase in I raises the wage rate in period 2 and therefore u^p.

---

[7] Note that Δ_1 on the LHS of (10.11) captures a multiplier effect. An increase in z directly increases the tax base by increasing $\theta(z)$ and thus the rental rate of capital. If we assume, as we shall do, that the multiplier term is less than unity then $\Delta_1 > 0$.

Substituting dz from (10.11) into (10.9) and (10.10), we derive the following two systems of equations whose analogs will be estimated in the following section:

$$\left[R_{33}^2 \, M^r + \frac{\beta_2 \, R_{32}^2 \, e \, M^p \, N^p \theta'}{\Delta_1} \right] dI = \left[\frac{R_3^2}{1-t} - \frac{R_{32}^2 \, e \, M^p \, N^p \theta'(1+r)z}{t\Delta_1} \right] dt$$

$$- R_{32}^2 \, M^p N^p \left[\frac{\beta_3 \, e\theta'}{\Delta_1} + (\theta - 1) \right] de, \quad (10.13)$$

$$\left[\Delta - \frac{\beta_1 \beta_3}{\Delta_1} \right] de = g' E_{22}^p \, du^p + \frac{\beta_1 (1+r)z}{t\Delta_1} dt$$

$$+ \left[\frac{\beta_1 \beta_2}{\Delta_1} + \frac{(\theta - 1) R_{32}^2 \, M^r}{1+r} \right] dI. \quad (10.14)$$

DATA AND EMPIRICAL SPECIFICATION

All data are from the *2001 World Development Indicators* CD from the World Bank. Data is averaged over the five-year period 1990–4 to mitigate the potential for a one-year aberration to skew the results. This period is chosen so as to include the largest number of observations in the sample.

The empirical specification stems form equations (10.13) and (10.14) of the previous section and is given as follows:

$$\text{INV} = a_0 + a_1 \cdot \frac{\text{ED}}{\text{GNI}} + a_2 . \text{SEC} + a_3 . \text{GDP} + a_4 . X + a_5 . Y + v$$

$$(10.15)$$

$$\text{SEC} = b_0 + b_1 \cdot \frac{\text{ED}}{\text{GNI}} + b_2 . \text{INV} + b_3 . \text{GDP} + b_4 . X + b_5 . Z + w,$$

$$(10.16)$$

where:
INV is the investment (gross fixed capital formation) per person ratio (in thousands), SEC is the gross enrolment rate in secondary education, ED/GNI is the government education expenditures to gross national income ratio, GDP is the natural log of GDP per capita measured using international dollars, X is a matrix of other variables common to both

equations, *Y* and *Z* are matrices of variables unique to their respective equation, *v* and *w* are unobservable components.

Enrolment in secondary education is used instead of primary education for two reasons. First, many countries have universal or nearly universal primary education and so primary education has less variation in the sample. Even after removing high-income countries, the median primary enrolment rate is 98 per cent as opposed to 58 per cent for secondary enrolment. The standard deviation for secondary enrolment is also larger than that for primary education. It is hoped that the increased variation will help to examine differences across countries better. Second, the model has agents becoming skilled labourers through previous schooling. It is more likely that one distinguishes skilled from unskilled by participation in secondary education rather than primary education.

In (10.15), ED/GNI is a proxy for the tax rate since it accounts for the fraction of income going to public education. The model predicts that a_1 is greater than zero since investment is decreasing with the tax rate. The sign of a_2 is also predicted to be positive because the return to physical capital is increasing with future human capital. INV is predicted to be increasing with GDP as higher-income countries can allocate more output towards investment. Matrix *X* contains the dummies AFRICA (sub-Saharan Africa) and LATAMER (Latin America) to control for regional effects that might influence the level of investment. Matrix *X* also contains INFMOR, infant mortality per 1000 births. This variable is included as a parsimonious, albeit imperfect, way to control for disparities of income. According to the model, only the income of the rich is relevant for investment levels. For any given level of income, a higher level of infant mortality suggests that more of this income is distributed among a smaller set of people.

Matrix *Y* contains two variables: INF and INFVOL. INF denotes the natural log of the average inflation rate as calculated from the GDP deflator. INFVOL denotes the natural log of the standard deviation of this inflation rate. Natural logs are taken to mitigate the impact that outliers having inflation rates in hundreds or thousands per cent have on the coefficient estimates. Both attempt to control for macroeconomic instability that might influence levels of investment. High or volatile inflation indicates instabilities that provide disincentives for investment. To identify the model, it is assumed that current inflation has no direct effects on school enrolment decisions once one takes into account the other control variables such as current income and public resources allocated to education.

The proxy for the tax rate, ED/GNI, is also included in (10.16). Large tax rates lower income for the poor and so households place more importance on the non-pecuniary benefit of education. This leads to higher enrolment. Larger tax rates also lead to greater education expenditures which raises the skill premium and so provides more incentive to attend school. As long as the increase in the supply of effective labour is not great enough to offset the increase in wages associated with the skill premium, the coefficient on ED/GNI in (10.16) should be positive. GDP is included since enrolment in education is predicted to be increasing with income. As in (10.15), INFMOR is included to capture how this income is distributed. SEC is predicted to be decreasing with INFMOR. The regional dummies are included, again to account for differences across regions. SEC is predicted to be increasing with INV because a larger capital stock raises the return to education. Matrix Z contains the single variable RURAL which denotes the fraction of the population living in rural areas. SEC is predicted to be decreasing with RURAL since the populace is more spread out in rural communities, thereby raising transportation costs to schools. The percentage of the population from rural areas is assumed not to directly influence investment levels, given the other controls.

Each of the unobservables v and w is assumed to have zero mean and finite but not necessarily identical variance. Because both endogenous variables appear in each equation, (10.15) and (10.16) will be estimated jointly using three-stage least squares.

Two groups of countries will be considered. The first group consists of the full sample. The second group removes those countries classified by the World Bank as high-income countries to determine if the results are robust to developing countries where enrolment in education might be more sensitive to macroeconomic policy. The countries are listed in the Appendix A10.1. Descriptive statistics are given in Table 10.1.

Table 10.1: Descriptive Statistics

Variable	Mean	Median	Std. Dev.
INV	150.31	96.94	151.25
	84.92	71.63	71.70
SEC	60.16	56.86	32.29
	49.83	48.95	27.08
ED/GNI	4.52	4.52	1.84
	4.34	4.16	1.84
GDP	8.29	8.27	1.06
	7.91	8.04	0.84
INFMOR	45.62	32.80	38.51
	55.57	45.67	37.23
INF	3.02	2.49	1.69
	3.40	2.91	1.68
INFVOL	2.31	1.82	2.13
	2.82	2.29	2.07
RURAL	46.11	45.78	22.89
	52.24	51.57	20.67
AFRICA	0.27		
	0.34		
LATAMER	0.14		
	0.17		

Note: Top row in each variable presents values for full sample (131 observations). Bottom row presents values for developing-country sample (104 observations).

RESULTS

The results are presented in Table 10.2. Columns 1 and 2 present findings for the full sample of countries and columns 3 and 4 consider only developing countries.

For the full sample, the coefficient on ED/GNI is negative and significant in the investment equation (–20.2). A one-standard deviation increase in ED/GNI (1.8) is associated with a decrease in investment of –36.4 or almost a quarter of a standard deviation. The coefficient on SEC is positive (5.93) and significant at the 10 per cent level. The coefficients for the regional dummies and GDP are positive but not significant. The coefficients on the inflation variables are negative but not significant although INFVOL is nearly so. However, the coefficient

Table 10.2: Results from Three-stage Least Squar Regressions

Group	Full Sample (1)	Full Sample (2)	Developing Countries (3)	Developing Countries (4)
Education	Investment Eqn. (10.15)	Enrolment Eqn. (10.16)	Investment Eqn. (10.15)	Enrolment Eqn. (10.16)
Constrant	−562.12[a]	−95.31[b]	−439.02[c]	−71.19
	(310.51)	(47.86)	(116.16)	(53.66)
ED/GNI	−20.20[c]	1.08	−6.16[a]	0.23
	(7.71)	(0.87)	(3.29)	(0.99)
SEC	5.93[a]		2.97[a]	
	(3.36)		(1.51)	
INV		−0.07[b]		−0.20[b]
		(0.04)		(0.08)
AFRICA	55.35	−7.17[a]	27.00	−5.37
	(37.32)	(4.29)	(17.65)	(4.66)
LATAMER	43.27	−22.28[c]	20.69	−24.75[c]
	(60.98)	(4.92)	(28.13)	(5.42)
GDP	48.37	22.46[c]	48.22[b]	22.51[c]
	(58.39)	(6.16)	(20.80)	(7.30)
INFVOL	−16.66		−12.91[b]	
	(10.47)		(6.45)	
INF	−10.46		−2.59	
	(16.46)		(9.79)	
INFMOR	2.09[b]	−0.19[b]	0.97[a]	−0.27[c]
	(0.94)	(0.09)	(0.54)	(0.09)
RURAL		−0.25[b]		−0.38[c]
		(0.10)		(0.12)
No. of Observations	131	131	104	104

Notes: Standard Errors in parentheses.

[a] denotes significance of 10 per cent level.
[b] denotes significance of 5 per cent level.
[c] denotes significance of 1 per cent level.

on INFMOR is positive and significant (2.09). Provided high infant mortality, given some income level, is a sign that this income is not evenly distributed, the positive coefficient on INFMOR implies that investment is higher where income is more concentrated.

In the enrolment equation, both sub-Saharan Africa and Latin America have lower enrolment rates than does the control group. Not surprisingly, the coefficient on GDP is positive and significant (22.46) suggesting that higher income is associated with greater participation in school. High infant mortality is associated with negative enrolment rates, indicating that a concentration of income lowers school enrolment. The coefficient on RURAL is also negative (−0.25) and suggests that rural communities have less access to schooling. The coefficient on ED/GNI (1.08) is positive but not significant at the 10 per cent level. The magnitude of the effect is also small. A one-standard deviation increase in ED/GNI is associated with an increase of SEC of only 2.0 percentage points or about one-sixteenth of a standard deviation.

Surprisingly, the coefficient on INV is negative and also significant (−0.07) suggesting that greater investment leads to lower school enrolment. A one-standard deviation increase in INV lowers SEC by 10 points or about one-third of a standard deviation. This finding runs counter to the model and implies that other factors are important. One possible explanation is that high investment for given levels of income is a signal of wealth inequalities that are not completely captured by including infant mortality in the specification. The negative coefficient on INV would then be interpreted to mean that wealth disparities imply a greater incidence of poverty and less opportunity for attending school. Under this interpretation, this finding should not be taken as causal in that greater investment actually lowers school enrolment. Future work will attempt to understand the negative coefficient on INV better.

Columns 3 and 4 remove the high-income countries form the sample. The results are somewhat altered. In the investment equation, higher income is now associated with greater investment. Findings regarding inflation and infant mortality are similar to those in column 1 although the magnitudes of the coefficients decrease. The coefficient on ED/GNI remains negative but its magnitude decreases by two-thirds and the economic impact of higher taxes for education on investment does not appear to be as strong. The magnitude of the coefficient on SEC is only half as great as it was before although it remains statistically significant.

In the enrolment equation, AFRICA is no longer significant but LATAMER remains so. Given the other controls, Latin American countries have lower enrolment rates than do even other developing countries. In fact, enrolment rates are lower by nearly a standard deviation. Higher income is again associated with higher enrolment. Findings regarding INFMOR and RURAL change little. However, there is now even less indication that higher tax rates lead to greater enrolment in secondary education. Its coefficient is 0.22, which is about 80 per cent smaller from that in column 2. Not only does the coefficient on INV remain negative and statistically significant, but it nearly triples. Raising INV by one-standard deviation (150) lowers SEC by 30 percentage points, almost one standard deviation.

These results provide some support for the theoretical model. Higher share of national income in public education expenditure are associated with lower investment but positively associated with enrolment, albeit not always significantly so. Barro (1991) found that other types of government expenditure were negatively associated with private investment. An implication for development policy is that there are potential trade-offs between investment in human capital and investment in physical capital, and policy markers should recognize this possibility. Sylwester (2000) reports that greater education expenditures are associated with lower economic growth concurrent with these expenditures (although future growth is higher). Our findings here suggest one explanation for this result, namely, the taxes induced by these greater expenditures lower investment.

No strong association between resources going to education and secondary enrolment is shown to be there. However, the model does suggest that there are offsetting effects from resources to enrolment. Devoting more resources to education raising the skill premium, given some number of skilled labourers, but it can also cause wages to fall in period 2 due to the greater supply of skilled labour and so discourage enrolment today. Perhaps these offsetting effects are behind the small coefficient in the empirical findings. A second possibility is that parents see other factors as more important for sending their children to school than government resources allocated to education. The Probe Team (1999) surveyed Indian villages and found reasons, other than economic as to why parents wanted to send their children to school.

CONCLUSION

In this paper, we examined the interactions between investments in physical capital and that in human capital when the latter is financed by taxing the group that makes the former. Our analysis has two parts.

In the first part, we develop theoretical relationships between the key variables of our model, and in the second we empirically estimate those relationships. In particular, we develop a two-period general equilibrium model in which there are two groups: rich and poor. The rich are responsible for investments in physical. The government decides on the quality of education by investing in schools financed by taxation of the rich. The poor families decide on the school participation rate.

The theoretical part of the paper examines all the general equilibrium channels via which a rise in the tax rate affects both the level of investments in physical capital and the school participation rate. The empirical part of the paper estimates these relationships econometrically using cross-country data for the year 2001.

Although the study is a first attempt at the problem and can be improved in a number of ways, it nonetheless confirms our prior belief that endeavours to increase the human capital stock by taxation can adversely affect investments in physical capital and thus long-term job opportunities for the poor, which in turn can affect investments in human capital. In other words, it is very important that the international community demonstrates its concern for child labour and low school participation rates in the developing countries by assisting those countries more in improving the quality of education.

Appendix A10.1

World Bank Income Groups

Developing Countries (104): Albania, Algeria, Angola, Argentina, Armenia, Azerbaijan, Bahrain, Bangladesh, Belarus, Belize, Bolivia, Botswana, Brazil, Bulgaria, Burkina Faso, Burundi, Cameroon, Cape Verde, Central African Republic, Chad, Chile, China, Colombia, Republic of Congo, Costa Rica, Cote d'Ivoire, Croatia, Dominican Republic, Ecuador, Egypt, El Salvador, Equatorial Guinea, Estonia, Ethiopia, Fiji, Gabon, the Gambia, Ghana, Guatemala, Guinea, Guyana, Haiti, Honduras, Hungary, India, Indonesia, Iran, Jamaica, Jordan, Kazakhstan, Kenya, Korea (South), Kyrgyz Republic, Latvia, Lebanon, Lesotho, Lithuania, Madagascar, Macedonia, Malawi, Malaysia, Malta, Mauritania, Mauritius, Mexico, Moldova, Mongolia, Morocco, Mozambique, Namibia, Nepal, Nicaragua, Niger, Nigeria, Pakistan, Panama, Paraguay, Peru, the Philippines, Poland, Romania,

Russia, Saudi Arabia, Senegal, Slovak Republic, South Africa, Sri Lanka, Suriname, Swaziland, Syria, Tanzania, Thailand, Togo, Trinidad and Tobago, Tunisia, Turkey, Uganda, Ukraine, Uruguay, Vanuatu, Venezuela, Yemen, Zambia, Zimbabwe.

High Income Countries (27): Australia, Austria, Belgium, Canada, Cyprus, Denmark, Finland, France, Greece, Hong Kong, Iceland, Ireland, Israel, Italy, Japan, Luxembourg, the Netherlands, New Zealand, Norway, Portugal, Singapore, Spain, Sweden, Switzerland, United Arab Emirates, the United Kingdom, the United States.

REFERENCES

ADDISON, T., S. Bhalotra and C. Heady, (1997), 'Child Labour in Pakistan and Ghana', mimeo, University of Warwick.

ASHAGRIE, K., (1993), 'Statistics on Child Labour', *Bulletin of Labour Statistics*, Issue no. 3, International Labour Organization, Geneva.

BALAND, J-M. and J. ROBINSON, (2000), 'Is Child Labour Inefficient'? *Journal of Political Economy*, 108, pp. pp. 663–79.

BARRO, R., (1991), 'Economic Growth in a Cross-section of Countries', *Quarterly Journal of Economics*, 106, pp. 407–43.

BASU, K., (1999), 'Child Labour: Cause, Consequences and Cure, with Remark on International Labour Standards', *Journal of Economic Literature*, 37, pp. 1083–119.

———, (2000), 'The Intriguing Relation Between Adult Minimum Wage and Child Labour', *Economic Journal*, 110, pp. C50–61.

———, (2002), 'A Note on Multiple General Equilibria with Child Labour', *Economics Letters*, 74, pp. 301–8.

BASU, K. and P.H. VAN, (1998), 'The Economics of Child Labour', *American Economic Review*, 88, pp. 412–27.

BHALOTRA, S., (1999), 'Is Child Labour Necessary'?, mimeo; Bristol: University of Bristol.

COCKBURN, J., (2000), 'Child Labour Versus Education: Poverty Constraints or Income Opportunities', mimeo, Oxford: Nuffield College.

DESSY, S.E., (2000), 'A Defense of Compulsory Measures Against Child Labour, *Journal of Development Economics*, 62, pp. 261–75.

DIXIT, A. and V. NORMAN, (1980), *Theory of International Trade*, Cambridge: Combridge University Press.

DRÈZE, J. and G. GANDHI-KINGDON, (2001), 'School Participation in Rural India', *Review of Development Economics,* 5, pp. 1–24.

GROOTAERT, C. and R. KANBUR, (1995), 'Child Labour: An Economic Perspective', *International Labour Review,* 134, pp. 187–203.

ILAHI, N., (1999), 'Children's Work and Schooling: Does Gender Matter? Evidence from the Peru LSMS Panel Data, Latin America and Caribbean Region', Washington DC: World Bank, Processed.

ILO, (1996), *Economically Active Populations: Estimates and Projections, 1950–2010,* Geneva: International Labour Organization.

JAFAREY, S. and S. LAHIRI, (2000), 'Food for Education and Funds for Education Quality: Policy Options to Reduce Child Labour', Discussion Paper No. 00–03, Department of Economics, University of Wales, Swansea.

_____, (2001), 'Child Labour: Theory, Policy and Evidence', *World Economics,* 2, pp. 69–93.

_____, (2002), 'Will Trade Sanctions Reduce Child Labour? The Role of Credit Markets', *Journal of Development Economics,* 68, pp. 137–56.

PROBE TEAM, (1999), *Public Report on Basic Education in India,* New Delhi: Oxford University Press.

RAVALLION, M. and Q. WOODON, (2000), 'Does Cheaper Schooling Mean Less Child Labour? Evidence from Behavioural Responses to an Enrollment Subsidy', *Economic Journal,* 110, pp. C158–C175.

RANJAN, P., (1999), 'Credit Constraints and the Phenomenon of Child Labour', *Journal of Development Economics,* 64, pp. 81–102.

RAY, R., (1999), 'Poverty, Household Size and Child Welfare in India', mimeo, University of Tasmania.

_____, (2000), ' The Determinants of Child Labour and Child Schooling in Ghana', mimeo, University of Tasmania.

SYLWESTER, K., (2000), 'Income Inequality, Education Expenditures, and Growth', *Journal of Development Economics,* 63, pp. 379–98.

WORLD BANK, (2001), *World Development Indicators CD-Rom,* Washington DC: World Bank.

11. Choice Under Uncertainty
Simple Proof, Illustration, and
Use of Some Result

Pradip Maiti

INTRODUCTION

How people should behave in uncertain situations is an important issue
in almost all branches of economics. However, theoretical discussion
on choice under uncertainty in the standard textbooks leaves much to
be desired. The analysis is either quite involved or very brief and the
results are often obtained in a way that is not well motivated. As a result,
students in general seem to feel uncomfortable with the treatment of the
topic. The purpose of the present paper is quite humble, namely, to try
to discuss this topic lucidly and at the same time prove the results
rigorously. In fact, proof of the Expected Utility Theory, the standard
theory of individual choice under uncertainty, can be well motivated by
using some results in linear algebra. The paper goes along this line. The
claim is not that some hitherto unknown results are proved here, but
that an attempt has been made to simplify and motivate the proofs of
the main results in this area.

In our usual theory of consumer behaviour, the choice which a
consumer is supposed to exercise is a choice over bundles of goods
which are sure things, that is, so many pounds of bread, so many

Sanjit Bose, in whose honour this volume is published, is my teacher as well as
my colleague. He inspired me greatly to work in linear economic models using tools
of linear algebra. This is a small tribute to an economist who has always impressed
me as well as others with his originality in economic thinking.

kilograms of fish, etc. Some amount of uncertainty may exist there also as, for example, one may not be sure about the quality of fish one is buying; yet the choices result in *certain* outcomes. However, many important economic decisions concern choices whose *outcomes* are *uncertain* at the time the choice is made. Thus one has to choose from among alternatives where some or each of these alternatives may result in some uncertain outcome. Apparently, it might seem difficult to theorize such choices. Fortunately, such uncertain alternatives have a special structure or one can model it having a special structure, which may simplify the analysis of consumer's demand for these kinds of alternatives.

Let us start with an example. Consider an individual who possesses some wealth (say, W dollars). However, there is a likelihood that a part of it (say, L) may be stolen. Let π be the probability of the latter event. Suppose further that he consumes whatever wealth remains with him. Thus the consumer is facing two states—a good state, with probability $(1-\pi)$, where wealth/consumption (C_g) is equal to W, and a bad state, with probability π, with wealth as well as consumption (C_b) equal to $W - L$. Thus his initial endowment point is E (Figure 11.1). Suppose now that he wants to improve upon his condition in the bad state, that is, increase his consumption in the bad state, by buying some insurance from an insurance company. If the rate of premium per unit of insurance is r and he buys I units of insurance, he has to pay rI amount of premium, but receives an amount I in the bad state (that is, in the state in which the loss occurs) so that his consumption in good state would be $W - rI$, and his consumption in bad state would be $W - L + (1 - r)I$, that is, $W - rI + I - L$. Thus his post-insurance endowment point is F (Figure 11.1), where the amount of insurance bought is AE/r (or, equivalently $AF/(1- r)$). To summarize, his initial endowment is point E, that is, the vector (W, $W - L$) and, if he buys an insurance I, his endowment is given by the point F, that is, the vector, ($W - rI$, $W - L + (1 - r)I$). Obviously, his post-insurance endowment depends on the amount of insurance he buys (I) as well as the rate of premium (r). The line joining points E and F in Figure 11.1 may be extended to meet the horizontal axis at a point, say B. The line BQFE gives endowment points corresponding to different amounts of insurance which are available to the consumer and hence, is his budget line. The consumer has to decide on an amount of insurance, that is, to choose a point on this line. The question is: how does he choose a point from among all feasible endowment points?

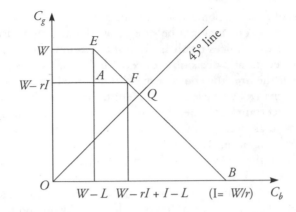

Figure 11.1: What is an Optimal Amount of Insurance?

This and numerous other cases involving uncertain outcomes are sought to be resolved through the Expected Utility Theory (EUT), the standard and the most popular theory of individual choice under uncertainty. The EUT, supposed to be the major paradigm in decision making since the Second World War, has been used prescriptively in management science (especially decision analysis), predictively in finance and economics, descriptively by psychologists, and has played a central role in theories of measurable utility (Schoemaker 1982: 529). The history of development of the EUT is quite interesting. When early mathematicians first formulated principles of behaviour in chance situations, they thought that the proper objective of a rational individual was to maximize expected money return. Thus, mathematicians such as Blaise Pascal and Pierre de Fermat assumed that if a gamble offers the pay-offs, say $(x_0, x_1, ..., x_N)$ with probabilities $(\pi(x_0), \pi(x_1), ..., \pi(x_N))$, a reasonable person, willing to enter the gamble, would pay anything up to its *expected value*, that is, $\bar{x} = x_0\pi(x_0) + x_1\pi(x_1) + ... + x_N\pi(x_N)$. However, it was later realized that the expected value is not the relevant criterion for choosing a gamble. This was demonstrated by Nicholas Bernoulli in 1728 through an example now known as the *St Petersburg Paradox*.

A fair coin is tossed repeatedly until a head is produced; if you enter the game, you receive \$2 if head comes up on the first toss, \$4 if it takes two tosses to land a head, \$8 if it takes three tosses—in short \$$2^n$ if it takes n tosses to land a head. The question is: what is the largest sure payment you would be willing to forgo in order to undertake a *single* play of this game? Note that the probability that a head appears first on the n-th toss is $1/2^n$. Therefore, this gamble offers a ½ chance of winning $2, a ¼ chance of winning $4 and so on, i.e. $1/2^n$ chance of winning 2^n. Since the expected value of this gamble is $\Sigma_{n=1}^{\infty}(2^n)(1/2^n)$, that is, infinite, it should be preferred to *any* finite sure gain. However, it is clear that few individuals would be willing to forgo more than a moderate amount for a one-shot play of the game. Even if we agree to limit the game to, say, at most 1000 tosses so that the expected value is $1000, many individuals will not be willing to pay more than $50 or $100 to play this game. Thus a typical individual's valuation of a gamble of this sort is much below its expected value.

This paradox was resolved independently by Gabriel Cramer and Nichola's cousin Daniel Bernoulli. Arguing that a gain of $200 was not necessarily 'worth' twice as much as a gain of $100, they hypothesized that rather than evaluating a gamble on the basis of its expected value, $\bar{x} = \Sigma x_i\, \pi(x_i)$, individuals will evaluate it on the basis of its *expected utility*: $\bar{u} = u(x_0).\pi(x_0) + u(x_1).\pi(x_1)+...+u(x_N).\pi_N$, which is calculated by weighting the *utility* of the i-th possible outcome $u(x_i)$ by its associated probability $\pi(x_i)$. The utility function, $u(x)$, which was proposed by Bernoulli was logarithmic, exhibiting diminishing increases in utility for equal increments in income. Bernoulli then proceeded to show that for a logarithmic function the game's expected utility, that is $\Sigma\{(1/2^n)(\log_e 2^n)\}$, is indeed finite (approximately equal to 0.346, Ingersoll Jr. 1987: 42)[1].

However, Bernoulli's theory is mostly a descriptive model since he addressed neither the issue of how to measure utility nor that of why his expectation principle would be rational. It was not until John von Neumann and Oscar Morgenstern (1944) that expected utility maximization was formally proved to be a rational decision criterion, that is, one derivable from several sensible axioms. Not only is von Neumann–Morgenstern (NM) utility theory quite different from what Bernoulli conceptualized, it is also more general in the sense that it is applicable to *any* type of outcomes of gambles, not merely monetary outcomes.

---

[1] Markowitz (1959: 207) gives another convincing argument against the expected return maxim from the field of portfolio selection. An investor who sought only to maximize the expected return would never prefer a diversified portfolio, since he would place all his funds in that security which had the highest expected return among all securities. Thus, if one considers diversification as a sound principle of investment, one must reject the objective of maximizing simply the expected return.

Specifically, the NM utility theory asserts that a few axioms about an individual's choice would guarantee the existence of a utility function yielding numerical utilities for different outcomes so that the expected utilities of different lotteries, when computed using these utility numbers, would preserve the individual's preference ordering over lotteries. Further, such a utility function is unique up to a positive linear transformation. All these results are derived in the following sections.

The plan of the paper is as follows. The second section introduces the basic structure of the theory along with the usual assumptions and definitions. The third secction states and proves the main theorem as well as a few lemmas and seeks to demonstrate some of these geometrically. The fourth section discusses briefly some important areas in economics in which EUT has been used extensively. Finally, the last section makes concluding observations.

THE BASIC STRUCTURE: DEFINITIONS, NOTATIONS, AND ASSUMPTIONS

To begin with, let us think of a basic set of 'prizes' or 'outcomes', χ, and a set of 'probability distributions' or 'lotteries', Δ, defined over the prizes in χ. The important point to note is that each lottery being a probability distribution may result in a number of possible outcomes and hence that, when one is choosing a lottery, one does not know which particular outcome of that lottery will materialize.

Lotteries, Simple and Compound, and Their Algebraic and Geometrical Representations

We shall assume that Δ consists of *probability distributions* that have a *finite* number of *outcomes*. We first give an example of a lottery and then go for a formal definition. Let $p = (\pi(x))$ denote a lottery in which the probability of receiving the outcome x is $\pi(x)$. Suppose that χ is the positive orthant in $\Re^3$ where $x = (\varepsilon_1, \varepsilon_2, \varepsilon_3) \in \chi$ represents ε_1 cans of beer, ε_2 pounds of bread, and ε_3 number of eggs. Consider two points $x_1 = (8, 2, 5)$ and $x_2 = (5, 4, 6)$ and a probability distribution $p = (\pi(x))$ representing 2/3rd chance of receiving x_1 and 1/3rd chance of receiving x_2. We say that the two points x_1 and x_2, which are a finite *subset* of χ, constitute a *support* of p in the sense that $\pi(x_1) = 2/3 > 0$,

$\pi(x_2)=1/3 > 0$, and $\pi(x_1) + \pi(x_2) = 1$. Let us now formally define a lottery—both a *simple* lottery as well as a *compound* lottery.

Simple Lottery

Definition 1: A simple lottery (that is, a simple probability distribution), $p = (\pi(x))$ defined on χ, where $\pi(x)$ gives the probability of receiving the prize x, is specified by

(a) a *finite* subset of χ, called the *support* of p and denoted by $\chi(p)$, and
(b) for each $x \in \chi(p)$, $\pi(x) > 0$ and $\Sigma_{x \in \chi(p)}\, \pi(x) = 1$.

The set of such simple lotteries on χ will be denoted by Δ.

Several points need to be noted in connection with this definition. *First*, the set of outcomes, $\chi = \{x\}$, over which a lottery is defined could be finite or even infinite[2] (as in the case of the previous example where it was the entire positive orthant of $\mathfrak{R}^3$). However, the number of outcomes of any given lottery is taken to be finite. *Second*, outcomes in χ need not be of the same form. For instance, one x could be a consumption bundle, another x a lottery itself, a third x a monetary pay-off, and so on. *Finally*, $\pi(x)$'s, the probabilities of receiving the different prizes in a lottery p, will be assumed to be *objectively* given (it may be pointed out that EUT has been demonstrated in the case in which $\pi(x)$'s are subjective probabilities; *see* Kreps 1992).

Geometrical Illustration

If χ is a finite set, a simple lottery can be represented as a point in the simplex of an appropriate dimension. For instance, lotteries yielding a maximum of three outcomes, x_0, x_1, and x_2, can be represented in a two-dimensional simplex—the triangle $e_{x_0}\, e_{x_1}\, e_{x_2}$—in Figure 11.2, where the probabilities of occurrence of the two outcomes x_1 and x_2 (that is $\pi(x_1)$ and $\pi(x_2)$) are measured on the two axes. Let the distance between a point e_{x_0} and another point e_{x_1} be denoted by $\vec{e}_{x_0}\, \vec{e}_{x_1}$. Now, let $\vec{e}_{x_0}\, \vec{e}_{x_1}$ and $\vec{e}_{x_0}\, \vec{e}_{x_2}$ each equal 1 and, let $e_{x_1}\, e_{x_2}$ be the straight line on which

---

[2] Mas-Colell et al. (1995:168) proves the EUT assuming a finite number of outcomes, but as Kreps (1992) argues, EUT could be demonstrated even with an infinite number of outcomes. We follow the latter.

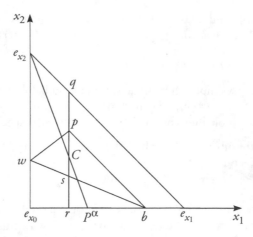

Figure 11.2:   Lotteries Depicted in a Probability Triangle

$\pi(x_1) + \pi(x_2) = 1$ so that distances $\vec{e}_{x_0}\,\vec{r}$ and $\vec{r}\,\vec{q}$ add up to unity. A point (such as p) inside the triangle represents a lottery, $p = (\pi(x_0), \pi(x_1), \pi(x_2))$, where the distances $\vec{e}_{x_0}\,\vec{r}$ and $\vec{r}\,\vec{p}$ equal respectively $\pi(x_1)$ and $\pi(x_2)$. However, as the $\pi(x)$'s sum up to unity, the distance $\vec{p}\,\vec{q}$ equals $\pi(x_0)$. A vertex, say e_{x_1}, is a simple lottery which yields the outcome x_1 as a certainty $(\pi(x_1)=1)$. Such simple lotteries may be called *degenerate lotteries*.[3] On the other hand, each interior point on the line $\vec{e}_{x_1}\,\vec{e}_{x_2}$ represents a lottery with its support consisting of x_1 and x_2 only.

Compound Lottery and its Simple Lottery Version

Once a simple lottery is defined, one may go for a more general variant, known as a *compound lottery*, whose outcomes are themselves simple lotteries.

To introduce this idea, take two simple lotteries $p = (\pi(x))$ and $s = (\sigma(x))$ with respective supports $\chi(p)$ and $\chi(s)$ and a number α between zero and one, inclusive. Consider now a compound lottery $\wp$

---

[3] Two other vertices, namely, the point e_{x_2} and the origin e_{x_0}, are the other two degenerate lotteries yielding respectively the outcome x_2 and x_0 as a certainty. In this context it may be pointed out that the use of the probability triangle such as the one depicted in Figure 11.2 goes back to Marschak (1950). However, Mark Machina popularized it in the 1980s to the extent that some would like to call this the 'Machina triangle' (Starmer 2000: 340, n. 12).

whose outcomes are p and s, occurring with the probabilities α and $(1-\alpha)$, respectively. To take an example, suppose p gives probabilities $\pi(x_0)$, $\pi(x_1)$ and $\pi(x_2)$ to the prizes x_0, x_1, and x_2, respectively and s gives probabilities $\sigma(x_1)$ and $\sigma(x_3)$ to the prizes x_1 and x_3, respectively (note that probabilities in a lottery add up to 1). Thus the *support* of the lottery p, $\chi(p) = \{x_0, x_1, x_2\}$ and similarly, $\chi(s) = \{x_1, x_3\}$. The compound lottery $\wp$, yielding the simple lottery p with probability α and the simple lottery s with the complementary probability $(1-\alpha)$, may, however, be *redefined* on the set of outcomes of simple lotteries, χ, whence it may be denoted by $C_{ps}^{\alpha} = (\gamma_{ps}^{\alpha}(x))$. The support of C_{ps}^{α} would be the set of outcomes $\{x_0, x_1, x_2, x_3\}$, that is, the *union* of $\chi(p)$ and $\chi(s)$. And the probabilities which it gives to these prizes are respectively, $\alpha\pi(x_0)$, $\alpha\pi(x_1) + (1-\alpha)\sigma(x_1)$, $\alpha\pi(x_2)$ and $(1-\alpha)\sigma(x_3)$. Such simple and compound lotteries are usually depicted as *chance nodes* (such as the one shown in Figure 11.3). Henceforth, without any confusion, we shall represent a compound lottery (such as $\wp$) by its simple lottery version defined on the *set of outcomes of simple lotteries* (that is, C_{ps}^{α}). Which version of a given compound lottery—whether its 'compound' version with lotteries as its different prizes or its 'simple' version with prizes defined on the set of outcomes of simple lotteries—is under discussion will be clear from the context. We now go for a formal definition below.

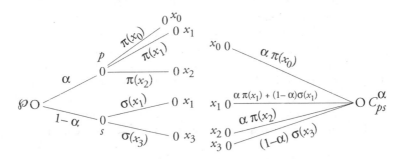

Figure 11.3: A Lottery Depicted by 'Chance Nodes'

Definition 2: A compound lottery yielding simple lotteries $p = (\pi(x))$ and $s = (\sigma(x))$ with probabilities α and $(1-\alpha)$, respectively —to be denoted by C_{ps}^{α}—is obtained in two steps:

(i) The support of C_{ps}^{α} is the union of supports of p and s [that is, $(C_{ps}^{\alpha}) = \chi(p) \cup \chi(s)$].

(ii)   The probability given by $C_{ps}^{\alpha} = (\gamma_{ps}^{\alpha}(x))$ to the outcome x is obtained as

$$\gamma_{ps}^{\alpha}(x) = \alpha\pi(x) + (1-\alpha)\sigma(x), \text{ for } x \in \chi(p) \cup \chi(s), \quad (11.1a)$$

where $\pi(x)$ is taken to be zero, if x is not in $\chi(p)$, and $\sigma(x)$ is taken to be zero, if x is not in $\chi(s)$.[4] Thus C_{ps}^{α} is, in fact, a convex combination of p and s:

$$C_{ps}^{\alpha} = \alpha p + (1-\alpha)s. \quad (11.1b)$$

where both p and s are to be defined on $\chi(p) \cup \chi(s)$ in the way specified above.

A few observations may be made now. First, a compound lottery may be generated by not merely two but *any* number of simple lotteries. Second, since we are considering lotteries with finite outcomes only, a simple lottery is nothing but a *vector* of probabilities of occurrence of different outcomes, and a compound lottery is nothing but a *convex combination* of two (or more) such vectors (that is, simple lotteries) in, say, an N-dimensional simplex, where the number of outcomes in the *support* of the compound lottery in question is $N + 1$. To demonstrate the point graphically, consider the two simple lotteries $p = (\pi(x))$ with the support $\{x_0, x_1, x_2\}$ and $r = (\rho(x))$ with the support $\{x_0, x_1\}$ in Figure 11.2. Now a compound lottery that yields p and r with probabilities α and $(1-\alpha)$ respectively is, in fact, a convex combination of p and r, and hence is given by the point C which lies on the line segment between p and r, where $\alpha = \vec{C}\,\vec{r}/\pi(x_2)$ and $(1-\alpha) = \vec{C}\,\vec{p}/\pi(x_2)$ (note that $\pi(x_2) = \vec{r}\,\vec{p}$). From the diagram it is clear that any compound lottery can be *represented* by (that is, *reduced*, so to say, to) a *unique* simple lottery.[5] This idea is used below to define a general compound lottery that has a number of simple lotteries as its different outcomes.

---

[4] Note that if we sum the above relation over all the x's in the support of C_{ps}^{α}, we get

$$\Sigma\gamma_{ps}^{\alpha}(x) = \alpha\Sigma\pi(x) + (1-\alpha)\Sigma\sigma(x) = \alpha\Sigma_{x \in \chi(p)}\pi(x) + (1-\alpha)\Sigma_{x \in \chi(s)}\sigma(x) = 1.$$

[5] However, the converse is not true, that is, a given simple lottery may be the simple lottery version of any one of a number of compound lotteries. This is clear from Figure 11.2 where, for instance, the point C can be expressed as a convex combination of *either* the three simple lotteries p, b, and w, or of the three degenerate lotteries e_{x_0}, e_{x_1}, and e_{x_2}, or even of a simple lottery e_{x_2} and a compound lottery p^{α}.

Definition 3:   Given a number of K simple lotteries, the k-th one being $p_k = (\pi_k(x)) \in \Delta$, a *compound lottery* which yields the simple lotteries p_1, p_2, ..., p_K with probabilities $\alpha_1, \alpha_2,..., \alpha_K$, respectively, is represented by $C = (\gamma(x)) \in \Delta$:

$$C = \sum_{k=1}^{K} \alpha_k p_k, \text{ (each } \alpha_k \geq \text{ and } \Sigma_{k=1}^{K} \alpha_k = 1), \qquad (11.2a)$$

where the support of C is the union of supports of p_K's [i.e. $\chi(C) = \chi(p_1) \cup \chi(p_2) ... \cup \chi(p_K)$] and the probability given by C to outcome x is obtained as[6]

$$\gamma(x) = \sum_{k=1}^{K} \alpha_k \pi_k(x), \text{ for } x \in \chi(C), \qquad (11.2b)$$

where $\pi_k(x)$ is taken to be zero, if x is not in $\chi(p_k)$.

Notations

We shall use the words 'outcome' and 'prize' interchangeably. Similarly, the words 'lottery', 'gamble', and 'probability distribution' will be used interchangeably. As noted in *Definition 1*, χ is the *set* of *outcomes* of simple lotteries and elements of χ will be denoted by x and z. All other lower-case letters p, q, r, s, b, w, etc., are used to denote simple lotteries in Δ. (Sometimes b and w will be used to denote the best and worst lottery, respectively.) A special class of simple lotteries is the set of *degenerate lotteries* (one for each outcome): e_x, which denotes a simple lottery yielding the outcome x for sure. In other words, e_x is a *unit vector* in Δ where 1 appears in the place corresponding to the outcome x.

The capital letters C and P will instead be used to represent (*simple lottery versions* of) compound lotteries and hence, will also belong to Δ. In particular, a compound lottery, which mixes a simple lottery $p = (\pi(x))$ with probability α and another simple lottery $s = (\sigma(x))$ with the complementary probability $(1 - \alpha)$, will be denoted by C_{ps}^{α} and is obtained as the *convex combination* of these two simple lotteries (with its component corresponding to x being equal to $\alpha \pi(x) + (1 - \alpha) \sigma(x)$):

---

[6] As in the case of *Definition 2*, here also the sum of $\gamma(x)$ over all $x \in \chi(C)$ can be shown to equal unity.

$$C_{ps}^{\alpha} = \alpha \, p + (1 - \alpha) \, s \qquad (11.3)$$

{for any $p, s \in \Delta$, and $\alpha \in [0, 1]$} C_{ps}^{α} will be called the α-*mixture* of p and s.

Since mixtures of two particular lotteries b and w will be needed frequently, we shall use a different notation for this. P^{α} will denote (the simple lottery version of) a compound lottery yielding the two lotteries b and w with probabilities α and $(1 - \alpha)$ respectively, and be called the α-*mixture* of b and w:

$$P^{\alpha} = \alpha b + (1 - \alpha) w, \text{ for any } \alpha \in [0, 1] \qquad (11.4)$$

Consequentialist Premise

We have observed earlier from Figure 11.2 that *different* compound lotteries may have the *same* simple lottery version.[7] Since compound lotteries having the same simple lottery version present exactly the same opportunity and since *any* compound lottery can always be reduced to a *unique* simple lottery version, it is not unreasonable to assume that an individual's perception of any lottery—simple or compound—depends only on its *simple* lottery *version* of receiving the prizes. Whether the probabilities ($\pi(x)$'s) of various prizes in χ arise as a result of a simple lottery C or of various compound lotteries having the same simple lottery version as C has no significance to him/her. And our premise is that although a decision maker may or may not regard all these lotteries as the same object, he/she may still view them as equivalent. This is sometimes called the *consequentialist premise* (Mas-Colell et al. 1995: 170) or *reduction of compound lotteries* (Varian 1992: 173).

Consequentialist Premise (C-premise): The decision maker is *indifferent* between a compound lottery and its corresponding simple lottery version, as well as among all compound lotteries having the same simple lottery version.

The above premise helps us to simplify our theoretical analysis, as one may assume, without any loss of generality, that the decision maker possesses a preference–indifference relation (denoted by $\succeq$) defined

[7] For instance, in Figure 11.2 a compound lottery yielding the three simple lotteries, b, w, and p, with probabilities ¼, ½, and ¼ respectively, and a compound lottery yielding simple lotteries p and s with equal probability, both have the *same simple* lottery version C.

over the space of simple lotteries (Δ) only—a relation in terms of which he or she can compare the different simple lotteries in the space Δ. Notations for this relation are clarified below:

Definition 4: Consider two lotteries p and r in the space Δ. Then we write:

$p \succeq r$: p is at least as good as, or *weakly preferred to*, r (Alternatively stated, the decision maker either *prefers* p to r, or is indifferent between p and r).

$p \succ r$: p is *strictly preferred* to r (i.e. $p \succeq r$ but not $r \succeq p$).

$p \sim r$: p is *indifferent* to r, that is, the decision maker is *indifferent* between p and r (which occurs when *both* $p \succeq r$ and $r \succeq p$).

Assumptions Underlying Preference–Indifference Relation

We state below the axioms that our preference–indifference relation $\succeq$ will be assumed to satisfy.[8]

(A1) *Completeness*: For any $p, r \in \Delta$, either $p \succeq r$, or $r \succeq p$, or both.

(A2) *Transitivity*: For any $p, r, s \in \Delta$, if $p \succeq r$, and $r \succeq s$, then $p \succeq s$.

(A3) *Continuity*: Given *any* $p, r, s \in \Delta$, partition the interval $[0,1]$ into the following two subsets: $B_{ps}(r) = \{\alpha \in [0, 1] | C_{ps}^{\alpha} \succeq r\}$, and $W_{ps}(r) = \{\alpha \in [0, 1] | r \succeq C_{ps}^{\alpha}\}$.

Each of these subsets is a closed set.

The first axiom requires that the decision maker is able to compare *any two* lotteries. While the axiom of transitivity is clear, that of 'continuity' in effect means that small changes in probabilities do not change the nature of the ordering between two lotteries.[9]

---

[8] Note that the lotteries p, r, or s may not have the same outcomes. However, C_{ps}^{α} or C_{rs}^{α} can be defined in the way spelt out in *Definition 2* or *Definition 3*.

[9] Given any $p = (\pi(x))$ and $s = (\sigma(x))$, and $\alpha \in [0, 1]$, consider compound lotteries: $C_{ps}^{\alpha} = \alpha p + (1-\alpha)s$. Our assumption of completeness (A1) implies that the decision maker can compare each lottery in this series with a third lottery r. Consider α's in the $[0, 1]$ interval and partition this interval into two subsets— to be called the better subset $B_{ps}(r)$ and the worse subset $W_{ps}(r)$—such that for the value of α in the better subset, we have $C_{ps}^{\alpha} \succeq r$, while α in the worse subset yields

(A4)   *Independence*: Consider two lotteries p, $r \in \Delta$. Take *any* α from the open interval $(0,1)$, and *any* other lottery $s \in \Delta$. Then $p \succeq r$, if and only if, $C_{ps}^{\alpha} \succeq C_{rs}^{\alpha}$.

The axiom of independence implies that if two lotteries p and r are each mixed with a third lottery s in such a way that in each of the resulting mixtures the consumer gets p with the same probability (say, α), then, because of this same part, the consumer's ordering of the two mixtures is *independent* of the particular third lottery used, and depends only on the ordering of p and r. Note that the usual theory of consumer behaviour may violate such an assumption.[10] Thus this axiom may appear to be quite restrictive. However, it is very crucial for many of the results in this area.

To simplify proof and demonstration of the expected utility theorem, we also introduce an additional assumption. We assume that Δ contains a *best* lottery b and a *worst* lottery w so that the decision maker weakly prefers b to *any* other lottery p in Δ, and also, *any* p to w. Obviously, if the decision maker were indifferent between b and w, that would imply his/her indifference among all the available lotteries. To rule out such a trivial case, we assume that $b \succ w$. We formalize these assumptions as follows:

(A5)   *Existence of best and worst lotteries*: There exist lotteries b and w in Δ such that $b \succ w$, and $b \succeq p \succeq w$, for any lottery $p \in \Delta$.

$r \succeq C_{ps}^{\alpha}$. The assumption of continuity stipulates that these two subsets are closed. In economic terms, the axiom of continuity states that an individual's preference ordering is continuous with regard to probability distributions; namely, that if we take a sequence of α_i's in $[0, 1]$ converging to α^* and if each $C_{ps}^{\alpha_i} \succeq r$, then we also have $C_{ps}^{\alpha^*} \succeq r$, that is, α^* also belongs to $B_{ps}(r)$; and similarly, if $\lim_{i \to \infty} \alpha_i = \alpha_0$ and each $\alpha_i \in W_{ps}(r)$, then $\alpha_0 = \in W_{ps}(r)$ as well (Herstein and Milnor 1953: 293). Now, the probability of the outcome x in C_{ps}^{α} equals $\alpha\pi(x) + (1-\alpha)\sigma(x)$. By varying α marginally we get lotteries in the series $\{C_{ps}^{\alpha}\}$ in which the probabilities of any given outcome change marginally. 'Continuity' means that such small changes in probabilities would not alter the ranking of C_{ps}^{α}'s vis-à-vis r.

[10]   A standard example is that a consumer may prefer coffee to tea, if each is served with milk, but may have the opposite preference, if milk is not added.

EXPECTED UTILITY THEOREM

In the standard theory of consumer behaviour it is assumed that the consumer is able to rank, in terms of preferences, different consumption bundles and that he chooses the most preferred bundle. Choices of this kind are axiomatized by assuming that ordinal numbers can be assigned to the various bundles, or to put it formally, that the consumer possesses a (*continuous*) *utility function* defined on the space of consumption bundles and that he chooses a bundle, which maximizes this utility function subject to a budget constraint. The theory of decision making under uncertainty rests on the assumption that a consumer's belief about uncertainty can be formulated in terms of probabilities and that his problem can be posed as one of choosing from among alternative probability distributions, that is, lotteries (each defined over a set of pay-offs or outcomes). Obviously, the consumer is assumed to possess a preference ranking over these probability distributions or lotteries and the theory builds up a system of assigning utility numbers to these different lotteries in a manner such that a consumer's preference ranking over such lotteries is preserved. In other words, the higher the utility number assigned to a lottery, the more preferred that lottery is to the consumer. Finally, the rational rule of behaviour is established as one of choosing that lottery, which has the highest measurable utility associated with it.

The structure we have stated above verbally constitutes the basic part of the path-breaking result in this area, namely, the *von Neumann–Morgenstern Utility Theorem*. Of course, as we shall see later, the theorem says much more than this. We now state and prove a few lemmas before we prove the main theorem.

A Few Lemmas and Geometrical Illustrations

Lemma 1: Let the preference–indifference relation $\succeq$ satisfy the Independence Axiom (A4).

Consider two lotteries p and $r \in \Delta$. Let α be any number from the open interval $(0, 1)$, and q be *any* other lottery from Δ. Then,

(a) $p \sim r$, if and only if, $C_{pq}^{\alpha} \sim C_{rq}^{\alpha}$,

(b) $p \succ r$, if and only if, $C_{pq}^{\alpha} \succ C_{rq}^{\alpha}$,

where the symbol $\succ$ signifies strictly preferred to.

Proof: (a) It is enough to prove the 'only if' part. Suppose that $p \sim r$. This implies that we have both (i) $p \succeq r$ as well as (ii) $r \succeq p$. The Independence Axiom then yields that for *any* $q \in \Delta$ and any $\alpha \in (0, 1)$, we have both (i) $C_{pq}^\alpha \succeq C_{rq}^\alpha$ and (ii) $C_{rq}^\alpha \succeq C_{pq}^\alpha$, and hence that $C_{pq}^\alpha \sim C_{rq}^\alpha$. (Recall that C_{pq}^α is the α-mixture of p and q.)

(b) To prove the 'only if' part, suppose that $p \succ r$. By definition, this implies that (i) $p \succeq r$ holds, but (ii) $p \sim r$ does not hold. Take now any $q \in \Delta$ and any $\alpha \in (0, 1)$. In view of the Independence Axiom, (i) implies that $C_{pq}^\alpha \succeq C_{rq}^\alpha$ holds, but in view of result (a) above, (ii) implies that $C_{pq}^\alpha \sim C_{rq}^\alpha$ does not hold (since, otherwise $p \sim r$, contradicting the given hypothesis). These two relations then imply that $C_{pq}^\alpha \succ C_{rq}^\alpha$. The converse may be proved in a similar way.

Corollary 1.1:

(a) $p \succ r$ implies that $p \succ C_{pr}^\alpha \succ r$, for any $\alpha \in (0, 1)$.

(b) Take a compound lottery $C = \Sigma_{k=1}^K \alpha_k\, p_k$, as defined in (3), and a simple lottery p. Then,

$$p \succ C \Rightarrow p \succ \lambda p + (1 - \lambda)C \succ C, \quad \text{for any } \lambda \in (0, 1)$$

Proof: It is enough to show (a). By definition, $C_{pr}^\alpha = \alpha p + (1 - \alpha)r$. Hence, we may write $p = (1 - \alpha)p + \alpha p = C_{pp}^{1-\alpha}$ and $r = \alpha r + (1 - \alpha)r = C_{rr}^\alpha$. Further, note that $C_{rp}^{1-\alpha} = (1 - \alpha)r + \alpha p$. Since $p \succ r$, we have now, by the Independence Axiom, $C_{pp}^{1-\alpha} \succ C_{rp}^{1-\alpha}$ (that is $p \succ C_{pr}^\alpha$) and $C_{pr}^\alpha \succ C_{rr}^\alpha$ (that is, $C_{pr}^\alpha \succ r$).

Corollary 1.2:   Consider a number of pairs of simple lotteries, (p_1, r_1), (p_2, r_2), ..., (p_K, r_K) such that $p_K \sim r_K$ for each pair k. For *any* set of non-negative α_k's satisfying $\Sigma_{k=1}^K \alpha_k = 1$, we then have,[11] $\Sigma_{k=1}^K \alpha_k\, p_k \sim \Sigma_{k=1}^K \alpha_k\, r_k$.

Remark 1: One interesting implication of *Lemma 1*(a) is noted below. With α varying between 0 and 1, C_{pr}^{α} represents the line segment between the two points p and r in the simplex of an appropriate dimension (e.g., Figure 11.2 for the case of three outcomes). *Lemma 1*(a) states that the two lotteries p and r are equally attractive, if and only if, all the lotteries on the line segment between p and r are equally attractive. This implies that an indifference curve giving the locus of lotteries, among which the decision maker is indifferent, is a straight line (in the case of three outcomes) and is a hyperplane, in general (when the number of outcomes exceeds three).

Lemma 2: Let P^{α} denote the simple lottery version of a compound lottery which mixes two simple lotteries b and w, with probabilities α and $(1-\alpha)$: $P^{\alpha} = \alpha b + (1-\alpha)w$. Suppose $b \succ w$, and suppose we take any $\alpha, \beta \in (0,1)$; then $P^{\alpha} \succ P^{\beta}$, if and only if, $\alpha > \beta$.

Proof: (a) To prove the 'if' part, observe that, by hypothesis, $b \succ w$, and by difinition, $P^{\beta} = \beta b + (1-\beta)w$. *Corollary 1.1* (a) ensures that $b \succ P^{\beta}$, whence *Corollary 1.1*(b) asserts that

(i) $\lambda b + (1-\lambda)P^{\beta} \succ P^{\beta}$, for any $\lambda \varepsilon (0,1)$.

(ii) Next observe that $\alpha > \beta$ implies that $P^{\alpha} > P^{\beta}$.

---

[11] The proof is by the method of induction. Obviously, the result holds for two pairs, since the repeated use of *Lemma 1*(a) yields that for any $\alpha \in [0,1]$, $\alpha p_1 + (1-\alpha)p_2 \sim \alpha r_1 + (1-\alpha)p_2 \sim \alpha r_1 + (1-\alpha)r_2$. Suppose now that it holds for m pairs, that is, $\Sigma_{k=1}^{m} \tilde{\alpha}_k p_k \sim \Sigma_{k=1}^{m} \tilde{\alpha}_k r_k$ (with $\tilde{\alpha}_k \geq 0$, and $\Sigma_{k=1}^{m} \tilde{\alpha}_k = 1$). If now, $p_{m+1} \sim r_{m+1}$, we get $\lambda \Sigma_{k=1}^{m} \tilde{\alpha}_k p_k + (1-\lambda)p_{m+1} \sim \lambda \Sigma_{k=1}^{m} \tilde{\alpha}_k r_k + (1-\lambda)p_{m+1} \sim \lambda \Sigma_{k=1}^{m} \tilde{\alpha}_k r_k + (1-\lambda)r_{m+1}$, for any $\lambda \in [0,1]$. The required result follows, if we set $\alpha_k = \lambda \tilde{\alpha}_k$, for each $k \leq m$ and $\alpha_{m+1} = 1-\lambda$. (Note that $\Sigma_{k=1}^{m+1} \alpha_k = \lambda \Sigma_{k=1}^{m} \tilde{\alpha}_k + 1-\lambda = \lambda + 1 - \lambda = 1$.)

This follows from (i), if we take $\lambda = (\alpha - \beta)/(1 - \beta)$. In this case, the LHS of (i) equals

$$[(\alpha - \beta)/(1 - \beta)]b + [(1 - \alpha)/(1 - \beta)]P^\beta$$
$$= [(\alpha - \beta)/(1 - \beta)]b + [(1 - \alpha)/(1 - \beta)][\beta b + (1 - \beta)w]$$
$$= [\{(\alpha - \beta) + \beta(1 - \alpha)\}/(1 - \beta)]b + (1 - \alpha)w$$
$$= \alpha b + (1 - \alpha)w$$
$$= P^\alpha \quad \text{(by the definition of } P^\alpha).$$

(b) To prove the 'only if' part, suppose $P^\alpha \succ P^\beta$, but $\beta \geq \alpha$. If $\beta = \alpha$, then $P^\alpha \backsim P^\beta$, contradicting the hypothesis. Assume then $\beta > \alpha$. However, proceeding as in (a) above, we would then obtain $P^\beta \succ P^\alpha$, which once again contradicts the given hypothesis.

Remark 2: Note that *Lemma 2* holds for *any* two lotteries b and w (not necessarily the best and the worst lotteries). The only condition is that $b \succ w$. The result may be demonstrated graphically. The distance of the line segment joining the lotteries (that is, the vectors) b and w in the two-dimensional simplex (say, in Figure 11.2), $| b - w |$, is positive, since b and w are different lotteries. This distance may be normalized to equal 1. (See Figure 11.4 below where the points labelled w and b may be taken to correspond to value 0 and 1, respectively.)

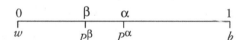

Figure 11.4: Distances Measuring Values of Lotteries

Consider now compound lotteries, each being a convex combination of the two lotteries b and w. Take one such lottery P^α, the α-*mixture*, which attaches a weight of α to b (and the complementary weight $(1 - \alpha)$ to w). P^α is then located at a distance of α from w. Since $b \succ w$, *Corollary 1.1*(a) asserts that $b \succ P^\alpha \succ w$. Now consider a second mixture P^β, which is a β-*mixture* of the same two lotteries and hence, is located at a distance of β from w. The lemma says that the α-*mixture* will be preferred *to* the β-*mixture*, if and only if, $\alpha > \beta$. As Figure 11.4 shows, when $1 > \alpha > \beta$, P^α can also be expressed as a mixture of b and P^β. In view of the fact that $b \succ P^\beta$, *Corollary 1.1*(b) then asserts that

$P^\alpha \succ P^\beta$. Thus one strictly prefers that compound lottery which has a higher probability of winning the better lottery, b.

Lemma 3: Suppose, $b \succeq p \succeq w$, for a lottery $p \in \Delta$. Then there exists a *unique* number $\alpha_p \in [0, 1]$ such that the decision maker is indifferent between p and the α_p-*mixture* of b and w:

$$p \sim P^{\alpha_p} \quad [\text{where } P^{\alpha_p} = \alpha_p b + (1 - \alpha_p)w].$$

Proof: First observe that if $p \sim b$ or $p \sim w$, the lemma holds trivially, since $\alpha_p = 1$, and $\alpha_p = 0$, will yield the required result in the two cases, respectively. Hence we consider a lottery p for which $b \succ p \succ w$. Recall that p^α stands for the α-*mixture* of b and w. We now try to partition the closed interval $[0, 1]$ into *two* sets of α's. One set—to be called the *better set*, $B(p)$—is such that for each α in that set the corresponding α-*mixture* is weakly preferred to the given p. On the other hand, for each α in the other set—called the *worse set*, $W(p)$—the given p is weakly preferred to the corresponding α-*mixture*. Thus we have

$$B(p) = \{\alpha \text{ in } [0, 1] \ni P^\alpha \succeq p\},$$

$$W(p) = \{\alpha \text{ in } [0, 1] \ni p \succeq P^\alpha\}. \quad [\text{where } P^\alpha = \alpha b + (1 - \alpha)w]$$

What we shall show is that $B(p) \cap W(p)$ contains *one and only one number*, say α_p.

(a) First observe that both $B(p)$ and $W(p)$ are closed (in view of the continuity Assumption $A(4)$) and, non-empty (since $1 \ \varepsilon \ B(p)$ and, $0 \ \varepsilon \ W(p)$).

(b) By the completeness property of the relation $\succeq$, any α in $[0, 1]$ belongs to at least one of the two sets, $B(p)$ and $W(p)$.

(c) Since $[0, 1]$ is connected and both $B(p)$ and $W(p)$ are non-empty and closed, they have a non-empty intersection, that is, there is some α, say α_p, which belongs to both the sets. Thus we have both $p \succeq P^{\alpha_p}$ and $P^{\alpha_p} \succeq p$ and hence, $p \sim P^{\alpha_p}$.

(d) To prove the uniqueness of α_p, suppose that $B(p) \cap W(p)$ contains two different α's say α_p and $\tilde{\alpha}_p$. The preceding argument would then yield both (i) $p \sim P^{\alpha_p}$ and (ii) $p \sim P^{\tilde{\alpha}_p}$. However, if they were different, one must be larger, say $\alpha_p > \tilde{\alpha}_p$. But then we have, by *Lemma 2*, $P^{\alpha_p} \succ P^{\tilde{\alpha}_p}$, yielding a contradiction to (i) and (ii) which state that the decision maker is indifferent between each mixture and p. Hence, there is a *single* intersection point of $B(p)$ and $W(p)$.

Corollary 3.1:   As in the case of *Lemma 2*, in the present case also the result holds good for *any* two lotteries b and w, provided $b \succ w$. However, if we assume (A5) and assume further that b and w are respectively the *best* and the *worst* lottery in Δ, then for every degenerate lottery e_x yielding outcome x as a certainty ($x \in \chi$) we have, $b \succeq e_x \succeq w$. The present lemma then asserts that for each such x, there exists a unique number $u(x) \in [0, 1]$ such that[12]

$$e_x \sim P^{u(x)} \quad [\text{where } P^{u(x)} = u(x)b + (1 - u(x))w]. \tag{11.5}$$

Note that $P^{u(x)}$ here is the compound lottery mixing the *best* lottery b with the probability $u(x)$ and the *worst* lottery w with the probability $1 - u(x)$. It may, therefore, be called the $u(x)$-*mixture* of the *best* and the *worst* lottery. (Note that the support of this compound lottery is the union of the supports of b and w: $\chi(P) = \chi(b) \cup \chi(w)$.)

Corollary 3.2:   For the $u(x)$ defined in (11.5), an individual is *indifferent* between a lottery $p = (\pi(x)) \in \Delta$ and the $\Sigma u(x)\pi(x)$-*mixture* of the *best* and the *worst* lottery.[13]

---

[12] By Lemma 3, for each $e_x \in \Delta$, there is a *unique* number $\alpha_{e_x} \in [0, 1]$ such that $e_x \sim \alpha_{e_x} b + (1 - \alpha_{e_x})w$. Setting $u(x) = \alpha_{e_x}$, we get the required result.

[13] Take a lottery $p = (\pi(x)) \in \Delta$. For each $x \in \chi(p)$, consider the degenerate lottery e_x. Consider now a compound lottery yielding each such degenerate lottery e_x with probability $\pi(x)$. The simple lottery version of this compound lottery is $\Sigma \pi(x)e_x$ (for this expression and the ones below, the sum considered is over all outcomes $x \in \chi(p)$). In view of the *C-premise*, we have

$p \sim \Sigma \pi(x)e_x$

$\quad \sim \Sigma \pi(x)\{u(x)b + [1 - u(x)]w\}$

$\qquad$ {by *Corollary 1.2* and relation (11.5), where $u(x) \in [0, 1]$}

$\quad \sim [\Sigma u(x)\pi(x)]b + [1 - \Sigma u(x)\pi(x)]w$.

The last equivalence follows from the *C-premise* and the fact that $\Sigma \pi(x) - \Sigma \pi(x)u(x) = 1 - \Sigma u(x)\pi(x)$. Further, note that $\Sigma u(x)\pi(x) \in [0, 1]$, as it is a weighted average of the $u(x)$'s and each $u(x) \in [0, 1]$.

$$p - \left[\sum u(x)\pi(x) \right] b + \left[\sum 1 - \Sigma u(x)\pi(x) \right] w, \qquad (11.6)$$

[the sum being over all $x \in \chi(p)$].

Remark 3: (Utility of a Prize and Utility of a Lottery) As the result (11.5) shows, the consumer is indifferent between an outcome x and the $u(x)$-*mixture* of the *best* and the *worst* lottery. The number $u(x)$ may be interpreted as a level of utility an individual obtains from the outcome x.

Similarly, α_p, defined in this lemma, may be interpreted as a level of utility an individual receives from the lottery $p = (\pi(x))$. To make this point self-explanatory, we shall use a different notation,[14] namely $v(p)$, to indicate the *value* or the *level of utility* obtained from the lottery p. The remarkable result demonstrated in *Corollary 3.2* is that this $v(p)$ (that is, α_p) can be expressed as a *weighted average* of the utility number $u(x)$'s assigned to the different outcomes, where the weights are the probabilities with which the different outcomes occur in the lottery:

$$(\alpha_p \equiv) v(p) = \sum u(x)\pi(x), \qquad (11.7)$$

where $p = (\pi(x))$ and the sum is over all $x \in \chi(p)$.

It is the most important result in the theory of choice under uncertainty and known as the von Neumann–Morgenstern expected utility representation.[15] This result states that if the decision maker's preferences over lotteries satisfy the continuity and independence axioms, such preferences are representable by a utility function with the expected utility form. We state and prove the result below.

Expected Utility Theorem (EUT)

(a) Suppose that the preference–indifference relation $\succeq$ defined on the space of simple lotteries Δ satisfies assumptions (A1) – (A4). Then

---

[14] Mas-Colell et al (1995) use two different notations namely $u(\cdot)$ and $U(\cdot)$ to distinguish levels of utility obtainable from an outcome and a lottery, respectively. We are using the notation $v(\cdot)$ for the latter.

[15] It may be noted that although one of the original modern developments of this theory appears in von Neumann and Morgenstern's *Theory of Games and Economic Behaviour*, the form goes back a good deal earlier to Daniel Bernoulli (Kreps 1992: 76).

$\succeq$ admits a utility representation of the expected utility form, that is, we can assign a number $u(x)$ to each outcome $x \in \chi$ in such a manner that for *any two* lotteries $p = (\pi(x))$, $r = (\rho(x)) \in \Delta$, we have[16]

$$p \succ r, \text{ if and only if, } \sum_{x \in \chi(p)} u(x)\pi(x) > \sum_{x \in \chi(r)} u(x)\rho(x). \quad (11.8)$$

(b) Moreover, if $\{u(\cdot)\}$ provides a representation of $\succeq$ in this sense, then so does a measure $\{\delta u(\cdot) + \theta\}$ where δ is *any positive* number and θ is *any* number. Further, if $\{u(\cdot)\}$ and $\{\tilde{u}(\cdot)\}$ provide a representation of $\succeq$ in this sense, then constants $\delta > 0$ and θ exist such that $\tilde{u}(\cdot) = \delta u(\cdot) + \theta$.

Proof: (a) The relation (11.6) states that for the lottery $p = (\pi(x)) \in \Delta$, we have $p \sim P^{\Sigma u(x)\pi(x)}$,

[where $P^{\Sigma u(x)\pi(x)} = \{\Sigma u(x)\pi(x)\}b + \{(1 - \Sigma u(x)\pi(x))\}w]$,

where $\Sigma u(x)\pi(x) \in [0, 1]$, the sum being over all $x \in \chi(p)$. Similarly, for the lottery $r = (\rho(x)) \in \Delta$, we have $\Sigma u(x)\rho(x) \in [0, 1]$, the sum being over all $x \in \chi(r)$ such that $r \sim P^{\Sigma u(x)\rho(x)}$ [where $P^{\Sigma u(x)\rho(x)} = \{\Sigma u(x)\rho(x)\}b + \{1 - \Sigma u(x) \rho(x)\}w]$. Further, *Lemma 3* asserts that the number $\Sigma u(x)\pi(x)$ (in case of p), or the number $\Sigma u(x)\rho(x)$ (in case of r) is *unique*. Now suppose,

$$p \succ r, \text{ that is, } P^{\Sigma u(x)\pi(x)} \succ P^{\Sigma u(x)\rho(x)}.$$

Lemma 2 then asserts that the above result holds, if and only if, $\Sigma u(x)\pi(x) > \Sigma u(x)\rho(x)$.

(b) Since the first part of the assertion is obvious,[17] we prove the second part. Let us note that *Corollary 3.1* asserts that for each $x \in \chi$, there exists a $u(x) \in [0, 1]$ such that $e_x \sim P^{u(x)}$,

---

[16] The converse is also true, namely that if $\succeq$ admits a utility representation of the expected utility form in the sense of (11.8), it satisfies properties (A1) – (A4) (Kreps 1992: 76). The proof is not difficult, but omitted here.

[17] Suppose $\{u(\cdot)\}$ provides an *expected utility* representation of the given preferences $\succeq$. This means then $p \succ r$, if and only if, $\Sigma u(x)\pi(x) > \Sigma u(x)\rho(x)$, that is, if and only if, $\delta\Sigma u(x)\pi(x) + \theta > \delta\Sigma u(x)\rho(x) + \theta$, that is, if and only if, $\Sigma \tilde{u}(x)\pi(x) > \Sigma \tilde{u}(x)\rho(x)$, for any measure $\tilde{u}(\cdot) = \delta u(\cdot) + \theta$, where δ is *any positive* number and θ is *any* number.

where $P^{u(x)}(=(\gamma(z)))$, say) is the $u(x)$-*mixture* of the *best* and the *worst* lottery, $b = (\beta(z))$ and $w = (\omega(z))$:

(i) $P^{u(x)} = u(x)b + (1-u(x))w$.

The z-th component of this mixture is given by

(ii) $\gamma(z) = u(x)\beta(z) + (1-u(x))\omega(z)$, [each $z \in \chi(P)$, where $\chi(P) = \chi(b) \cup \chi(w)$].

Suppose now $\{\tilde{u}(\cdot)\}$ also provides an expected utility representation of the same preferences, so that the *values* of lotteries, $b = (\beta(z)) \in \Delta$ and $w = (\omega(z)) \in \Delta$, are given by $\tilde{v}(b)$ $= \Sigma_{z \in \chi(b)} \tilde{u}(z)\beta(z)$ and $\tilde{v}(w) = \Sigma_{z \in \chi(w)} \tilde{u}(z)\omega(z)$, respectively. Since we already have $e_x \sim P^{u(x)}$, the new measure should also represent this equivalence for each $x \in \chi$. Thus, using the measure $\{\tilde{u}(\cdot)\}$, we get

$\tilde{u}(x) =$ the value of $x =$ value of $e_x =$ the value of $P^{u(x)}$

[since $e_x \sim P^{u(x)}$]

$= \Sigma\tilde{u}(z)\gamma(z)$, [since $\{\tilde{u}(\cdot)\}$ is of the *expected utility* form ; the sum is over all $z \in \chi(P)$]

$= \Sigma\tilde{u}(z)\{u(x)\beta(z) + (1-u(x))\omega(z)\}$,

[using (ii) above]

$= u(x)\{\Sigma\tilde{u}(z)\beta(z)\} + (1-u(x))\{\Sigma\tilde{u}(z)\omega(z)\}$

$= u(x)\tilde{v}(b) + (1-u(x))\tilde{v}(w) = [\tilde{v}(b) - \tilde{v}(w)]u(x) + \tilde{v}(w)$

$= \delta u(x) + \theta$, [where $\delta \equiv \tilde{v}(b) - \tilde{v}(w) > 0$,

(since $b \succ w$) and $\theta \equiv \tilde{v}(w)$].[18]

---

[18] The utility function referred to in the theorem is usually called a von Neumann–Morgenstern (NM) utility function, after its originators. The relation $\tilde{u}(\cdot) = \delta u(\cdot) + \theta$ (for $\delta > 0$) is called an increasing affine transformation of $u(\cdot)$. There is an interesting implication of this result, namely that a von Neumann–Morgenstern utility function is a 'cardinal' measure. That is, unlike ordinal utility the numerical value of utility has a precise meaning (up to a scaling) beyond the simple rank of the numbers. This can be easily demonstrated as follows. Suppose χ consists of the three outcomes: $x_0 = 0$, $x_1 = 4$, and $x_2 = 9$. Consider a lottery p which pays x_0 and x_2 with equal probability and a degenerate lottery e_1 which pays x_1 with certainty. Under the utility function $u(x) = x$, the expected utilities of p and e_1 are respectively, $v(p) = (1/2) \{u(x_0) + u(x_2)\} = (1/2)(x_0 + x_2) = (1/2).9 = 4.5$ and $v(e_1) = x_1 = 4$ and hence, $p \succ e_1$.

Implication, Amplification, and Illustration of EUT

Before we proceed further let us try to understand the importance of the result contained in the above theorem. The theorem seeks to establish the existence of a numerical representation for preferences on Δ. That is, it shows that the assumptions (A1)–(A4) guarantee that there exists a function v: $\Delta \rightarrow \Re$ ($\Re$ being the real line) such that $p \succ q$ if and only if $v(p) \geq v(q)$. The theorem, however, establishes a good deal more, since it asserts that one can construct a real-valued function on χ, that is, assign a utility level $u(x)$ to each possible prize $x \in \chi$ such that this function v can be shown to take the form of expected utility of prizes: $v(p) = \Sigma u(x) \pi(x)$. In other words, it is possible to get a set[19] of *real numbers* $\{u(x)\text{'s}\}$ for the different prizes—which may be interpreted as utility levels yielded by these prizes—so that each probability distribution p can be drawn over the real line and the *expected value* of this distribution then measures the *utility* from the lottery p, that is, $v(p)$.

The above result can be demonstrated conveniently in a diagram for a lottery having, say, five outcomes, x_0 to x_4; utility numbers assigned to these outcomes are as shown in the Figure 11.5. A lottery $p = (.3, .1, .1, .3, .2)$ is drawn as a probability distribution on the real line measuring the utility numbers of outcomes. The value of the lottery $v(p)$ is given by the *expected value* of the distribution, namely, 0.4.

There are many advantages of the EUT. One advantage is its *analytic simplicity.* To compare two lotteries, one has just to compare the means, that is, the expected values, of the two probability distributions. This simplicity probably accounts for its pervasive use in economics. It is easy to work with, and difficult to do without, expected utility. The other advantage is *normative.* Expected utility may provide a valuable guide to action. People often find it hard to think systematically about risky alternatives. But if an individual believes that his choices should satisfy the axioms on which the theorem is based (notably, the independence axiom), the theorem can be used as a guide in his

---

However, if we apply the increasing transformation $\tilde{u}(x) = \sqrt{x}$, then under $\tilde{u}(\cdot)$, the expected utility of lottery p is $\tilde{v}(p) = \frac{1}{2}\{\sqrt{\tilde{u}(x_0)} + \sqrt{\tilde{u}(x_2)}\} = 3/2$, and that of the lottery e_1 is $\tilde{v}(e_1) = \sqrt{x_1} = 2$, so that $e_1 \succ p$. This shows that arbitrary monotone transformations of the NM utility function do not preserve ordering over lotteries.

[19] In fact, as the result (b) of the theorem demonstrates, an infinite *number* of such *sets* of real numbers like $\{u_i\}$, $\{\tilde{u}_i\}$, etc., can be obtained. However, there is at least one set of u_i's in which each $u_i \in [0, 1]$.

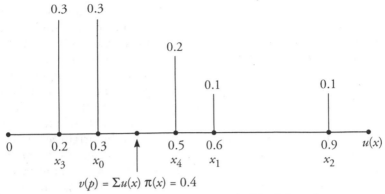

Figure 11.5: A Lottery Drawn on the Line Measuring
Utilities of Different Outcomes

decision-making process. A *third* feature is that it is not required that outcomes of lotteries be expressed in nominal values or be of the same dimension. As indicated in the section on algebraic and geometric representation of simple and compound lotteries, outcomes (x's) of a lottery could be of different forms. One outcome (say x_0) may be a consumption bundle, another, a monetary pay-off, a third, a physical capital, and so on. By assigning utilities, that is numbers $u(x)$'s, EUT translates the different types of outcomes onto the real line—the *real line* on which the different lotteries (that is, probability distributions) can be redefined. A comparison of these lotteries may then be facilitated by considering one or two moments of these distributions. What the EUT does is to rank these lotteries by considering their first moment (that is, expectation) only. Thus the most specific implication of the EUT stems from its form or the *preference function*: $u(x_0).\pi(x_0) + u(x_1).\pi(x_1) + ... + u(x_N).\pi(x_N)$, which is linear in the probabilities. Once the origin and the unit of the utility scale are chosen, utility numbers of different outcomes $u(x)$'s get fixed and hence the expected utility $\Sigma u(x)\pi(x)$ of a lottery $p = (\pi(x))$ is linear in the $p(x)$'s. The implication is that an indifference curve or iso-(expected) utility curve, being the locus of lotteries yielding a given level of utility, is a hyperplane.

The indifference curves as well as utility levels of various lotteries can be shown graphically in the case of three outcomes. With a finite number of outcomes, one of the prizes would be the best prize and one, the worst, in the sense that for *any* $x \in \chi$, the former $\succeq x$ and $x \succeq$ the latter. Given the result (b) of the EUT, there are two degrees of freedom in the choice of a utility function here. Hence, the origin and the unit of the utility scale may be set arbitrarily. Suppose, x_0 is the worst outcome and x_1, the best. Let us fix $u(x_0) = 0$ and $u(x_1) = 1$, or equivalently, $v(e_{x_0}) = 0$ and $v(e_{x_1}) = 1$. The utility of outcome x_2, or for that matter, of any lottery, will then lie between 0 and 1, that is, on the line segment between the points labelled $u(x_0)$ and $u(x_1)$ in Figure 11.6 (which replicates Figure 11.2). However, its horizontal axis is used to measure not only the probability of x_1, but the utility of a lottery as well,[20] since both lie between 0 and 1. Thus the origin $u(x_0)$ also represents lottery e_{x_0} and the point $u(x_1)$ also is the same as the lottery e_{x_1}. Consider now e_{x_2}. *Corollary 3.1* asserts that a real number, say $u(x_2) \in [0, 1]$ exists such that $e_{x_2} \sim u(x_2)e_{x_1} + \{1 - u(x_2)\}e_{x_0}$, and that this $u(x_2)$ may be called the utility of x_2. Let us mark this point on the horizontal axis and note that all the lotteries on the line segment $e_{x_2}u(x_2)$ are equally attractive (in view of *Remark 1*) and hence, have the same utility level $u(x_2)$.

Probability of x_2

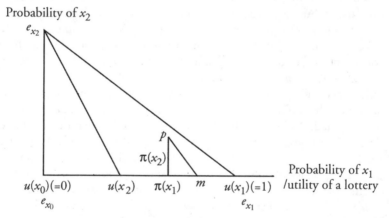

Figure 11.6: Triangle Showing Lotteries and their Corresponding Utilities

Consider now a lottery $p = (\pi(x))$. The straight line through p, drawn *parallel* to the line $e_{x_2}u(x_2)$, cuts the horizontal axis at a point say m. We assert that m measures the *level of utility* of the lottery p. To show this, note that the slopes of the line $e_{x_2}u(x_2)$ and the line pm are

[20] We have modified the so-called 'Machina triangle' slightly. Here an eastward movement yields higher utility. The advantage is that utility of any lottery can also be measured on the horizontal axis.

the same and hence, we have $\left[\dfrac{u(x_2)}{e_{x_0}e_{x_2}}\right] = \dfrac{u(x_2)}{1} = \dfrac{m - \pi(x_1)}{\pi(x_2)}$

or, $m = \pi(x_1) + u(x_2)\,\pi(x_2)$
$\quad\quad = u(x_0)\pi(x_0) + u(x_1)\pi(x_1) + u(x_2)\pi(x_2)$ (since $u(x_0) = 0$, $u(x_1) = 1$)
$\quad\quad = v(p)$, the *expected utility* from p.

Observe that all the lotteries on the line *pm* or even its extension up to the frontier (not shown in the diagram) have the same utility level, *m*. Thus we can measure the utility level of any lottery, once that of outcome x_2 (that is $u(x_2)$) and hence the slope of the indifference curve are determined.

Illustration

To illustrate the use of EUT, let us try to solve the insurance problem we started with. Each lottery (say, p_I) here involves a particular amount of insurance bought (say, I), having two possible outcomes: C_b (= $W - L + I - rI$) with probability π and C_g (= $W - rI$) with probability $(1-\pi)$. The pair of outcomes C_b and C_g depends on the level of I and hence, is different for different lotteries. Further, the set of outcomes, χ, consists of all the points on the budget line *EB* in Figure 11.1. The expected value of the lottery p_I depends on the level of I and is given by

$$v(p_I) = (1 - \pi)u(C_g) + \pi u(C_b), \{C_g = W - rI; C_b = W - L + I - rI\}.$$

The standard assumption is that the utility function $u(\cdot)$ is concave: $u'(\cdot) > 0$, $u''(.) < 0$. This means that an indifference curve (between C_g and C_b) giving constant expected utility is convex to the origin and that its slope is given by $dC_g/dC_b = -\{\pi.u'(C_b)/(1-\pi).u'(C_g)\}$[21]. As shown in Figure 11.1, the slope of the budget line is: $dC_g/dC_b = -r/(1-r)$. Optimality requires the equality of these two slopes, that is, $u'(C_b)/u'(C_g) = \{r.(1-\pi)\}/\{(1-r).\pi\}$. Now, an insurance contract is said to be *actuarially fair*, if the cost of one unit of insurance (r) is equal to the probability of loss (π). Hence, in this case, an optimal insurance is one where $u'(C_b) = u'(C_g)$, that is, $C_b = C_g$ (the point Q at which the

---

[21] It is easy to check that $d^2C_g/dC_b^2 > 0$ (*see* Sargent 1987: 142–50, for a similar exercise in the context of selection of an optimal portfolio with a given investible fund). We have not drawn the indifference curve in Figure 11.1. Note that the concavity of the utility function means that the consumer is risk-averse (Mas-Colell et al. 1995: 185–7).

budget line cuts the 45° line), which occurs when $I = L$. In this case the consumer insures *completely* and consumes $W - rL$, regardless of the occurrence of the loss. If, on the other hand, the insurance contract is actuarially *unfair* (that is, $r > \pi$), optimality is attained at a point (such as F in Figure 11.1) where $u'(C_b) > u'(C_g)$. But this implies $C_b < C_g$, that is $I < L$. Thus, in the case of an actuarially unfair contract the consumer insures only *partially*.

OTHER USES OF EUT

We begin by mentioning some extensions of the EUT. We have developed the EUT considering the probabilities of outcomes to be given *objectively*. But the approach taken by Savage (1954) views probability assessments about the different states of nature by an investor to be purely *subjective*, and the EUT has been demonstrated with this assumption. Again, we have so far considered probability distributions with finite support only. But the EUT can be extended to the case of continuous probability distributions as well (*see* Kreps 1992: 79–81, 98–110). Further, the basic tools and results of the EU analysis can be carried to cases where the independence axiom is violated provided certain condition is satisfied. This has been shown by Machina (1982). In addition, this theory is very helpful for understanding the concepts of risk and risk aversion, for example, Arrow–Pratt measures of absolute and relative risk aversion (*see* Varian 1992: 177–89 and Ingersoll, Jr., 1987: 37–41 and ch. 5). It has also been used to define stochastic dominance of one probability distribution over another (*see* Mas-Colell et al. 1995: 194–9). Since all these concepts are well analysed in the textbooks, we shall not discuss them here any further. We shall rather turn to some of the other important applications of the theory.

In fact, the EUT is used extensively in economic policy and decision-making. We have already demonstrated in the preceding section how this theory helps one in finding an optimal insurance policy. To economize on space, we shall point out only two other important uses here—one in the theory of financial decision-making and the other in the theory of growth and fluctuations.

Use in Portfolio Analysis

Perhaps the most widespread use of this theory is in portfolio analysis and capital asset pricing model, which investigates how an individual, faced with the problem of choosing current and future consumption over a horizon of, say, T periods (that is, C_0, C_1, ... , C_{T-1}), would put his investible financial wealth into a given number of securities in each period so as to maximize discounted present value of expected utility, conditional on information at time zero:

$$\text{Max } E_0 \left[\Sigma_{t=0}^{T-1} \beta^t \, U(C_t) \right]. \tag{11.9}$$

The notation $E_t[\cdot]$ denotes an expectation conditional on information at time t, and β is the discount factor (the reciprocal of one plus the rate of discount). The utility function in any period $U(\cdot)$ is NM utility function, which is strictly increasing and concave (reflecting consumer's aversion towards risk). The budget constraint of the consumer who is assumed to be uncertain about both future labour income and returns on assets is given by

$$A_{t+1} = (A_t + Y_t - C_t)[(1 + r_{t+1})w_{ot} + \Sigma_{i=1}^n (1 + z_{it+1})w_{it}],$$
$$\text{for any } t < T \quad (11.10)$$

A_t is financial wealth at the beginning of the period t, Y_t is labour income, which is random but known as of time t. Given consumption C_t, the consumer has gross savings of $(A_t + Y_t - C_t)$, which he can put into n risky assets and a risk-free asset. The i-th risky asset earns a rate of return between periods t and $t+1$ $(z_{i,t+1})$ which is random and not known as of time t. The risk-less asset has a return r_{t+1} which is a deterministic function of time. The share of the portfolio invested in period t in the i-th risky asset is w_{it} and that in the risk-free asset is w_{ot} ($w_{0t} + w_{1t} + ... + w_{nt} = 1$). The expression in brackets in (11.10), therefore, gives the realized rate of return on the portfolio $w_t = \{w_{0t}, w_{1t}, ... , w_{nt}\}$.

The convenient method to solve such dynamic decision problems under uncertainty is one of stochastic dynamic programming.[22] This

---

[22] *See* Ljungqvist and Sargent (2000: Chs 2–4, 10). For a rigorous and comprehensive discussion, *see* Stokey et al. (1989). A lucid discussion can be found in Blanchard and Fischer (1989: 279–83). Our presentation is based on the latter, (in particular, Chs 6 and 10). It may be pointed out that apart from the first-order conditions stated in (11.11) –(11.12), the maximization problem must also satisfy some terminal conditions.

method would yield the following set of first-order optimality conditions, or the so-called *Euler equations* ($(n + 1)$ in number, in the present case):

$$U'(C_t) = \beta E_t [U'(C_{t+1})(1 + z_{i,t+1})], \quad (i = 1, 2, ..., n) \quad (11.11)$$

$$U'(C_t) = \beta E_t [U'(C_{t+1})(1 + r_{t+1})]. \quad (11.12)$$

Although we have not shown the derivation, these conditions can be obtained by intuitive arguments. The rational individual must choose consumption such that, along an optimal path, small reallocation of wealth between consumption and investment in any asset will not alter the value of the programme (11.9). For instance, suppose that the consumer decreases consumption by one unit at time t, invests that unit in the i-th asset and consumes the proceeds at time $t + 1$. The decrease in utility at time t is $U'(C_t)$ while the increase in expected utility at time $t + 1$, viewed as of time t, is equal to $\beta E_t[U'(C_{t+1})(1 + z_{i,\,t+1})]$. Along an optimal path these two must be the same (otherwise, there would exist a path yielding a higher EU). As (11.12) shows, similar result holds good for the risk-free asset as well. One may now manipulate these equations further to yield a number of interesting concepts and issues.

Measure of Risk Premium

One of the important issues in financial economics is the quantification of the trade-off between risk and expected return. Commonsense suggests that investment in risky assets such as those in the stock market should yield higher expected returns than in risk-free asset in order to induce people to hold those assets. However, it was only with the development of the Capital Asset Pricing Model (CAPM) that economists were able to quantify risk and the reward for bearing it. We shall first discuss the consumption CAPM based on the marginal utility of consumption. Subtracting (11.12) from (11.11), we have,

$$\begin{aligned}
0 &= E_t[U'(C_{t+1})(z_{i,\,t+1} - r_{t+1})] \\
&= E_t[U'(C_{t+1})z_{i,\,t+1}] - r_{t+1}E_t[U'(C_{t+1})]
\end{aligned}$$

The last equality follows from the fact that r_{t+1} is deterministic. Dropping the time index (that is, $E_t[\cdot]$ is denoted by $E[\cdot]$, etc.) and noting that Cov $(X, Y) = E(XY) - E(X).E(Y)$, the above equation may be rewritten as

$$O = E[U'(C_{t+1})]\ E[z_{it+1}] + Cov\{U'(C_{t+1}), z_{it+1}\} = r_{t+1}E[U'(C_{t+1})] + ... \tag{11.13}$$

In equilibrium, the expected return on an asset i, therefore, satisfies

$$E[z_{i,t+1}] = r_{t+1} - \{1/E[U'(C_{t+1})]\}.Cov\{U'(C_{t+1}), z_{i,t+1}\} \tag{11.14}$$

Thus the expected rate of return on any asset can be written as the sum of two components: the risk-free rate plus the *risk premium*, which depends on the covariance of the asset's return with the marginal utility (MU) of consumption. When this covariance is negative, the asset's return will be low when MU of consumption is high, that is, when consumption itself is low (since risk aversion implies MU of consumption decreases with consumption). Such an asset is risky in that it fails to deliver wealth precisely when it is most valuable to the investor (that is, MU is high). Hence, such an asset must have an expected return that is higher than the risk-free rate in order to compensate for its risk. On the other hand, an investor may hold an asset even when its expected return is less than the risk-free rate, provided the asset's returns are positively correlated with MU of consumption. Such an asset pays off more in situations when consumption is low, that is, MU of consumption is high. Hence, individuals will be induced to hold such an asset as a hedge against low consumption.

Although we have derived a measure of risk premium from the point of view of consumption CAPM, the standard and the traditional CAPM derives such a measure in a different way, by casting the investor's problem in terms of expectation and variance of returns. Markowitz (1959) laid the groundwork for this approach by arguing that investors would optimally hold a mean-variance efficient portfolio, that is, a portfolio with the smallest variance for a given level of expected return. Subsequently, it was shown by Sharpe and Lintner in the 1960s that if investors have homogenous expectations and hold mean-variance efficient portfolios, then, in the absence of market frictions, the portfolio of all invested wealth or the market portfolio will itself be mean-variance efficient portfolio. The standard CAPM result is that the expected return on any asset is equal to the risk-free rate plus a 'risk-premium' that depends on the covariance of the asset's return with some efficient portfolio of risky assets. Since market portfolio of risky assets is usually supposed to be efficient, this result may be stated as

$$E[z_{i,t+1}] - r_{t+1} = \beta_i \left(E[z_{m,t+1}] - r_{t+1} \right). \tag{11.15}$$

Here, $z_{m,t+1}$ is the return on the market portfolio of risky assets (which is a potentially observable portfolio as long as one can measure the aggregate (market) holdings of risky assets) and β_i (or the asset's 'beta') is the ratio of $Cov\,(z_{i,t+1},\,z_{m,t+1})$ to $Var\,(z_{m,t+1})$. It may be noted that β_i has the interpretation of a regression coefficient of $z_{i,t+1}$ on $z_{m,t+1}$ and that the (11.15) can also be derived from (11.14) by making a special assumption, namely, that the MU of consumption and the return on the market portfolio are perfectly correlated (Blanchard and Fischer 1989: 506–9). Further (11.15) is known in finance as the *security market line*[23] or an asset's 'beta'. It is interesting to note that the 'risk-premium' for an asset does not depend on the asset's 'own risk' (that is, variance of its own return), but depends on its 'beta', that is, how the holding of this asset affects the riskiness of the market portfolio.

Stochastic Discount Factor

By dividing (11.11) throughout by $U'(C_t)$ which is positive, we get

$$\begin{aligned} 1 &= E_t[(1+z_{i,t+1})\beta U'(C_{t+1})/\{U'(C_t)\}] \\ &= E_t[(1+z_{i,t+1}) \cdot M_{t+1}], \end{aligned} \tag{11.16}$$

where $\beta U'(C_{t+1})/\{U'(C_t)\}$ is denoted by M_{t+1}. In the literature M_{t+1} is known as the *stochastic discount factor* (Campbell et al. 2000: 294 and also Ljungqvist and Sargent 2000: 152). To explain the meaning of this concept, suppose that there are S possible states of nature (and, suppose, π_{t+j}^s is the probability of occurrence of state s in period $t+j$). The value of the stochastic discount factor in state s in period $t+j$ (to be denoted by M_{t+j}^s) depends on the MU of consumption in that state in period $t+j$: $M_{t+j}^s = \beta U'(C_{t+j}^s)/\{U'(C_t)\}$. If the rate of return (in state s) of the i-th asset held between periods t and $t+1$ is $z_{i,t+1}^s$, then the expectation indicated in the second line of the (11.16) is given by, $\Sigma_{s=1}^s\{\pi_{t+1}^s(1+z_{i,t+1}^s)M_{t+j}^s\}$.

Such stochastic discount factors are used to derive a number of important results. For instance, it is used to find the *value of a firm* in

---

[23] For the derivation of (11.15) from the mean-variance approach and for references, *see* Huang and Litzenberger (1988: Ch. 3, 4); Varian (1992: Ch. 20, 371–5), and Campbell et al. (1997: Ch. 5).

period t (say, V_t) as the expected discounted value of stream of its cash flows f_{t+j} (that is, its profit net of its investment): $V_t = E_t[\Sigma_{j=1}^{\infty}(M_{t+j}f_{t+j})]$. It is also used to derive the famous *Modigliani–Miller Theorem* regarding the irrelevance of the debt–equity division of the financial structure of a firm. In other words, the value of the firm is invariant to whether the firm finances itself through bonds or equities. Finally, it is also used to find the price of a share in period t (p_t) as the expected discounted stream of its dividends ($y_t + {}_j$): $p_t = E_t[\Sigma_{j=1}^{\infty}(M_{t+j}y_{t+j})]$ (*see* Blanchard and Fischer 1989: Ch. 6, 292–6 and Ch. 10, 510–12 ; Ljungqvist and Sargent 2000: Ch. 10, 229–40).

Equity Premium Puzzle

Assume that consumers have constant relative risk-aversion utility:

$$U(C_t) = C_t^{1-\theta}/(1-\theta),$$

where θ, the absolute value of the elasticity of MU of consumption with respect to consumption, is the coefficient of relative risk-aversion. Here (11.11) now becomes

$$C_t^{-\theta} = \beta E_t(C_{t+1}^{-\theta}(1+z_{i,t+1})], \text{ or dividing throughout by } C_t^{-\theta} \text{ and}$$

β, one gets

$$
\begin{aligned}
1/\beta &= E_t[(1+z_{i,t+1})(C_{t+1}/C_t)^{-\theta}] \\
&= E_t[(1+z_{i,t+1})(1+g_{t+1})^{-\theta}] \\
&= E[(1+z_i)(1+g)^{-\theta}] \text{ (omitting the time subscript),}
\end{aligned}
$$

where g_{t+1} is the proportional rate of growth of consumption ($= C_{t+1}/C_t - 1$). By taking a second-order Taylor approximation of the right-hand side around $r = g = 0$, Romer (1996: 330–2) shows that

$$E[z_i] - r \cong \theta \operatorname{cov}(z_i, g). \tag{11.17}$$

In a famous paper Mehra and Prescott (1985) show that it is difficult to reconcile observed asset returns with (11.17). As reported in Ljungqvist and Sargent (2000: 260–3), if one considers the same data for the US economy as used by Mehra and Prescott for the period 1890–1979, the *difference* between the average annual return on the stock market and the return on the relatively risk-less bonds—the so-called *equity premium*—is about 0.06 while over the same period, the covariance between g and the market rate of return is 0.00219. These would then imply that the value of θ has to be 27 in order that (11.17) is satisfied. But this amounts to an extraordinarily high level of risk-aversion on the part of the individuals, which is difficult to reconcile with the household behaviour. This inconsistency is known in the literature as the *equity premium puzzle*. This puzzle has stimulated a large body of studies (for references, Romer 1996: Ch. 7; Campbell et al. 1997: Ch. 8; Ljungqvist and Sargent 2000: Ch. 10).

Use in the Theory of Growth and Fluctuations

The stochastic version of models of growth and fluctuations is another important area where EUT has been used extensively. The economic models of business cycles which were developed after the publication of Keynes' General Theory were based on the interaction of the multiplier–accelerator mechanism (e.g., Samuelson 1939; Hicks 1950). These models viewed fluctuations as being driven by aggregate demand, mainly unstable investment expenditure, with supply-side factors like full employment and the persistence of some autonomous investment providing the constraints that gave rise to the turning points in the cycles. The earlier literature also contains two other features. The *first* is its view about the dynamic behaviour of an economy. The view was that an economy grows along a smooth-trend path from which it gets frequently disturbed by cyclical fluctuations. *Second*, these models looked upon the sharp fluctuations in output and employment as prima facie evidence of major market imperfections and explored what these imperfections might be. However, over the last two decades some economists have been strongly arguing that this is a misguided research strategy, since macroeconomic fluctuations can be explained without invoking imperfections. The proponents of what is now termed the *Real Business Cycle* (RBC) theory argue that an economy even in perfectly competitive general equilibrium can experience sustained fluctuations in outputs and other macro variables. RBC models seek to demonstrate that, cycles can arise even in equilibrium situations through optimal responses of economic agents to real disturbances (such as random changes in technology or productivity). RBC theorists further emphasize that such models are capable of mimicking the salient empirical regularities displayed by business cycles. What we shall try to do here is to outline the basic structure of a stochastic growth model and then to indicate some important features of the RBC theory.[24]

---

[24] *See* Stokey et al. (1989: 16–21) for a description of the basic structure of a

Consider the following version of the Ramsey model. There is no population growth and the population size is normalized to one. Let Y_t, C_t, K_t be respectively the output, consumption, and (beginning-of-period) capital stock at time t. Assume that capital depreciates fully after one period and that output is given by the Cobb–Douglas production function:

$$Y_t = Z_t K_t^\alpha, \qquad (0 < \alpha < 1) \tag{11.18}$$

where Z_t is a random variable (with given properties), representing productivity or technology shocks. The feasibility constraint of the economy is that the output in any period is either consumed or invested (to be used as capital stock in the next period) :

$$K_{t+1} + C_t = Y_t; \tag{11.19}$$

Assume that the households in this economy rank stochastic consumption sequences according to the expected utility they deliver, where their underlying (common) utility function is additively separable as before:

$$E[u(C_0, C_1, C_2, ...)] = E_0[\Sigma_{t=0}^{\infty} \beta^t U(C_t)], \tag{11.20}$$

where $E[\cdot]$ denotes expected utility from the probability distribution of the random variables $(C_0, C_1, C_2, ...)$. The problem facing a social planner in this stochastic environment is to maximize the objective function (11.20) subject to (11.18) and (11.19). We have used a similar objective function earlier in (11.9), of course, in the context of a finite-horizon problem. Let us try to explain the meaning of such an objective function. Note that the pair (K_t, Z_t) and hence Y_t [via (11.18)] is known when the planner decides on its division between C_t and K_{t+1}. The planner in period zero is supposed to choose, in addition to the pair (C_0, K_1), an infinite sequence of $\{(C_t, K_{t+1})\}_{t=0}^{\infty}$ describing all future consumption and capital pairs. Note that this is not a sequence of numbers, but a sequence of *contingency plans*, one for each period. Specifically, (C_t, K_{t+1}) chosen in each period t is contingent on the realization of shocks $Z_1, Z_2, ..., Z_t$. Hence, the planner chooses among sequences of functions, where the t-th function in the sequence has as

---

stochastic growth model. A lucid presentation of RBC theory can be found in Plosser (1989: 51–77). Mankiw (1989) provides, what may be called, a Keynesian critique of the RBC theory. Our discussion of this theory follows mainly Blanchard and Fischer (1989: 320–6).

its arguments the $(Z_1, Z_2, \ldots, Z_t)$ of shocks realized between the time the planning is drawn up and the time the decision is carried out. The feasible set for the planner is the set of pairs (C_0, K_1) and the sequence of functions $\{(C_t(\cdot), K_{t+1}(\cdot))\}_{t=0}^{\infty}$ that satisfy (11.18) and (11.19) for all periods and all realizations of shocks.

To get an explicit solution, we shall also assume that the utility function is logarithmic: $U(C_t) = \ln C_t$. The first-order conditions now read as[25] $U'(C_t) = E_t[\beta U'(C_{t+1})(\partial Y_{t+1}/\partial K_{t+1})]$, or using the logarithmic utility function,

$$(1/C_t) = E_t[(\beta/C_{t+1})\alpha Z_{t+1}K_{t+1}^{\alpha-1}]. \tag{11.21}$$

An explicit solution of (11.21) is derivable and is given by

$$C_t = (1-\alpha\beta)Z_t K_t^{\alpha}, \text{ and } K_{t+1} = \alpha\beta Z_t K_t^{\alpha}. \tag{11.22}$$

Using (11.18) and (11.22), one gets, $K_{t+1} = \alpha\beta Y_t$ and hence, $Y_t = Z_t K_t^{\alpha} = Z_t \alpha\beta Y_{t-1}$. Taking logarithm of both sides of the last relation, one finally gets that the logarithm of output follows a first-order auto-regressive process with random shock, $\ln Z_t$ and that the auto-regressive coefficient is α, the share of capital in output. The path of Y_t depends on the behaviour of productivity shock, $\ln Z_t$. As shown in Romer (1996: Ch. 4) and Blanchard and Fischer (1989: Ch. 7), a transitory productivity disturbance gives rise to interesting output dynamics, and changes in productivity shocks lead to fluctuations in output. In fact, when the productivity shock follows a random walk with drift (say, δ), that is, $\ln Z_t = \delta + \ln Z_{t-1} + \varepsilon_t$ (where ε_t is a white noise), the level of output will be raised permanently even if there is a one-time productivity shock (that is, ε_t is some positive amount at a given time, say t_0, and zero for all other periods).

CONCLUSION

In conclusion we shall point out some critique of the EUT. As a descriptive theory the EUT, in particular its Independence Axiom (IA), has always been questioned. A growing body of empirical evidence

---

[25] The interpretation of the first relation is obvious. A reallocation of one unit of output from consumption to investment in period t reduces utility by $U'(C_t)$, but raises utility in the next period (by allowing higher output to be produced) by $U'(C_{t+1})(\partial Y_{t+1}/\partial K_{t+1})$. Along an optimal path, the expected value of the latter, when discounted, must equal the former.

exists which reveals patterns of choice behaviour inconsistent with the EUT or even the IA. One of the earliest examples of this is the well-known *Allais Paradox* which consists of choosing a lottery from each of the two pairs (e_1, p) and (r, s), where each lottery is defined on the three outcomes: 0, 1 million dollars, and 5 million dollars. These lotteries are described in Table 11.1 (in which we have also included two other lotteries, q and e_0).

Table 11.1: Allais Paradox

Outcome	Lottery					
(in million dollars)	e_1	p	r	s	q	e_0
$x_0 : 0$	0	.01	.90	.89	1/11	1
$x_1 : 1$	1	.89	0	.11	0	0
$x_2 : 5$	0	.10	.10	0	10/11	0

Researchers have given this problem to several hundred people and the modal preference has been found to be for e_1 in the first pair and r in the second pair. But this behaviour contradicts both the EUT and the IA. To show the first, note that under the EUT, $e_1 \succ p$ implies $u(x_1)$ > 0.01 $u(x_0)$ + 0.89 $u(x_1)$ + 0.10 $u(x_2)$. Now, adding 0.89 $u(x_0)$ to both sides, one gets 0.89 $u(x_0)$ + 0.11 $u(x_1)$ > 0.90 $u(x_0)$ + 0.10 $u(x_2)$, which yields $s \succ r$. To show its inconsistency with the IA, observe that $e_1 \succ p$ implies $e_1 \succ q$. [If not, one would have $q \succeq e_1$ yielding, in view of the IA and CP, 0.11q + 0.89 $e_1 \succeq$ 0.11e_1 + 0.89 e_1, that is, $p \succeq e_1$, (since $p \sim 0.11q + 0.89e_1$), a contradiction.] However, $e_1 \succ q$ implies, once again in view of the IA and the CP, that 0.11 e_1 + 0.89 $e_0 \succ$ 0.11 q + 0.89 e_0, that is, $s \succ r$.

There are other types of evidence. Researchers have responded to this growing body of evidence by developing *nonlinear (non-expected utility)* functional forms for individual preference functions or lotteries.[26] Finally, we should also point out that some economists have reservations against using EUT. They prefer using an ordinal utility function defined over the mean and standard deviation (and also higher moments) of the distribution of returns of a security/portfolio.[27] This in fact belongs

---

[26] *See* Machina (1989, 1997) and Starmer (2000) for discussion on both the Non-expected Utility Theory and the kinds of evidence contradicting EUT.

[27] One of the early exponents of such an approach is Hicks (1967: Chs 2, 3, and 6).

to the mean-variance approach to portfolio analysis that has already been referred to.

REFERENCES

BLANCHARD, O.J. and S. FISCHER, (1989), *Lectures on Macroeconomics*, Cambridge, Massachusetts: MIT Press.

CAMPBELL, J.Y., ANDREW W. LO and A. CRAIG MACKINLAY, (1997), *The Econometrics of Financial Markets*, Princeton, New Jersey: Princeton University Press

HERSTEIN, I.N. and J. MILNOR, (1953), 'An Axiomatic Approach To Measurable Utility', *Econometrica*, 21, pp. 291–7; reprinted in the collected volume Omar P. Hamuda and J. C. R.Rowley (eds), (1997), *Expected Utility, Fair Gambles and Rational Choice*; *Foundations of Probability, Econometrics and Economic Games 1*, UK: Hants, Aldershort.

HICKS, SIR J., (1950), *A Contribution to the Theory of Trade Cycles*, London: Oxford University Press.

——, (1967), *Critical Essays in Monetary Theory*, London: Oxford University Press.

HUANG, CHI-FU and R.H. LITZENBERGER, (1988), *Foundations for Financial Economics*, New Jersey: Prentice Hall, New Jersey.

INGERSOLL, J.E. Jr., (1987), *Theory of Financial Decision Making*, Maryland, USA: Rowman & Littlefield.

KREPS, D.M., (1992), *A Course in Microeconomics Theory*, New Delhi: Prentice-Hall of India Pvt. Ltd.

LINTNER, J., (1965), 'The Valuation of Risk Assets and the Selection of Risky Investments in Stock Portfolio and Capital Budgets', *Review of Economics and Statistics*, 47, pp. 13–37.

LJUNGQVIST, L. and T.J. SARGENT, (2000), *Recursive Macroeconomic Theory*, Cambridge, Massachusetts: MIT Press.

MACHINA M.J., (1982), 'Expected Utility Analysis Without the Independence Axiom', *Econometrica*, 50, pp. 277–323.

——, (1987), 'Choice under Uncertainty : Problems Solved and Unsolved', *Journal of Economic Perspectives*, 1, pp. 121–254.

——, (1989), 'Dynamic Inconsistency and Non-Expected Utility Models of Choice under Uncertainty', *Journal of Economic Literature*, XXVII, pp. 1622–68.

———, (1997), 'Choice under Uncertainty: Problems Solved and Unsolved'; in Partha Dasgupta and Karl-Goran Maler (eds), *The Environment and Emerging Development Issues*, 1, Oxford: Clarendon Press.

MANKIW, N.G., (1989), 'Real Business Cycles : A New Keynesian Perspective', *Journal of Economic Perspective*, 3(3) (summer), pp. 79–90.

MARKOWITZ, H.M., (1959), *Portfolio Selection: Efficient Diversification of Investments,* Yale: Cowles Foundation for Research in Economics, Yale University Press.

MARSCHAK, J., (1950), 'Rational Behaviour, Uncertain Prospects, and Measurable Utility', *Econometrica*, 18, pp. 111–41.

MAS-COLELL, A., M.D. WHINSTON, and J.R. GREEN, (1995), *Microeconomic Theory*, Oxford: Oxford University Press.

MEHRA, R. and E.C. PRESCOTT, (1985), 'The Equity Premium: A Puzzle', *Journal of Monetary Economics*, 15(2), pp. 145–61.

PLOSSER, C.I., (1989), 'Understanding Real Business Cycles', *Journal of Economic Perspective*, 3(3) (summer).

ROMER, D., (1996), *Advanced Macroeconomics*, New York: McGraw-Hill.

SAMUELSON, P.A., (1939), 'Interactions between the Multiplier Analysis and the Principle of Acceleration', *Review of Economic Studies*, 21, May pp. 75–8.

SARGENT, T.J. (1987), *Macroeconomic Theory*, 2nd edition, San Diego, California: Academic Press.

SAVAGE, L., (1954), *The Foundation of Statistics*, New York: John Wiley and Sons (revised and enlarged edition, (1972), New York: Dover Publication).

SCHOEMAKER, P.J. H., (1982), 'The Expected Utility Model: Its Variants, Purposes, Evidence And Limitations', *Journal of Economic Literature*, XX, pp. 529–63.

SHARPE, W., F., (1964), 'Capital Asset Prices: Theory of Market Equilibrium under Conditions of Risk', *Journal of Finance*, 19, pp. 425–42.

STARMER, C., (2000), 'Developments in Non-expected Utility Theory: The Hunt for a Descriptive Theory of Choice under Risk', *Journal of Economic Literature*, XXXVIII, June, pp. 332–82.

STOKEY, N.L., R. LUCAS JR., with E. Prescott, (1989), *Recursive Methods in Economic Dynamics*, Cambridge, Massachusetts: Harvard University Press.

VARIAN, H.R., (1992), *Microeconomic Analysis*, 3rd edition, New York: W.W. Norton & Co.

VON NEUMANN, J. and O. MORGENSTERN, (1944), *Theory of Games and Economic Behaviour*, Princeton, New Jersey: Princeton University Press.

Part III: GLOBAL ECONOMY AND ECONOMIC POLICY

12. Some Macroeconomic Aspects of Foreign Trade

A Structuralist Perspective

Mihir Rakshit

The capital of the merchant exchanges the surplus produce of one place for that of another, and thus encourages the industry, and increases the enjoyments of both... without such exportation, a part of the productive capacity of the country must cease, and the value of its annual produce diminish.

Adam Smith 1776: 342, 353

INTRODUCTION

Economists have identified three routes through which international trade impinges on the domestic economy. First, in Keynesian models removal of barriers to trade may raise or lower the level of aggregate output and employment. Second, neoclassical theories subsume full employment and indicate how trade affects allocation of resources in different lines of production. Third and perhaps the most important in the long run, unfettered movements of goods across national boundaries promote division of labour, enable firms to exploit scale economies, and induce technological improvements over time. In the present paper we abstract from the last two effects and concentrate on the possible short-run expansionary or contractionary effects of trade on the level of economic activity. Note that if the economy does not enjoy full employment, not only does the macroeconomic impact of trade dominate the effects, but there also occurs serious disincentive to invest in machinery or research and development. Hence the importance of resolving the first set of issues before coming to the second and the third.

Since the focus of the paper is on the levels of income and employment, our natural point of departure would seem to be the Keynesian theory of foreign trade multiplier. What is not commonly recoginzed is that in Smithian analysis as well, trade[1] plays a crucial role in determining levels of output and employment. However, while Smith is quite unequivocal in claiming that foreign trade raises production and employment in *all* countries,[2] in neo-Keynesian theories the sign of the foreign trade multiplier is the same as that of the balance of trade, so that the effect will be contractionary for some, but expansionary for other countries.[3] The paper develops a general framework for examining the economic consequences of alternative patterns of international trade. The framework provides a resolution of the apparently conflicting stands of Smith and Keynes, helps in understanding the economic impact of North–South or other forms of trade, and brings to the fore the role of inter-sectoral differences in operation of demand and supply constraints in governing both the pattern of international exchange and the sign of foreign trade multiplier.

FOREIGN TRADE MULTIPLIER IN THE VENT FOR SURPLUS MODEL: A KEYNESIAN INTERPRETATION OF SMITH

The first step towards development of a general framework is to recognize that both the neoclassical situation of full employment everywhere and the Keynesian world of no supply constraint anywhere are two polar cases that do not generally correspond to conditions under which international trade takes place. Again, even within the same country, output may be demand-constrained in some sectors, but limited by supply-side factors in others.[4] Indeed, explicit modelling of

---

[1] Apart from its role in enhancing long-term productivity through scale economies and division of labour.

[2] For textual evidence regarding the role of demand in governing the level of employment in Smith, the interested reader is referred to Smith (1976: 342, 353, 359, 415).

[3] Remembering that positive trade balance of a country implies negative trade balance for the rest of the world.

[4] A situation considered typical of developing countries (Taylor 1983; Rakshit 1982).

such dualistic patterns of production within and across countries constitutes the key to the resolution of conflicting views on the impact of trade on the level of economic activity. Consider, first, Smith's perception that by providing a vent for surplus[5] domestic production, international trade raises the level of output and employment in *all* countries.

The simplest way of modelling the Smith-type situation is to consider a world consisting of two countries, *A* and *B*, both producing two commodities *X* and *Y*. In order to highlight the basic Keynesian mechanism operating under the Smithian pattern of trade, we take the exchange rate, money prices, and hence the relative price *p* of *Y* in terms of *X* to be fixed and identical in the two countries under both autarky and free trade—an assumption we shall presently relax. We assume further that the sectoral demand and supply conditions are such that under autarky, while *Y* is demand-constrained and *X* supply-constrained in *A*, the situation is the reverse in *B*. In formal terms, the autarky equilibrium levels of output in the two countries are given by the following relations:

$$Y_a = Y^{da}(Y_a, \bar{X}_a, \bar{p}) < \bar{Y}^{sa}$$

$$1 > Y_1^{da} > 0; \, Y_2^{da} > 0; \, Y_3^{da} < 0 \tag{12.1}$$

$$X_a = \bar{X}^{sa}(=\bar{X}_a) < X^{da}(Y_a \bar{X}_a, \bar{p})$$

$$X_1^{da} > 0; \, 1 > X_2^{da} > 0; \, X_3^{da} > 0 \tag{12.2}$$

$$Y_b = \bar{Y}^{sb}(=\bar{Y}_b) < Y^{db}(\bar{Y}_b, X_b, \bar{p})$$

$$1 > Y_1^{db} > 0; \, Y_2^{db} > 0; \, Y_3^{db} < 0 \tag{12.3}$$

$$X_b = X^{db}(\bar{Y}_b, X_b, \bar{p}) < \bar{X}^{sb})$$

$$X_1^{db} > 0; \, 1 > X_2^{db} > 0; \, X_3^{db} > 0 \tag{12.4}$$

where superscripts *da*, *db*, *sa*, and *sb* attached to *Y* and *X* denote their respective demand and supply in the two countries *A* and *B*; Y_a, X_a, etc., stand for equilibrium output levels; and bar upon a variable denotes that the variable is fixed (in the short run).

---

[5] For an alternative interpretation of the vent for surplus approach, *see* Myint (1958, 1977). Rakshit (1993) provides a critique of Myint.

Note that in (12.1)–(12.4) the surplus productive capacity of $Y(X)$ in $A(B)$ coexists with excess demand for $Y(X)$ in $B(A)$—a situation ripe for inter-country exchange of goods, once barriers to trade are dismantled.[6] When trade opens up, a Keynes-type expansionary process is set in motion, with both countries experiencing an increase in demand for the good in excess supply in the domestic market. Assuming that the free trade global equilibrium is demand-constrained, Y_a and X_b are now given by two Keynesian equations:[7]

$$Y_a = Y^{da}(Y_a, \bar{X}_a, \bar{p}) + Y^{db}(\bar{Y}_b, X_b, \bar{p}) - \bar{Y}_b \tag{12.5}$$

$$X_b = X^{db}(\bar{Y}_b, X_b, \bar{p}) + X^{da}(Y_a, \bar{X}_a, \bar{p}) - \bar{X}_a. \tag{12.6}$$

In order to keep the algebra uncluttered and appreciate the expansionary impact of the Smithian pattern of trade we make the simplifying assumption that

$$\eta_{yb} = Y^{db} - \bar{Y}_b > 0; \text{ but } \eta_{xa} = X^{da} - \bar{X}_a = 0,$$

where η denotes excess demand under autarky. Linearizing (12.5) and (12.6) around the autarky equilibrium values of Y_a and X_b, we obtain the increments in output in the two countries (dY_a and dX_b) due to opening up of trade:

$$dY_a / \eta_{yb} = 1 / s_y > 1 \tag{12.7}$$

$$dX_b / \eta_{yb} = [X_1^{da} / (1 - Y_1^{da})] / s_x > 0, \tag{12.8}$$

where

$$s_y = 1 - [Y_1^{da} + \frac{X_1^{da}}{1 - X_2^{db}} Y_2^{db}] \tag{12.9}$$

and

$$s_x = 1 - [X_2^{db} + \frac{Y_2^{db}}{1 - Y_1^{da_+}} X_1^{da}]. \tag{12.10}$$

The relations (12.7) and (12.8) indicate the foreign trade multipliers per unit of pre-existing excess demand for Y in B. If this excess demand

[6] Note that the autarky equilibrium abstracts from the spillover effects of excess demand from one market to another.

[7] Remembering that even under free trade $X_a = \bar{X}_a$ and $Y_b = \bar{Y}_b$.

is unity, the initial impact of trade is to raise Y_a by one unit. However, this sets in motion a cumulative expansionary process in *both* the countries as there occurs additional demand for Y and X in successive rounds of income generation. Note that the expression within third brackets on the RHS of (12.9) is nothing but the additional expenditure on Y generated in the two countries following a unit increase in Y_a. In country A the extra demand is Y_1^{da}; in B however, the additional expenditure on Y_a due to a rise in X_b which is $X_1^{da}/(1-X_2^{db})$ times Y_2^{db}, as A raises its demand for X by X_1^{da} and causes thereby an increase in the production of X_b by a multiple, $1/(1-X_2^{db})$. Similarly, the expression within the third brackets in (12.10) denotes the direct plus indirect marginal propensity to spend on X with respect to a unit increase in the production of the commodity in B. Hence s_x and s_y are nothing but the marginal leakages from the income–expenditure streams of the two commodities.[8]

The two (vent for surplus) multipliers, given by the reciprocal of respective marginal leakages, thus admit of a fairly straightforward Keynesian intepretation in terms of an initial impulse and the feedback effects over successive rounds of production of Y_a and X_b. With $\eta_{yb} > 0$ and $\eta_{xa} = 0$, while the foreign trade multiplier in the Y_a sector operates on η_{yb}, that in the X_b sector is triggered off by the additional demand for X originating in Y_a sector. Quite clearly, a positive η_{xa} will also produce similar expansionary effects in the two countries.

Foreign Trade without Initial Excess Demand

Our analysis of the Smithian form of trade may appear unduly contrived in that the pre- and the post-trade prices are taken to be the same in both the countries, so that excess demand under autarky forms the basis of international trade.[9] Abandonment of this assumption makes the algebra somewhat complicated, but does not alter the basic results of the simple framework. In order to capture the role of prices we make

[8] As in the simple Keynesian model, stability requires that the marginal leakages, s_x and s_y, are positive. For proof, *see* Appendix A12.1.

[9] The purpose of the simplifying assumption has been to highlight the basic neo-Keynesian expansionary process in the Smithian model of trade. The assumption becomes less preposterous when, from an initial situation of free trade with no inter-country price differences, the government imposes quantitative restrictions on trade, but prices do not change (for a variety of resons like inertia or cost of revisions or oligopolistic practices.)

the neo-Keynesian assumption that prices remain constant so long as there is excess capacity, but they become market-clearing once demand deficiency disappears. Autarky equilibrium in A is now given by the following relations:

$$Y_a = Y^{da}(Y_a, \bar{X}_a, p_a) \tag{12.11}$$

$$X_a = \bar{X}_a = X^{da}(Y_a, \bar{X}_a, p_a), \tag{12.12}$$

where p_a, the ratio of money prices, $\bar{P}_y^a$ and P_x^a, is now a variable, with P_y^a remaining fixed and P_x^a adjusting to eliminate excess demand in the X market.

The autarky equilibrium in A determines Y_a and p_a, and is characterized by underutilized capacity in Y and market-clearing price in X. Opposite is the nature of autarky equilibrium in B, given by (12.13) and (12.14):

$$Y_b = \bar{Y}_b = Y^{db}(\bar{Y}_b, X_b, p_b) \tag{12.13}$$

$$X_b = X^{db}(\bar{Y}_b, X_b, p_b), \tag{12.14}$$

where p_b is the ratio of money prices, P_y^b and $\bar{P}_x^b$.

Now the basis of trade is the difference in prices and not the coexistence of excess demand for and excess supply of the same commodity in different parts of the world before trade opens up. Let the free trade equilibrium be still demand-constrained, so that equalization of prices across countries makes the free trade price ratio p^* equal to $\bar{P}_y^a / \bar{P}_x^b$. With $\bar{X}_a$ and $\bar{Y}_b$ remaining unchanged, the free trade equilibrium levels of Y_a and X_b are now given by:

$$Y_a = Y^{da}(Y_a, \bar{X}_a, p^*) + Y^{db}(\bar{Y}_b, X_b, p^*) - \bar{Y}_b \tag{12.15}$$

$$X_b = X^{db}(\bar{Y}_b, X_b, p^*) + X^{da}(Y_a, \bar{X}_a, p^*) - \bar{X}_a. \tag{12.16}$$

Linearization of (12.15) and (12.16) yields the effects of trade on production in the two countries:

$$dY_a = [(Y_3^{da} dp_a + Y_3^{db} dp_b) + \frac{Y_2^{db}(X_3^{da} dp_a + X_3^{db} dp_b)}{(1 - X_2^{db})}]/s_y \tag{12.17}$$

$$= [\{Y_3^{da} + \frac{X_3^{da} Y_2^{db}}{(1 - X_2^{db})}\} dp_a + \{Y_3^{db} + \frac{Y_2^{db} X_3^{db}}{(1 - X_2^{db})}\} dp_b]/s_y \tag{12.17a}$$

$$dX_b = [(X_3^{da}dp_a + X_3^{db}dp_b) + \frac{X_1^{da}(Y_3^{da}dp_a + Y_3^{db}dp_b)}{(1 - Y_1^{da})}]/s_x, \quad (12.18)$$

where dY_a and dX_b stand for changes in Y_a and X_b respectively due to opening up of trade, while dp_a and dp_b denote the difference between the free trade and autarky price ratios in the two countries (remembering that $dp_a > 0$, but $dp_b < 0$).

In spite of the somewhat cumbrous look of (12.17) and (12.18), the results are quite unambiguous and admit of a simple economic interpretation. The denominators, as we have already seen, are the marginal leakages from the two income streams. The numerators, on which the multipliers ($1/s_y$ and $1/s_x$) operate, show the additional expenditure following the equalization of prices through trade. Note that while the first part of the numerator on the RHS of 12.17 (12.18) denotes the change in the demand for $Y(X)$ operating directly through variations in relative prices, the second part indicates the additional demand for $Y(X)$ due to the rise in $X_b(Y_a)$ generated through the direct price effect and the *sectoral* multiplier[10] operating thereon.

What about the signs of dY_a and dX_b? Since both s_x and s_y are positive, the signs will be the same as that of the numerator. The problem however is that the effects on the demand for Y_a or X_b operating through dp_a and dp_b do not pull in the same direction. Thus with $dp_a > 0$ and $dp_b < 0$, the initial impact on the demand for Y_a will be positive from B, but negative from A. However, as we show in Appendix A12.1, stability conditions ensure that the impact of an increase in p_a on the demand for Y_a, given by the coefficient of dp_a in (12.17a), is positive; but that of a rise in p_b is negative. This also brings forth the mechanism of foreign trade multiplier in this model: increase in Y_a or X_b will be a multiple of the initial increase in demand generated through inter-country equalization of the price ratio. Hence the unambiguity regarding the expansionary effects of trade in the vent for surplus model, irrespective of whether the effect is triggered off by some pre-existing excess demand, or through a rise in the relative price of the commodity facing a demand constraint in the domestic market. It may also be easily verified that the expansionary effects are the greater, (i) the larger the marginal propensities to spend with respect to an increase in production of the two goods, (ii) the greater the price responsiveness of demand

---

[10] Thus the sectoral multiplier for $X_b, 1/(1 - X_2^{db})$, refers to its equilibrium increment due to a unit increase in the demand for X_b, where Y_a *remains unchanged.*

for the imported product, and (iii) the lower the price elasticity of home demand for the exportable—conclusions that clearly bear the Keynesian stamp.[11]

FOREIGN TRADE MULTIPLIER UNDER ALTERNATIVE PATTERNS OF TRADE

The vent for surplus case considered above was perhaps the most important form of international trade in olden days. However, the model does not capture the forces operating under trade between developed and developing countries. Indeed, economic history has been replete with instances where patterns of trade were non-Smithian. It was not uncommon for countries like India to import industrial goods, production of which was demand-constrained, against exports of commodities in short supply. The important point to note in this connection is that trade pattern can well be contra-Smithian due to (a) inter-country differences in the patterns of demand, factor endowment, and technical conditions; and (b) variations in money wages across sectors. Turning the algebra and the economics of the first section on their head, it is easy to show that under the Contra-Smithian patterns of exchange, foreign trade multipliers in both the countries are unambiguously negative.[12]

North—South Trade

There is no inter-country conflict of interest in the two forms of trade considered so far, Smithian and contra-Smithian: exchange of goods either enriches or impoverishes all the trading nations. This cannot be said of the North–South or colonial form of trade under which advanced countries import food or primary products in exchange for industrial goods. The distinguishing feature of this form of trade is that in both sets of countries agricultural production is mostly supply-constrained, but non-agricultural output is more often than not limited by demand conditions.

---

[11] Note that we have ignored the effects of interst rate due to lowering of *absolute* level of prices and changes in money supply associated with positive or negative trade balance.

[12] We leave it to the interested reader to verify the result.

Let X stand for farm products and Y for non-agricultural output. Before trade opens up, industrial goods are cheaper in B (Britain) and agricultural goods in A (India):

$$\bar{P}_y^a > \bar{P}_y^b \text{ and } P_x^b > P_x^a, \text{ so that } p_a > p_b. \tag{12.19}$$

Free trade wipes out the Y-sector in A which imports industrial goods at price $\bar{P}_y^b$ against export of its agricultural products.[13] The post-trade equilibrium values of Y_b and $p (= \bar{P}_y^b / P_x)$ are given by the following pair of equations:

$$Y_b = Y^{db}(Y_b, \bar{X}_b, p) + Y^{da}(Y_a = 0, \bar{X}_a, p) - Y_a(= 0) \tag{12.20}$$

$$X^{db}(Y_b, \bar{X}_b, p) + X^{da}(Y_a = 0, \bar{X}_a, p) = \bar{X}_a + \bar{X}_b, \tag{12.21}$$

where production of agricultural goods is assumed to be price-inelastic. Let $p_a - p_b = h > 0$ [by (12.19)], and $dp_b = p - p_b$ so that $dp_a = p - p_a = dp_b - h$.

Relations (12.20) and (12.21) yield dp_b and the change in Y_b ($= dY_b$) due to opening up of trade:

$$dY_b = \frac{[\{(1 - Y_1^{da})Y_a^* + \frac{Y_a^* X_1^{da}(Y_3^{da} + Y_3^{db})}{(X_3^{da} + X_3^{db})}\} + \{\frac{h(Y_3^{db} X_3^{da} - Y_3^{da} X_3^{db})}{(X_3^{da} + X_3^{db})}\}]}{s_{yb}^*} \tag{12.22}$$

$$dp_b = \frac{[(X_1^{da} Y_a^* + h X_3^{da}) - X_1^{db} dY_b]}{(X_3^{da} + X_3^{db})}, \tag{12.23}$$

where

$$s_{yb}^* = 1 - Y_1^{db} + (Y_3^{da} + Y_3^{db}) \frac{X_1^{db}}{(X_3^{da} + X_3^{db})} \tag{12.24}$$

remembering that $-dY_a = Y_a^*$ = autarky equilibrium value of Y_a.

---

[13] Imperfect substitutability in consumption between machine-made goods and artisans' wares did enable parts of Indian handicrafts to survive the onslaught of (post-Industrial Revolution) Indo-British trade. Our assumption regarding nominal prices is in accord with the metallic standard prevalent in those days—an assumption we relax in the next section. For an alternative analysis of the impact of trade on developing countries with balance of trade equilibrium, *see* Rakshit (1982).

With price-inelastic supply of X_a, the impact of trade[14] on the level of economic activity in A is unambiguously negative. In fact, the impact may be contractionary even for B, though this will be more an exception than a rule.[15] With $s^*_{yb} > 0$ (for stability, Appendix A12.1), verify that both dY_b and dp_b will be unambiguously positive when the marginal propensities to spend with respect to changes in income and prices are the same in A and B; in fact, in this case dY_b exactly equals Y^*, so that world production of Y remains unchanged.

It is the wide divergence in the spending propensities of two countries that gives rise to the possibility of a negative foreign trade multiplier for both A and B. With the opening up of trade the demand for Y originating in the X_a sector is directed towards Y_b. Again, cheapening of Y also induces an increased demand for Y_b from producer of X_a. However, there is also a decline in demand for Y_b originating from X_b sector due to a decline in its price. Hence arises the possibility of a negative dY_b, when Y^{db} is highly sensitive to p_b, and price-insensitivity of X^{da} and X^{db} makes dp_b relatively large.

IMPACT OF BALANCED TRADE

The models considered so far are characterized by a surplus in trade balance of one country along with a deficit in the other—a state of affairs that cannot continue for long, and must trigger off some corrective mechanism sooner or later. Given other features of the models, the simplest way of introducing the mechanism is to assume that trade

[14] However, factors engaged in X_a do gain through a fall in p. In interpreting (12.22) note that (*a*) the numerator on the RHS indicates additional demand for Y_b due to fall in production of Y_a (by Y_a^*)and to the closing of the price gap ($p_a - p_b$), with the opening up of trade; and (*b*) s^*_{yb} is the marginal leakage from the income stream of Y_b operating through changes in production and relative prices. Relation (12.23) shows the extent of change in p_b required to neutralize the change in demand for X by A and B under the influence of trade (remembering that aggregate supply of X remains unchanged).

[15] There could also have been some decline in agricultural output in Britain following her large-scale import of farm products (due to diminishing returns in agriculture and money wage rigidity). The findings of economic historians (Ashworth 1960: 68–9; Lewis 1978: 260–2) that agricultural production of Britain remained practically stagnant in this period is in conformity with our assumption, though its explanation may perhaps be sought in improved techniques. We have chosen to ignore these complications in order to highlight the major effects of colonial trade.

becomes balanced through adjustments in e, the amount of A's currency per unit of B's currency (e, assumed to be fixed so far, was set at unity by choice of units). In order to appreciate the way the earlier results are modified under balanced trade we discuss in some detail only the Smithian model, since changes in other cases are then not difficult to perceive.

Conditions for autarky equilibrium (and stability) in A and B are still given by (12.1)–(12.4), though the pre-trade price ratios p_a and p_b may now differ. However, the free trade equilibrium values of Y_a, X_b and $p(\bar{P}_y^a / e\bar{P}_x^b)$ are now given by:

$$Y_a = Y^{da}(Y_a, \bar{X}_a, p) + Y^{db}(\bar{Y}_b, X_b, p) - \bar{Y}_b \qquad (12.25)$$

$$X_b = X^{da}(Y_a, \bar{X}_a, p) + X^{db}(\bar{Y}_b, X_b, p) - \bar{X}_a \qquad (12.26)$$

$$X^{da}(Y_a, \bar{X}_a, p) - \bar{X}_a = p[Y^{db}(\bar{Y}_b, X_b, p) - \bar{Y}_b], \qquad (12.27)$$

where the LHS and the RHS of the balance of trade equilibrium condition (12.27) denotes A's imports and exports respectively, both measured in terms of X.

Algebraic results relating to stability and the impact of trade are relegated to Appendix A12.1. As one would expect, with $p_b > p_a$ under autarky, the equilibrium p under free trade with a flexible exchange rate lies between p_b and p_a. However, we no longer have unambiguous results for the production effects with:

$$sign(dY_a) = sign(Y_3^{da} + X_3^{da}/p_b) \qquad (12.28)$$

$$sign(dX_b) = sign\{-(p_b Y_3^{db} + X_3^{db})\}. \qquad (12.29)$$

With demand for Y and X moving in opposite directions with respect to a change in the price ratio, the impact of balanced trade on production can be positive or negative, and the sign may also differ from one country to another.

A Widow's Cruse Theory of Imports

The interesting point to note in this connection is that the sign (though not the magnitude) of foreign trade multiplier of a country depends on its own preferences alone, and is positive or negative according as its own import demand is more sensitive or less sensitive to price changes than its demand for exportables. Since in the vent-for-surplus model scarcity makes importables items of luxury consumption, both dY_a and dY_b are likely to be positive: Smith is vindicated for the fix as also the flex exchange regime!

How do we interpret the queer and seemingly anti-Keynesian result that a country stands to gain by spending more lavishly on imports when trade opens up? The clue to the resolution of the paradox is also Keynesian! The RHS of (12.28) is nothing but the price-induced change in *aggregate* expenditure by A (measured in Y). With balance of trade equilibrium, this expenditure equals domestic production $(Y_a + \bar{X}_a/p)$. Hence if the RHS of (12.28) is positive, international trade provides a boost to Y_a through an increase in p_a following trade. Similar is the case for (12.29). Under balanced trade, it is thus clear, an increase in import demand will produce an expansionary impact on the country's exportables: hence the widow's cruse theory of imports under the vent-for-surplus model.

The conclusion for the contra-Smithian pattern of trade is immediate: with imports equalling exports, a country will be blessed (cursed) with a positive (negative) foreign trade multiplier if its own demand for exportables is relatively more (less) sensitive to price changes than that for importables.

North–South Trade with a Flexible Exchange Rate

In the North–South trade model comprising (12.20) and (12.21), there is no room for attaining trade balance through adjustments in the exchange rate in as much as production levels and terms of trade p are obtained uniquely from the two relations. However, given our assumption of fixed $\bar{P}_y^b$ and money wages in the two countries, variations in the exchange rate at a given p (and hence a given P_b^x) affect real wages in A and produce thereby both a demand- and supply-side impact. Thus a depreciation reduces real wages and tends to improve thereby A's trade balance with an increase in agricultural output (X_a) and (a probable) shift of income distribution against workers (remembering that marginal propensity to save is generally larger for workers than for non-workers). Hence the balance-of-trade equilibrium condition (with incorporation of e as an additional argument in Y^{da}, X^{da}, and X_a) provides the required closure of the North–South model.

Even without going into mathematical details of the modified model it is clear that balanced trade cannot prevent demise of A's manufactures since at the equilibrium exchange rate e^*, $\overline{P}_y^a > e^* \overline{P}_y^b$ (otherwise, British industries are wiped out). Note that with balance-of-trade equilibrium

$$Y_b = Y^{db} + [X^{db} - X_b (p)]/p, \tag{12.30}$$

where production of X_b is taken to be negatively related to p. It is thus clear that Y_b registers an increase under (balanced) free trade, if an increase in p raises *aggregate* excess demand in the domestic sector. The economic interpretation of the condition is fairly simple. The change in excess demand consists of (a) additional demand for Y and (b) the increase in X^{db} less the extra output of X_b (measured in terms of Y). While (a) directly adds to the demand for Y_b, balanced trade also ensures that extra imports, indicated by (b), produce a one-for-one feedback effect on the demand for B's exportables. Indeed, dY_b will be a multiple of the excess demand due to the difference between the free trade and autarky price ratios in B, and this multiple, as one would expect, is nothing but the reciprocal of the leakage from the domestic income stream due to a unit increase in Y_b.

CONCLUSION

1. The paper suggests that the most important factor determining the sign of the foreign trade multiplier is the nature of the constraint operating on production of exportables and importables. The foreign trade multiplier is positive for all countries if each nation imports goods that are supply-constrained in the domestic market against commodities, production of which is limited by demand. This was precisely the type of trade that Smith had in view. However, there is no reason why trade should be universally beneficial; more often than not, it is expansionary for some and contractionary for other countries. Indeed, under the North–South or colonial forms of trade, the multiplier may be negative for both nations in spite of the fact that in one country (but not in both) export industries have excess capacity, and there is no excess supply of importables.

2. For simplicity of exposition we have abstracted from non-tradables. What is important, however, is the degree of substitutability in demand for various types of goods: imports that are close substitutes of products (tradables or non-tradables) of industries facing demand constraint will generally have adverse impact, and

exports of goods in excess supply a favourable impact on the level of domestic production.

3. Under balance-of-trade equilibrium the sign (though not the magnitude) of foreign trade multiplier of a country depends entirely on its own propensity to spend: the multiplier is positive or negative according as the change in the domestic price ratio due to trade raises or lowers the *aggregate* excess demand in the domestic sector. In other words, the impact of balanced trade is expansionary for a country when price responsiveness of its own demand for importables is larger than that for exportables.

Appendix A 12.1

Stability of the Vent-for-Surplus Model

Consider the equilibrium values of Y_a and X_b given jointly by (12.5) and (12.6) in the text. Assuming adjustments in production of Y_a and X_b to have the same sign as their respective excess demand, standard methods yield the following two stability conditions:

$$(1 - Y_1^{da}) + (1 - X_2^{db}) > 0 \tag{A12.1}$$

$$\Delta_1 \equiv (1 - Y_1^{da})(1 - X_2^{db}) - Y_2^{db}.X_1^{da} > 0. \tag{A12.2}$$

The conditions imply that $Y_1^{da} < 1$ and $X_2^{db} < 1$ (as assumed in the text). Hence stability requires that

$$s_y \equiv \Delta_1/(1 - X_2^{db}) > 0 \text{ and } s_x \equiv \Delta_1/(1 - Y_1^{da}) > 0 \tag{A12.2a}$$

STABILITY OF TRADE EQUILIBRIUM WITHOUT INITIAL EXCESS DEMAND

Autarky equilibrium in A and B is given respectively by (12.11)–(12.12) and (12.13)–(12-14) in the text. In A a disequilibrium sets in motion quantity adjustments in the Y markets, but price adjustments in the market for X. Differential equations obtained by linearizing the adjustment functions in the two markets around autarky equilibrium values of Y_a and p_a yield the corresponding stability conditions in A:

$$(1-Y_1^{da})+X_3^{da}>0 \tag{A12.3}$$

$$\Delta_a \equiv X_3^{da}(1-Y_1^{da})+X_1^{da}Y_3^{da}>0. \tag{A12.4}$$

Stability of autarky equilibrium in B can similarly be shown to require:

$$(1-X_2^{db})-Y_3^{db}>0 \tag{A12.5}$$

$$\Delta_b \equiv -[Y_3^{db}(1-X_2^{db})+Y_2^{db}X_3^{db}]>0. \tag{A12.6}$$

However, since the free trade equilibrium relations (12.13) and (12.14) are the same as (12.5) and (12.6) the stability conditions in this case also will be given by (A12.1) and (A12.2) or (A12.2a).

In evaluating dY_a from (12.17a), note that

$$Y_3^{da}(1-X_2^{db})+X_3^{da}Y_2^{db} = Y_2^{db}[X_3^{da}+Y_3^{da}(1-X_2^{db})/Y_2^{db}]$$

$$> Y_2^{db}[X_3^{da}+Y_3^{da}X_1^{da}/(1-Y_1^{da})] \quad \text{[with } Y_3^{da}<0 \text{ and (A12.2)]}$$

$$> 0 \text{ [by (A12.4)]}. \tag{A12.7}$$

Relations (A12.7), (A12.6), and (A12.2a) along with the fact that $dp_a>0$ and $dp_b<0$ ensure that dY_a, as given in (12.17a) is positive. Similarly for the positivity of dX_b.

NORTH—SOUTH TRADE

The post-trade equilibrium values of Y_b and p are given by (12.20) and (12.21) in the text. Assuming that disequilibrium in Y-market leads to production adjustments while that in X-market leads to price changes, we obtain the following conditions for stability of post-trade equilibrium:[16]

$$(1-Y_1^{db})+(X_3^{da}+X_3^{db})>0 \tag{A12.8}$$

$$\Delta_c \equiv (1-Y_1^{db})(X_3^{da}+X_3^{db})+X_1^{db}(Y_3^{da}+Y_3^{db})>0 \quad ..(A12.9)$$

$$s_{yb}^* \equiv \Delta_c/(X_3^{da}+X_3^{db})>0 \tag{A12.9a}$$

remembering that $X_3^{da}+X_3^{db}>0$.

[16] While deriving (A12.8) and (A12.9) we have made the perfectly harmless assumption that the speed of adjustments in both the markets is unity.

BALANCED TRADE

The vent-for-surplus model with balance-of-trade equilibrium is given by (12.25), (12.26), and (12.27) in the text, which yield values of Y_a, X_a, and p (or e). For deriving stability conditions it is appropriate to assume that while a disequilibrium in Y_a and X_a markets gives rise to quantity adjustments, that in the balance of trade causes adjustments in p (or e) with $p = \bar{P}_y^a / e\bar{P}_x^b$. Of the four stability conditions the most important one for our purpose is:

$$\Delta \equiv \begin{vmatrix} -(1-Y_1^{da}) & Y_2^{db} & (Y_3^{da}+Y_3^{db}) \\ X_1^{da} & -(1-X_2^{db}) & (X_3^{da}+X_3^{db}) \\ -X_1^{da} & p_bY_2^{db} & E_p \end{vmatrix} < 0 \qquad (A12.10)$$

where

$$E_p \equiv (Y^{db} - \bar{Y}_b) + pY_3^{db} - X_3^{da} \qquad (A12.11)$$

Linearization of (12.25), (12.26), and (12.27) around the autarky equilibrium values of Y_a, X_b, p_a, and p_b yields the effects of trade:

$$dY_a = -h\Delta_b(p_bY_3^{da} + X_3^{da})/\Delta \qquad (A12.12)$$

$$dX_b = h\Delta_a(p_bY_3^{db} + X_3^{db})/\Delta \qquad (A12.13)$$

$$dp_a = -h\Delta_b[p_b(1-Y_1^{da}) - X_1^{da}/p_b] \qquad (A12.14)$$

where h is the difference between autarky values of p_a and p_b.

The expression within third brackets in (A12.14) is positive with marginal propensity to spend out of Y_a falling short of unity. Hence stability conditions (A12.4), (A12.6), and (A12.10) imply that $dp_a > 0$. In other words, the equilibrium price ratio lies between p_a and p_b. Again, (A12.11) and (A12.12) along with these three stability conditions yield (12.28) and (12.29) in the text. We no longer have unequivocal conditions concerning the production effects: signs of dY_a ahd dX_b depend on the relative price sensitivity of exportables and importables in the two countries.

REFERENCES

ASHWORTH, W., (1960), *An Economic History of England, 1870–1939*, London: Methuen.

LEWIS, W.A., (1978), *Growth and Fluctuations*, London: Allen and Unwin.

MYINT, H., (1958), 'The Classical Theory of International Trade and Underdeveloped Countries', *Economic Journal*, June.

——, (1977), 'Adam Smith's Theory of International Trade in the Perspective of Economic Development', *Economica*, August.

RAKSHIT, M., (1982), *The Labour Surplus Economy: A Neo-Keynesian Approach*, Delhi: Macmillan and New Jersey: Humanities Press.

——, (1993), *Trade, Mercantile Capital and Economic Development*, Delhi: Orient Longman.

SMITH, A., (1776), *An Enquiry into the Nature and Causes of the Wealth of Nations*, New York: Modern Library.

TAYLOR, L., (1983), *Structuralist Macroeconomics*, New York: Basic Books.

13. Complementarity and International Trade

On Some Recent Developments in Structural General Equilibrium Models

INTRODUCTION

The 2 × 2 Heckscher–Ohlin–Samuelson (HOS) model of international trade has served as the major workhorse of pure theory of international trade. Two-country, two-good structure is the most natural way of abstraction and the associated simple production structure, exhibiting neoclassical technology, provides the right kind of framework to analyse distributional consequences of trade policy. One particular characteristic of a two-good structure embedded in a full-employment environment is that it does not allow for 'complementarity' in production. An increase in the production of one must be matched by a decline in the production of the other. Therefore, it is difficult to analyse situations where trade pattern involves more than one export good and/or import-competing products. Those policy analyses, which work wonders in a two-good structure, may fail to hold in models where import-competing goods and exportables are complementary. In 1970, Fred Gruen and Max Corden wrote a paper to argue that a tariff

This is a humble effort to mark my deep respect for Prof. Sanjit Bose. I was fortunate to have him as my colleague for a few years. I am indebted to Ronald Jones and Hamid Beladi for allowing me to draw from our joint work. I am also grateful to Saibal Kar for research assistance. The usual disclaimer applies.

imposed by the Australian government might worsen the terms of trade, a result that belied the fundamental intuition underlying the idea of protection. A tariff, in this model, could promote production of an import-competing good as well as an export good at the cost of another product, possibly an exportable. Rising supply of exportables could depress prices too much and hence the result. What they had in their model was an example of 'complementarity' and that was what was driving the result. As it has turned out later that such complementarity can generate a fairly rich variety of interesting results unattainable in the standard two-good structure.

In this paper I intend to survey some of these results starting off with the general theoretical perspective developed in Jones and Marjit (1992) which characterizes the class of models that contains Gruen and Corden (1970) as an example. Once the theoretical discussion is over, we shall identify a few areas where such models have been used to derive new insights. We broadly define three such areas of analyses. The first and foremost has to do with trade policy, foreign investment, and factor returns in the standard full-employment models of trade. The second set refers to an area in development economics dealing with unemployment and wage differential. The third category deals with political–economic issues.

As we shall demonstrate, this class of models is essentially a hybrid of the 2 × 2 HOS framework and the specific-factor model developed in Jones (1971) and Samuelson (1971). However, the structure we are interested in is likely to emerge from a broader set-up and is obtained as a consequence of opening up to trade. In a way it is international trade, which generates such a pattern of incomplete specialization and hence such a production structure is endogenous.

The plan of the paper is as follows. In the second section we summarize Jones and Marjit (1992) and the theoretical implications therein. In the third section we talk about the applicability of the theoretical framework in handling issues such as trade policy, foreign investment, and national welfare. The fourth brings to the fore some issues related to migration, unemployment, and informal labour markets. The fifth adds a bit of the political–economic angle to the structure and discusses possible applications. The last section concludes.

One point I would like to make at the very outset. Since I shall be drawing heavily from already published papers, the algebraic proofs are not reproduced here. Instead we try to trace the basic arguments underlying the results. Interested readers may go beyond and read the specific articles highlighted in the text.

A 3 × 3 ENDOGENOUS PRODUCTION STRUCTURE

It is well known that free trade can drastically alter production and specialization pattern of the small economies. This is primarily reflected in the fact that if there are more goods than factors, free trade equilibrium will not allow many of them to be produced in a country (Jones 1971). The specific factor (SF, henceforth) model of trade where each sector has a specific factor, possibly capital, attached to it and a single mobile factor, labour, can be easily extended to tackle a large number of goods with the caveat that the number of factors must exceed the number of goods by one. While in $n \times n$ HOS-type models, under a set of assumptions, commodity prices uniquely solve for factor prices, it is not possible in SF models simply because we have one less equation to solve for the factor prices. In this structure one needs to take account of the full-employment conditions as well. As a consequence of that, the factor endowments, given the set of commodity prices, affect the factor prices. The end result is a non-validation of the well-known factor-price equalization theorem. These are pretty well known in the literature. For a survey of related issues one can refer to Ethier (1984).

With this backdrop let us start with a general SF model. Suppose we have n types of capital and labour. Each type of capital and labour can produce a particular good, but in lots of varieties. Hence, for each sector, employing the specific factor, we have a number of varieties say m_1 for the first, m_2 for the second and m_n for the n-th sector. The general equilibrium system looks as follows:

$$w a_{Li}^v + r_i a_{Ki}^v = P_i^v \tag{13.1}$$

$$\sum_v a_{Ki}^v X_i^v = K_i \tag{13.2}$$

$$\sum_i \sum_v a_{Li}^v X_i^v = L, \tag{13.3}$$

where w, r, P, K, L, and a's have usual interpretations. Here (13.1) represents a competitive condition in the i-th sector for the v-th variety. Equation (13.2) represents the full-employment condition for the i-th type of capital, the specific factor used in sector i, and (13.3) denotes the full-employment condition for labour.

To start with we have a closed economy where every variety of each type has positive demand and hence produced. Next, we open up this economy for trade and let the free trade prices be determined in the rest of the world. In other words we have a small open economy. Then, one can write down the following proposition.

Proposition 1: (Jones and Marjit 1992): The free-trade production structure of the small economy will be characterized by either (a) a pure SF structure with single variety being produced in each sector or (b) where a single variety is produced in $(n-1)$ sectors and two varieties are produced in the rest.

Outline of the Proof: First, note that two or more sectors cannot produce more than one variety under competitive conditions. Suppose they do; then, given the prices of the variety, one can solve for w and return to the specific capital from one of the sectors. Given such a w, return to the other specific factor can be easily determined from a single variety in each sector. Now for all other varieties the average cost as well as price, which is given exogenously, will be predetermined. If varieties are distinct, in the sense that their technologies and demands are not linearly dependent on others, only that variety, which promises the highest return to the specific factor, will survive. Therefore, at most one sector will produce two varieties.

Also no sector can produce more than two varieties because for that sector one would have more goods than factors and therefore competitive conditions will rule out production of at least one of them.

Hence, at most one sector will produce a maximum of two varieties. This leaves us with two possible scenarios (a) and (b) as in the proposition. QED.

It is obvious that each sector must produce at least one variety; else the specific factor used in this sector will remain unemployed. Possibility (a) gives us the standard SF model. Possibility (b) is more interesting in the sense that it allows one sector to produce two varieties and the rest will produce one each.

Let us focus on the sector, which produces two varieties. This can be any of the n we have. Without any loss of generality let us suppose this is the n-th sector, which produces the first and second variety. Therefore, the following must hold,

$$wa^1_{Ln} + r_n a^1_{Kn} = P^1_n \qquad (13.4)$$

$$wa^2_{Ln} + r_n a^2_{Kn} = P^2_n. \qquad (13.5)$$

Given P^1_n, P^2_n, one can determine w and r_n, and then $r_1, ..., r_{n-1}$ from the other competitive price conditions valid for each sector. If technologies are the same across countries, those producing 'same' varieties must have their factor prices equalized. Also note that the n-th sector is crucial in the sense that w gets determined in this sector and $r_1, ..., r_{n-1}$ are derived as residuals. n-th sector presents a 2×2 HOS subsystem within a broad SF framework. We have an $n \times n$ model where $(n{-}1)$ represents a typical SF structure whereas within the n-th we have an HOS. Amalgamation of these two structures gives us, in principle, a 3×3 model with 'complementarity' to which we turn now.

Since both the HOS and SF-type structures usually deal with two goods and we have stated at the very beginning that our primary purpose is to look for complementarity, a minimal framework needed for such exploration must have at least three goods. We have three goods, X, Y, and Z. While X and Y use labour and capital, Z uses labour and land. The structure here is exactly similar to the one we have been discussing so far. The structure is basically recursive while land is used only in Z, capital in X and Y, and labour in X, Y, and Z. What we have argued so far is that such a structure is not purely ad hoc, it can be an outcome of the process of trade. The intriguing feature is that such a 3×3 model captures both the HOS and SF models at the same time. This is exactly the model that Gruen and Corden (1970) talked about. Now, let us look into the aspect of complementarity we are interested in.

Proposition 2: An increase in the price of $Z(X)$ must expand both $Z(X)$ and $X(Z)$, *if* X is capital intensive.

Outline of the Proof: An increase in the price of Z draws labour away from X and Y for producing more of Z. As labour leave X and Y, the HOS subsystem is left with same capital and less labour. Hence, due to the well-known Rybczynski effect, X must expand and Y must contract.

An increase in P_X, other things being equal, will increase r and reduce w due to the well-known Stolper–Samuelson result. As w goes down, workers leave for sector Z and output expands there. Output of X expands first, given the amount of Z, as P_X increases. Then as Z expands, there is a second round of Rybczynski effect that increases it further. QED.

Complementarity in production between Z and X does lead to interesting results as would be demonstrated in the forthcoming sections. But before we leave this section, let me comment briefly on patterns of trade in this framework.

We have three factors of production: land, capital, and labour. Had it been an SF model, larger stock of land would reduce capital-based output. Here, clearly a country having more land will also draw a lot of labour into the production of Z and hence promote production of X through the Rybczynski effect. Therefore, such an economy may end up exporting both Z and X. Similarly, unproductive agriculture will release workforce towards X and Y. In the process Y will expand and X will contract. We may end up having a country with unproductive agriculture, but a massive labour-intensive manufacturing sector. If one interprets K as 'skill' or human capital, countries may be great producers of agricultural products such as Z and skill-intensive manufacturing such as X.[1] On the other hand, a country exporting Y may be importing goods which are more capital-intensive such as X, as well as those which are less so, such as Z. It is straightforward to show that the essence of the arguments remains valid even if Z uses a bit of capital. Therefore, the so-called Leontieff Paradox may not be a paradox after all. A country may export both capital-intensive and labour-intensive products.

TRADE POLICY, COMPLEMENTARITY, AND FOREIGN INVESTMENT

A voluminous literature exists describing the link between foreign investment and national welfare particularly when foreign capital flows into the protected import-competing sector. A well-known result is due to Brecher and Alejandro (1977) which states that growth in the protected sector induced by foreign capital, in the face of full repatriation of capital income, must reduce national welfare. This particular result has been decoded and clarified time and again. Jones (1984, 2001) suggests that tariff-induced endogenous flow of capital hurts national welfare independent of the location of foreign capital. In case foreign capital is employed in the exportables, an increase in capital flow into the import-competing sector should drive away foreign capital from the exportables.

---

[1] For a discussion on HOS trade pattern in a multi-commodity framework, *see* Jones, Beladi, and Marjit (1999). In fact such a trade pattern is consistent with the Indian experience in recent years.

The idea of complementarity we have developed earlier works in a different way to modify the welfare result in a three-good model. In this context we invoke two results from the literature.

The first one deals with the case where an increase in foreign capital in an export sector reduces national welfare even if capital does not flow into the distorted import-competing sector. This alters the earlier results in two ways. First, the decline in welfare is not a consequence of increased capital flow in the protected sector. Second, it is associated through an expansion in the export sector, a consequence absent in the earlier models.

The second one produces a fairly counter-intuitive result. We show that there are situations when production in the import-competing sector and volume of imports can both go up at the same time. If this is the outcome, it puts to serious test the conventional wisdom on foreign investment and welfare.

Proposition 3: (Beladi and Marjit 1992): Growth in the export sector (Z) induced by foreign capital must reduce national welfare if X is protected.

Outline of Proof: Let us interpret the specific factor in Z as foreign-owned capital. As Z expands, X automatically expands due to complementarity. Since X is protected, this leads to a decline in the volume of imports. This reduces welfare for a small open economy as the entire capital income is repatriated.   QED.

Complementarity allows similar welfare results even if foreign capital does not directly flow into the import-competing sector. The message of such results in a two-good structure seems to suggest the essentiality of location of capital. More reasonable policy seems to be to induce an expansion in the exportables, which cuts back the size of the protected sector. Complementarity suggests that location might be unimportant. The fact that output of an import-competing good and an export good can move together is ruled out by construction in a two-good framework.

The foundation of negative welfare results lies with a decline in the volume of imports. Consumption distortion is magnified whenever the tariff-ridden sector is allowed to grow and as a consequence, volume of imports is reduced. Negative relation between an expanding import-competing sector and volume of imports is absolutely essential for the welfare result. This is a well-known and accepted norm in the standard trade models. Complementarity can alter such a perspective drastically when one deals with intermediates.

Proposition 4: (Marjit and Beladi 1996): In the presence of complementarity with intermediate goods, volume of imports can expand along with the size of import-competing production.

Outline of the Proof: Interpret Z as an intermediate good which is also imported from abroad. Now X uses labour, capital, and Z, the intermediate good, while Y uses only labour and capital. The system of equations looks as follows:

Competitive price conditions:

$$wa_{LX} + ra_{KX} + P_Z a_{ZX} = P_X \tag{13.6}$$

$$wa_{LY} + ra_{KY} = P_Y \tag{13.7}$$

$$wa_{LZ} + Ra_{TZ} = P_Z. \tag{13.8}$$

Full-employment conditions:

$$a_{LX}X + a_{LY}Y + a_{LZ}Z = L \tag{13.9}$$

$$a_{KX}X + a_{KX}Y = K \tag{13.10}$$

$$a_{TZ}Z = T. \tag{13.11}$$

Also note that import of Z, call it Z_m, is nothing but

$$a_{ZX}X - Z = Z_m \tag{13.12}$$

Given (P_X, P_Y, P_Z), (w, r, R) are determined from (13.6)–(13.8) and then given (L, K, T), (X, Y, Z) are determined from (13.9)–(13.11). Then Z_m is determined from (13.12).

As T grows Z expands. It draws labour away from X and Y. As X is capital-intensive, it expands due to the Rybczynski effect creating additional demand for Z. From (13.12), $a_{ZX}X$ increases as well as Z. Hence, it is quite likely that Z_m can expand as well. QED.

It is pretty unusual that secular growth in the import-competing sector helps growth in import demand for the same product as well. Since Z and X are complementary, there is a natural way why this can happen. Of course, the fact that we are dealing with the intermediate good matters as well. While supply-side shocks can affect the derived demand for an intermediate, in case of pure final goods it is very unlikely

...at a growth in one sector stimulates demand so much that an excess demand for the good produced in this sector is stimulated further. A more general result is derived in Marjit and Beladi (1999).

We now turn to the application of complementarity relationship in some familiar areas of research in development.

MIGRATION WAGE DIFFERENTIAL AND INFORMAL LABOUR

In this section we provide two theoretical examples which exploit the complementarity relationship for deriving two interesting results.

A long-discussed and well-known issue in the standard Harris–Todaro model of migration has been the impact of urban wage subsidy on aggregate unemployment. In fact, the interesting result was that an effort to increase employment would attract people from the rural sector and open unemployment would increase, defeating the initial purpose of the policy. A host of papers starting with Harris and Todaro (1970) and followed by Bhagwati and Srinivasan (1974), Basu (1997), Gang and Gangopadhyay (1985), and others have dealt with this issue and the 'paradox' of wage subsidy and unemployment.

Marjit (1991) has proposed a simple model where the rural sector produces food and cash crop, which in turn is processed in the urban sector with the help of urban labour. Here, the rural sector is characterized by a 2 × 2 HOS subsystem using land and labour. The third sector is located in the urban area. Note that an increase in the price of the processed manufacturing must increase the price of the intermediate or the cash crop and also its production. The agro-based industrial product and the cash crop exhibit the 'complementary' relationship. Then the following proposition is immediate.

Proposition 5: Urban wage subsidy must reduce aggregate unemployment if the cash crop is labour-intensive.

Outline of Proof: Wage subsidy reduces cost and increases the price of the cash crop given the final good's price (under small-economy assumption). This must increase rural wage via the Stolper–Samuelson argument and also increase employment there, since the cash crop is labour-intensive. This in turn helps to reduce urban unemployment.

QED.

The idea here is to find a 'complementary' segment of the rural sector which is automatically stimulated by urban wage subsidy. If this is the labour-intensive sector, subsidization unambiguously reduces unemployment and paradox does not seem to be an outcome.[2] Marjit (1991) also suggests that besides labour, there may be something else which also moves between the sectors. Disaggregating the rural sector into food and cash crop allows us to explore the resource allocation in the resultant 3 × 3 complementary system.

Marjit (2003) develops a model to analyse the impact of economic reform on the wage of workers employed in the informal sector of an economy. This is a very sensitive issue in transition economies since deregulation and dismantling of protectionary policies tend to cut back the size of the formal sector. As displaced formal workers enter the informal market, concern for a dampening real wage in this sector seems to be a real one. Anyway, Marjit (2003) observes that this may not be the case. In fact, Marjit (2003) is a more complex version of Marjit (1991). In a way Marjit (1991) can be stretched a bit to highlight the direction of the results.

Consider that initially the good produced in the urban sector is protected. As one removes protection it must reduce the price of the cash crop. Since cash crop is labour-intensive, this must mean a decline in the rural wage. If cash crop is land-intensive, rural wage in fact would go up. If flexible rural wage proxies the notion of informal wage, here is a case where freeing up trade would increase rural wage. The main idea is that protection, to start with, must artificially raise the price of the non-labour-intensive product. Again the complementarity plays a role.

Marjit (2003) uses a 'full-employment' model with wage differential, where a fixed-wage 'formal' sector uses labour, capital, and an informal intermediate. The informal sector in turn has two segments; one produces a final good and the other the intermediate good. The competitive conditions look like the following:

$$\bar{w}a_{LX} + ra_{KX} + P_M a_{MX} = P_X \tag{13.13}$$

$$wa_{LM} + ra_{KM} = P_M \tag{13.14}$$

$$wa_{LY} + ra_{KY} = P_Y. \tag{13.15}$$

Note that, if M is capital-intensive, r would be an increasing function of P_M From (13.13), a fall in P_X must reduce P_M and r, and raise w, the

---

[2] In fact, many so-called 'paradoxes' in the Harris–Todaro model are results of a violation of an interesting 'envelope' property. For this result, *see* Marjit and Beladi (2003).

informal wage. Contraction in X contracts M, the capital-intensive informal segment. If X is protected, it definitely hurts the informal workers even if a part of the informal segment also benefits from such protection. Therefore, the following proposition is immediate.

Proposition 6: (Marjit 2003): A decline in P_x must increase w.

Standard general equilibrium models have been used time and again to highlight policy outcomes for the developing countries. A notable work came up in terms of the Harris–Todaro model. It was supposed to capture two crucial features of a developing country, namely, rural–urban migration and open unemployment. It had all the derived features, three major factors—land, labour, and capital—and a dual economic structure. The need for a further-break up of the two-good framework seemed to be redundant at that stage.

More recently, researchers have questioned the idea of open unemployment among the poor because they cannot afford to remain unemployed. Several authors have repeatedly asserted that the formal-informal divisioning of the urban sector is absolutely essential to capture the essence of a developing world as, on average, more than 60 to 70 per cent of the developing country workforce is absorbed in the informal segment. If enough jobs are not available in the formal sector, people find something to hang on to in the informal. One should not ignore agriculture as well, since it continues to provide livelihood to a substantial chunk of population.[3]

Note that the necessity to break down the urban sector into formal and informal components and clubbing them with agriculture immediately opens up the possibility of using the idea of complementarity. In fact, the three-good generic model we have been talking about fits it rather well. Here is some excerpt from an ongoing work by Marjit, Sarkar, and Kar (2002).

Let us get back to the basic three-good model developed in the last section. Consider X, a product from the formal segment of urban manufacturing and Y from the informal segment. Both use labour and capital. While wage is fixed through negotiations with the unions in the formal sector, competition among workers determines the wage in the informal. Z is produced in agriculture with land and labour. Labour

---

[3] Literature on this is voluminous. A survey paper by Agenor (1996) is a good starting point. For some recent discussions one could go through Marjit (2003) and Kar and Marjit (2001).

moves freely among the three sectors; earns more in the form.
albeit the same, in the other two sectors. Clearly, this is a ⸱
complementarity. As price of X increases, more workers are draw
the informal into the formal manufacturing. Returns to capital inc⸱
informal wage drops, and hence production of Z is stimulated. Her
X and Z are complementary.

There are three interesting results, which may be highlighted here.
First, if the unionized wage is indexed to prices, a Stolper–Samuelson
type outcome between (P_X, P_Y) and (w, r) is a must *independent of the
factor intensity ranking between X and Y* (Marjit and Beladi 2002).

Second, consider the case where the formal manufacturing is initially
protected by a tariff. A decline in tariff, in that case, must increase the
informal wage. Since wage in the formal sector is fixed, a drop in its
price must reduce the return to capital, r. As r drops, given P_Y, w must
go up. This also leads to a contraction in agriculture. The result changes
drastically if capital does not move between X and Y. However, if
capital does not move between X and Y, an increase in P_Z helps the
informal workers, otherwise not. In any case, an increase in P_Y must
increase the real wage of the informal workers, whereas a rise in P_Z
does not.

These results are related to the impact of economic reform on
informal real income in transitional economies. Marjit, Sarkar, and Kar
(2002) try to accomplish this by utilizing the data on informal
manufacturing in India. The bottom line is that a hybrid of an HOS
system and a pure SF sector seems to be a natural candidate for such
analyses.[4]

POLITICAL ECONOMY ISSUES

It is now well recognized that political factors are crucial in determining
equilibrium policy outcomes. Politics driven by vested interests prevents
the 'first-best' outcomes and generates policies that may be clearly
undesirable from a welfare-maximizing perspective. Earlier works by
Mayer (1984) and Hillman (1989) provide the basic starting point in
political–economic perspective on international trade. More recently,
Grossman and Helpman (1994) have led to the renewal of interest in
this literature. A classic book by Dixit (1996) is also a very valuable

---

[4] Complementarity in Harris–Todaro framework can break the positive
relationship between trade and employment. *See* Beladi and Marjit (1996).

on in this area. SF models have been used repeatedly to
the relationship between trade policy and factorial income
ution and to focus on the incentive for political lobbying when
its anticipate favourable or unfavourable outcomes associated with
particular policy. Clearly, the interests of protectionary lobbies are
captured by the rent enjoyed by the protected specific factor.

If agriculture is protected, landlords will lobby for higher tariffs and
workers may or may not support this depending on their taste pattern.
While we get an overall view of the problem in a two-good model by looking
at the single import-competing sector, we may lose sight of interesting
situations that are likely to emerge when there are more than one import-
competing sectors. We may ask the following question in this context. Is
uniform tariff politically sustainable? Since uniform tariff does away with
the incentive for inter-sectoral lobbying and is believed to be less distortionary, it is mandated to be a judicious policy. However, in our three-
good model with complementarity, one can invoke an interesting result.

Consider an economy which imports Y and Z, that is, the labour-intensive
manufacturing and agriculture. X, the capital-intensive product, is
exported. This seems to be a well-accepted trade pattern for a typically
developed country.

Proposition 7: (Marjit 1993) Uniform tariffs on Y and Z must reduce
the real income of the farmers.

Outline of Proof: A tariff on Y must increase the wage rate more than
in proportion to the tariff due to the Stolper–Samuelson effect. If wage
goes up by more than tariff and Z is protected by the same tariff rate,
real return to land must fall.   QED.

This result suggests that farmers will definitely lobby for higher rate
of protection than labour-intensive manufacturers. Therefore, uniform
tariffs do not provide the same incentive to the lobbyist in each sector.
If real wage has to go up in terms of Z, real return cannot go up. In fact,
landowners will love an export subsidy on X since that will increase r and
reduce w. An export subsidy will work as a protectionary device for
agriculture. The Gruen and Corden (1970) outcome is also a clear
possibility here. A tariff on Z will increase production of X and therefore
terms of trade may worsen for a large economy.

For a small economy, capitalists are likely to be indifferent to a tariff
on Z. Since given (P_X, P_Y), (w, r) are determined; a rise in P_Z only
increases return to land, but does not do anything to the wage or rate
of return to capital.

Another example concerns the policy problem for a develop economy, which cannot cut back tariffs drastically, but has the optic of inviting foreign investment into the new export-processing zones. If we interpret Z as the new exportable produced with local labour and foreign capital, and X as the one which is protected by a tariff, politics of allowing joint ventures between local and foreign capital clearly comes up as a better option than pure foreign ownership. The argument runs as follows.

Suppose, return to capital is higher in X than in Z, that is, cost of capital is greater if local capital is involved in the production of Z. Higher return is due to the fact that X is protected and for some political reason tariff cannot be reduced any further. A joint venture is defined to be a process in which both types of capital are hired for production. Clearly, if local capital is relatively expensive, it makes sense to use only foreign capital. But if more local capital is directed to sector Z, import of X will increase and the distortionary effect of a tariff will be reduced. Such a move pacifies the resistance against drastic cutback in tariffs, but at the same time reduces the impact of existing distortions.

CONCLUDING REMARKS

International trade theory has drawn incessantly from the HOS and the SF models of general equilibrium. However, the popular two-good structure seems to be inadequate in studying the interrelationship between similar types of tradables. Once there are more than one exportable or importable, a notion of complementarity surfaces and this paper is a survey of a class of models which highlight this issue. We have demonstrated the usefulness of such models in the literature on trade and development. The structure we deal with is somewhat endogenously generated through international trade. It is essentially a three-good mix of HOS and SF structures. We have elaborated how this class of models helps us to develop new insights into the pattern of trade, trade policies, growth and national welfare, migration and unemployment, formal–informal labour, and political–economic considerations. We believe it has particular significance as a workable and realistic framework to address policy issues in the contemporary developing world.[5]

[5] In this paper I have drawn mainly from my own work and that of my co-authors. Here is a list of some other papers, which have dealt with such structures. Ali Khan (1993), Chandra and Ali Khan (1993), Findlay (1995), Chao and Yu (1993), and others.

ـFERENCES

AGENOR, P.R., (1996), 'The Labor Market and Economic Adjustment,' IMF Staff Papers, 32, pp. 261–335.

ALI KHAN, M., (1993), 'Trade and Development in the Presence of an Informal Sector: A Four Sector Model' in Kaushik Basu et al. (eds), *Capital Investment and Development: Essays in Memory of Sukhamoy Chakravarty*, Part II, 7, Cambridge: Massachusetts: Basil Blackwell.

BASU, K., (1997), *Analytical Development Economics: The Less Developed Economy revisited*, Cambridge and London: MIT Press.

BELADI, H. and S. MARJIT, (1992), 'Foreign Capital and Protectionism', *Canadian Journal of Economics*, 25(1), pp. 233–8.

____, (1996), 'An Analysis of Rural–Urban Migration and Protection', *Canadian Journal of Economics*, 29(4), pp. 930–40.

BHAGWATI, J. and T. N. SRINIVASAN, (1974), 'On Re-analyzing the H–T Model: Policy Rankings in the Case of Sector Specific Sticky Wages', *American Economic Review*, 64, pp. 502–8.

BRECHER, R. and C. DIAZ-ALEJANDRO, (1977), 'Tariff, Foreign Capital and Immiserizing Growth', *Journal of International Economics*, 7(4), pp. 317–22.

CHANDRA, V. and M. ALI KHAN, (1993), 'Foreign Investment in the Presence of an Informal Sector', *Economica*, 60(237), pp. 79–103.

CHAO, C.C. and E. YU, (1993), 'Content Protection, Urban Unemployment and Welfare', *Canadian Journal of Economics*, May, pp. 481–92.

DIXIT, A., (1996), *The Making of Economic Policy: A Transaction Cost Politics Perspective: Munich Lectures in Economics*, Cambridge: Massachusetts: MIT Press.

ETHIER, W., (1984), 'Higher Dimensional Issues in Trade Theory', in R.W. Jones and P. Kennen (eds), *Handbook of International Economics*, Vol. 1, Amsterdam: North-Holland.

FINDLAY, R., (1995), 'Factor Proportions, Trade and Growth', *Ohlin Lectures*, Vol. 5, Cambridge and London: MIT Press.

GANG, I. and S. GANGOPADHYAY, (1985), 'A Note on Optimal Policies in Dual Economies', *Quarterly Journal of Economics*, 100 (5), pp. 1067–71.

GROSSMAN,G. and E. HELPMAN, (1994), 'Protection for Sale,' *American Economic Review*, 84, pp. 833–50.

GRUEN, F. and M. CORDEN, (1970), 'A Tariff that Worsens Terms of

Trade', in I.A. McDougall and R.H Snape (eds), *Studies . International Economics*, Amsterdam: North-Holland.

HARRIS, R. and M. TODARO, (1970), 'Migration, Unemployment and Development: A Two -Sector Analysis', *American Economic Review*, 60, pp. 126–42.

HILLMAN, A., (1989), 'The Political Economy of Protection', in *Fundamentals of Pure and Applied Economics Series*, Vol. 32, *International Trade Sector*, Chur, Switzerland; London; New York; and Camberwell, Australia: Harwood Press.

JONES, R.W., (1971), 'A Three-factor Model in Theory, Trade, and History', in J. Bhagwati et al. (eds), *Trade, Balance of Payments, and Growth: Papers in International Economics in Honor of Charles Kindleberger*, Amsterdam: North-Holland.

——, (1984), 'Protection and the Harmful Effects of Endogenous Capital Flows', *Economics Letters*, 15, pp. 325–30.

——, (2001), 'Globalization and the Theory of Input Trade', *Ohlin Lectures*, Vol. 8, Cambridge, Massachusetts : MIT Press.

JONES, R.W. and S. MARJIT, (1992), 'International Trade and Endogenous Production Structure', in W. Neuefeind and R. Reizman (eds), *Economic Theory and International Trade: Essays in Honor of J. Trout Rader*, Springer Verlag.

JONES, R.W., H. BELADI and S. MARJIT, (1999), 'The Three Faces of Factor Intensities', *Journal of International Economics*, 48(2), pp. 413–20.

KAR, S. and S. MARJIT, (2001), 'Informal Sector in General Equilibrium: 'Welfare Effects of Trade Policy Reforms', *International Review of Economics and Finance*, 10, pp. 289–300.

MARJIT, S., (1991), 'Agro-based Industry and Rural–Urban Migration: A Case for an Urban Employment Subsidy', *Journal of Development Economics*, 35(2), pp. 393–8.

——, (1993), 'Uniform Tariffs in General Equilibrium: A simple model', *Journal of Economics*, 55(2), pp. 193–207.

——, (2003), 'Economic Reform and the Informal Wage: A General Equilibrium Analysis', *Journal of Development Economics*, 72(1), pp. 371–8.

MARJIT, S. and H. BELADI, (1996), 'Protection and Gainful Effects of Foreign Capital', *Economics Letters*, 53, pp. 311–16.

——, (1999), 'Complementarity Between Import Competition and Export Promotion', *Journal of Economic Theory*, 86, pp.280–5.

——, (2002), 'The Stolper–Samuelson Theorem in a Wage Differential Framework, *The Japanese Economic Review*, 53(2), pp. 177–81.

___, (2003), 'Possibility and Impossibility of Paradoxes in a Small-Economy Harris–Todaro Framework—A Unifying Analysis', *Journal of Development Economics*, 72(1), pp. 379–85.

MARJIT, S., P. SARKAR and S. KAR, (2002), 'Capital, Labour and Wages: Informal Sector in a Transition Economy', mimeo., Centre for Studies in Social Sciences, Calcutta.

MAYER, W., (1984), 'Endogenous Tariff Formation', *American Economic Review*, 74(5), pp. 970–85.

SAMUELSON, P., (1971), 'An Exact Hume–Ricardo–Marshall Model of International Trade', *Journal of International Economics*, 1(1), pp. 1–18.

Index